Assessing Academic Library Collections for Diversity, Equity, and Inclusion

Assessing Academic Library Collections for Diversity, Equity, and Inclusion

Karen Kohn

BLOOMSBURY ACADEMIC

NEW YORK • LONDON • OXFORD • NEW DELHI • SYDNEY

BLOOMSBURY ACADEMIC
Bloomsbury Publishing Inc, 1385 Broadway, New York, NY 10018, USA
Bloomsbury Publishing Plc, 50 Bedford Square, London, WC1B 3DP, UK
Bloomsbury Publishing Ireland, 29 Earlsfort Terrace, Dublin 2, D02 AY28, Ireland

BLOOMSBURY, BLOOMSBURY ACADEMIC and the Diana logo are trademarks of
Bloomsbury Publishing Plc

First published in the United States of America 2025

A catalog record for this book is available from the Library of Congress.

HB: 978-1-5381-9573-4
PB: 978-1-5381-9574-1
ePDF: 979-8-7651-5422-9
eBook: 978-1-5381-9575-8

Typeset by Deanta Global Publishing Services, Chennai, India
Printed and bound in the United States of America

For product safety related questions contact productsafety@bloomsbury.com.

To find out more about our authors and books visit www.bloomsbury.com and sign up
for our newsletters.

Contents

Contents

List of Figures

List of Tables

List of Text Boxes

1

Assessing Collections for Diversity, Equity, and Inclusion

If you read journals related to academic librarianship or attend conferences, you have probably noticed a number of articles and sessions in recent years related to diversity, equity, and inclusion (DEI). Some authors and presenters describe projects to expand library collections, while others detail attempts to better understand strengths or gaps in existing holdings. Many of these projects focus on a subset of the collection, often children's literature, while others are concerned with a particular population, such as African Americans or the lesbian, gay, bisexual, transgender, and queer or questioning (LGBTQ) community.

For every article or presentation, anecdotally there seem to be twice as many librarians who have a sense that they should be conducting some type of diversity assessment or audit but are unsure how to do it or are overwhelmed. Academic librarians wonder if they should be analyzing their entire collections and, if so, how they would find the time. Other questions include what the targets should be for the number of works dealing with diverse populations, and do these works need to be written by members of the population in question? What if there is no information available on the author's identity?

This book does not answer those questions but rather lays out questions you should ask when planning an assessment and offers possible ways to answer them. It aims to be flexible enough to allow you to develop your own project using the approach and scope that make the most sense to you while offering enough structure to make that work feel manageable.

WHAT IS DIVERSITY, EQUITY, AND INCLUSION

There are a variety of terms academic librarians and others in higher education use to talk about their goals of changing spheres that have long been dominated by straight, able-bodied, white men into those that incorporate a wider range of identities. This book uses what appears to be the most common phrase currently: diversity, equity, and inclusion. Each term has a different meaning, though they are interrelated. Using these three terms, with the initials DEI as shorthand, has the benefit of making explicit the goals and values involved in this work.

In Sara Ahmed's book *On Being Included: Racism and Diversity in Institutional Life*, she observes that the term "diversity" has become popular in recent years partly because it has a celebratory connotation as well as implications that serve business interests; it "evokes the pleasures of consumption."[1] She says it has replaced terms such as "equal opportunity" or "antiracism," which can be less palatable due to their suggestions of legal obligation or negativity. While the term "diversity" can be simplistic and obscure issues of inequality, the higher education staff Ahmed interviewed felt that the positive tone of the word diversity was sometimes helpful in making the topic more appealing for others to discuss, and it is undoubtedly a very heavily used term at this point in time.

Officially, the word "diversity" refers simply to variety, or in the case of collections, the presence of works that are different from each other in some way. In discussions of the diversity of library collections, the type of variety that is usually under consideration is that of people and identities represented by the works in the collection. Though library materials can vary in other ways, such as political stance and discipline, and libraries generally aim for these types of diversity as well, these differences are not usually the focus of DEI work.

While necessary for the creation of truly representative collections, diversity alone is inadequate. Diversity does not necessarily imply a commitment to justice or to investigating the systems that have led to its lack. Equity, the second word in the common DEI initialism, points to the power structures that have led to the current lack of diversity within institutions and collections. A task force at the University of Washington Libraries specifies that equity requires that "structures of systemic racism and classism [are] mitigated to maximize fairness to those who have been historically marginalized."[2] When considering library collections, equity could pertain to the subject matter of library materials, that is, having works that address discriminatory social structures, and it could also mean being aware of the structures that have kept library collections from being more diverse.

The third part of DEI, inclusion, has been interpreted in different ways. Susan Iverson, in her study of diversity action plans at U.S. flagship universities, sees the term "inclusion" as potentially problematic, as it implies "including (adding) others to the existing (or dominant) cultural project."[3] Similar to the word "diversity," it can mean addition without real change. This is certainly a danger at academic libraries, which usually contain many older works by white men. The purchase of newer books by more diverse authors will not significantly change a collection that has been built over decades. The University of Washington Libraries task force offers a definition that is more transformative, describing inclusion as relating to input from stakeholders and to shared power. In terms of collections, that could mean finding ways to allow people from marginalized groups to offer input into selection, even if these people are not on your staff, or it might mean acquiring materials that would not be discovered using your usual selection methods due to their format, type of publisher, or country of origin.

When taken together, DEI can describe an intention to make real changes. The three terms are sometimes implied even when the word "diversity" is used alone. In higher education at large, Iverson notes that "diversity action plans" commonly include dedication to equity and inclusion as well. At its best, the word "diversity" functions as shorthand for diversity, equity, and inclusion, and that is how it should be understood here.

WHY DIVERSITY MATTERS

In the past few decades, library employees have increasingly been thinking about DEI from a variety of angles: who we hire, how we serve our patrons, and what materials we acquire. While strategies for achieving diversity goals are still being developed, in a sense the goals themselves are an extension of the long-standing values of the profession. Most librarians are familiar with S. R. Ranganathan's laws of library science, originally published in 1931, which include as their second precept "every reader his book." In a 1957 article, Ranganathan expanded on this law to note the need for books for the blind, illustrated books for those with low literacy, "speaking-books" for patrons with intellectual disabilities, and materials for working-class artisans.[4] Though the specific types of patrons that Ranganathan describes are not always found in universities, the values he is known for infuse the library profession as a whole. The American Library Association's (ALA) Library Bill of Rights offers a similar set of values, intended to apply to all libraries. The document begins with the assertion that "books and other library resources should be provided for the interest, information, and enlightenment of all people of the community the library serves."[5]

While Ranganathan was focused mostly on the format of books and to some extent the subject matter (he notes an obligation to serve "the stray specialist in any subject"), today's concept of serving all patrons has expanded to mean reflecting diverse identities. A 2006 Interpretation of the Library Bill of Rights states, "[a] diverse collection should contain content by and about a wide array of people and cultures," particularly "content created by and representative of marginalized and underrepresented groups."[6] The guidance adds to, rather than supersedes, Ranganathan's directives, as it also mentions diversity of formats and attention to patrons with disabilities.

As DEI is central to libraries' traditional goals of serving all patrons, its importance to collections may seem obvious. Reasons for building diverse collections are multiple, however, and are worth enumerating, as different reasons may be most salient for different libraries and situations. Your motivation for building a diverse collection can also influence which traits you will attempt to measure. Some rationales for diversifying collections have the goal of teaching white, able-bodied, non-immigrant students about people different from them, while others are more geared toward allowing students of a range of races, orientations, and abilities to see themselves reflected. Both of these goals matter, but it can be offensive to treat a diverse collection as existing primarily for those in the dominant group. Among children's librarians, diversity in collections is often understood with reference to Rudine Sims Bishop's metaphor of "mirrors, windows, and sliding glass doors."[7] Books can serve these roles for college students as well, allowing readers to see a reflection of their own lives, learn more about others' lives, and step through a "door" to enter someone else's world temporarily. Though Bishop's life's work was the study of children's literature, her metaphor provides a useful reminder that diverse works serve both the people who are represented in them and those who are not.

At university libraries, one of the most common goals of building a diverse and inclusive collection is supporting the curriculum. Many universities include in their undergraduate requirements coursework related to different cultures, and the library should have materials to support these classes. Area studies programs or interdisciplinary programs such as disability studies also need library resources. Universities can have a range of reasons for offering these courses and programs, from the belief that exposure to other cultures can make students more employable and competitive to a desire to educate students about inequalities that they might later work to diminish. These different rationales could affect which courses are offered and therefore which materials the library would provide as curricular support. An assessment related to the curriculum would likely focus on the traits that are mentioned in course or program descriptions. It could also include analysis of intersectional identities within the population in question, for instance asking whether the Latin American Studies collection includes works on LGBTQ people.

Reasons for building an inclusive library collection go beyond supporting coursework. Improving the library's holdings can be a way to enhance a sense of belonging by allowing the diverse student body to see itself reflected in the collection. A common criticism of institutional diversity efforts is their focus on recruitment rather than on improving the climate for students who are already enrolled. Laying the foundation for a sense of belonging can affect retention rates and therefore benefit the university, but there is also an inherent good in making students feel comfortable and valued. A goal of enhancing belonging could lead to a broad review of the variety of identity characteristics that could be in the collection, ranging from the oft-studied race to less commonly studied traits such as immigration or disability status. You may choose to measure representation of identities that are especially prevalent among your students. For instance, a Hispanic Serving Institution would want to see if the books in its collection were by or about various Hispanic peoples and might also be interested in immigration.

Another goal of introducing diversity within a university is to prepare students to participate in society. This goal can have an international focus, which the library could support by assessing where different books and journals in the library were published and purchasing more materials from other countries. In their chapter about the discourses of diversity in higher education, Leah Hakkola and Rebecca Ropers-Huilman describe the "internationalization discourse" as preparing students for work in a globalized world.[8] They note as limitations to this discourse that it can overlook the need to acknowledge diversity within one's own country and ignore issues of inequality. A broader view of diversity that is still focused on participation in society is the "pluralistic democratic education discourse." This model, as described by Hakkola and Ropers-Huilman, considers both internationalism and diversity within the country and has a goal of promoting democracy and justice rather than business interests. Such a goal could be especially relevant to schools that are more homogeneous, where the library and the institution may want to offer opportunities to learn about other cultures that the institution's demographics don't facilitate. In addition, some academic programs are designed to prepare students for service professions, where knowledge of the experiences of populations they serve can be key. While doing diversity with the goal of preparing students to participate in society could lead to treating diverse collections as a resource for students from dominant groups to improve their employment prospects, the pluralistic democratic education discourse can also be conceptualized as a way to educate about power structures in hopes of promoting change.

BARRIERS TO BUILDING DIVERSE COLLECTIONS

Despite these motivations for building diverse collections and the call from ALA to do so, there are many structural and societal barriers that impede collections diversity. The whiteness of the publishing world means that many traditional methods of collecting will by default build collections that underrepresent people of color. Penguin Random House (PRH) recently published a report on their own progress toward DEI and found the publishing industry in the United States was 76.4 percent white, despite white people making up only

60 percent of the U.S. population.[9] The authors whose work PRH published between 2019 and 2021 were 74.86 percent white. Lee & Low, an independent publisher of multicultural children's books, began surveying publishing houses in 2015 and has repeated their study every four years. Most recently in 2023, their Diversity Baseline Survey found the industry overall to be 72.5 percent white, 68.7 percent straight, and 83.5 percent nondisabled. Editorial departments, which decide which books to publish, were 71.6 percent white.[10]

In addition to lack of diversity among those who determine what books are published, librarians' methods for identifying and purchasing books can also influence the homogeneity of the collection. Many libraries rely on large-scale selection processes such as approval plans, which rely on a vendor to track what is being published and compare newly published books to criteria set by the library. Vendors do not track every smaller publisher and may not handle books that are not in English. Another common purchase and selection strategy is demand-driven acquisitions (DDA), which involves loading records for ebooks into the catalog prior to purchasing them and then making a purchase after patrons have accessed the book a certain number of times. While appealing to libraries for financial reasons, DDA can exacerbate the problem of representation by privileging books that will appeal to large numbers of people. In a DDA program, titles with a focus on minority populations could see less demand and therefore be less likely to trigger a purchase.

Firm ordering, the most straightforward selection method, in which librarians choose specific titles to purchase, can allow for more attention to diversity. These purchases are not fully inclusive, however, according to the way the term was defined above, as involving input from stakeholders or from the people whose identities you want represented in your collection. The most recent demographic survey conducted by ALA in 2012 reported that 86.1 percent of credentialed librarians in higher education were white.[11] Just under 4 percent had a disability, though it is not clear which disabilities the survey counted. Of course, white librarians can and should buy books about non-white people, and able-bodied librarians can and should buy books about disabled people, but selectors may still unintentionally center their own identities. Even those who attempt to be inclusive may not be doing as much as they perceive they are, and assessment can help keep librarians' efforts on track.

WHY ASSESSMENT MATTERS

While there are many reasons for attempting to build diverse collections, the value of assessing collections for diversity may be less evident. Amanda Rybin Koob and colleagues at the University of Colorado Boulder offer as one of multiple reasons for not assessing their collections for diversity, "It was clear to us that our collections were dominated by white voices and perspectives. How could they be otherwise?"[12] The same could likely be said of any predominantly white institution. It could certainly be argued that assessment does not need to be the first step in a project to improve the equity of one's collection.

It can be useful, however, to include assessment as a piece of your library's DEI efforts for several reasons. One argument is that simply knowing something is being measured naturally causes you to pay attention to it and makes you more likely to try to improve. Annabelle Mortensen makes a comparison to the way fitness trackers encourage people to be more active.[13] An additional reason to rely on data is to avoid overestimating the effects of your diversification projects. The natural tendency of people to overestimate the numbers of minoritized people present in communities and in memories of situations is likely to play a role in collection-building as well. A recent series of experiments by Rasha Kardosh and colleagues asked Israelis and Americans to estimate the percentage of people in a given setting (a memory, a matrix of headshots, or a photo of a realistic scene such as a subway station) who were from a minority group in their country. Participants overestimated the prevalence of the minority group, whether the observer belonged to that group or to the majority. The authors explain that humans naturally notice what is uncommon, and a minority in any society is by definition less common.[14] Though the implications of this tendency for collection development have not been studied, it is easy to imagine a selector who believes that she is frequently buying books about various underrepresented populations when in fact these purchases make up a small percentage of the total. Alternately, you may be doing well at buying books about non-white people, but there may be a particular group of people of color missing from your collection. Assessment can counteract this tendency to overestimate the presence of what is less common by replacing that estimate with a measurement.

Assessment can serve as a prompt to do better. In Sara Ahmed's study of diversity officers in higher education, she found that "being shown to have done badly has more value than being shown to have done well," as such findings motivate action.[15] Even if you have an intuitive sense that your collection is not very diverse, or you have heard as much from students, having a measure of how homogeneous the collection is can increase the drive to do better.

In libraries where hand-picked titles make up only a small percentage of purchases, there would naturally be a discrepancy between how much effort librarians feel they are pulling into surfacing non-dominant voices and how well these voices are actually represented in the collection. If your library primarily relies on approval plans or ebook packages, then even if you add BIPOC-owned publishers to your approval plan, purchase DEI-related ebook packages, and place firm orders that support your DEI goals (all good steps!), the majority of your purchases are still not being reviewed for representation and inclusivity. An assessment project therefore gives the library staff the chance to learn how their main selection methods are performing with regard to DEI and to make adjustments where necessary.

HOW TO USE AN ASSESSMENT

An academic library may decide to conduct a collection assessment project for a variety of purposes. In the case of assessment for diversity and inclusion, a common goal is simply to establish a baseline. While librarians may be familiar with their own collection in certain ways, if thinking about the collection in terms of representation is a new focus, it is good to take a deeper look into the strengths and weaknesses. As noted above, perceptions are likely to be off when it comes to the presence of minority identities, and data can provide a more accurate picture. The findings of an audit could help you figure out where your collection is weakest, thus indicating where to place your initial focus. Identifying gaps can also help subject librarians, collection managers, or administrators set new goals, whether these goals pertain to acquiring particular books, earmarking spending, or identifying new selection strategies.

Data from an assessment often functions as a communication tool. Any findings showing areas of relative strength can demonstrate support for research and curricular needs, for instance if you are trying to help an area studies program apply for reaccreditation. Demonstrated areas of weaknesses provide justification for reallocating the existing budget or can help make the case for more money.

Lastly, if your library already has some DEI collections projects underway, an audit could be a way of seeing if your efforts have made a difference. The findings could affirm to selectors that their efforts are having a positive effect, help make the case that more work is needed, or guide further adjustments to your selection strategies. Assessment does not imply that there is an endpoint at which a collection will be fully diversified and the work will be done. On the contrary, the work will never be done. Assessment can help keep that work on track while also recognizing improvements to the collection.

WHAT'S IN THIS BOOK

This book is written for academic librarians who are interested in assessing their collections for any of the reasons noted above. You might be a collections strategist who is trying to decide where to start in developing DEI-focused collection projects, or a subject librarian wanting to learn more about your library's holdings in your disciplinary areas. Because the book deals with concepts such as how to determine the scope of an assessment and create an operational definition of diversity, the methods described are adaptable to a variety of DEI assessment projects.

The methods presented here differ from those typically presented in works on collection assessment that do not have a DEI focus, and therefore the organization of this book is specific to DEI assessment as well. Traditionally, collection assessment has been classified as either collection-focused or user-focused. Peggy Johnson's classic book *Fundamentals of Collection Development and Management* provides a two-by-two matrix with columns designating if the assessment method is use-based or collection-based and rows designating quantitative and qualitative methods.[16] The methods in this book would all belong in the "collection-based" column. This book does not include any user-focused assessment methods, as creating a more equitable collection may involve deliberately buying niche works that may not be heavily used. It is of course important to listen to the populations that you want your collection to represent, and this will be discussed in the final chapter, on strategies for moving forward. When a population is small within your university, however, looking at usage statistics is not the best way to listen to its members, as their low numbers mean their interests may not be reflected in usage statistics.

Another tool this book deliberately eschews is benchmarking one's own library in comparison to others. There won't necessarily be a peer group whose collection is inclusive at an ideal level, and any comparison of your own library to others influenced by the same trends in publishing and librarianship won't necessarily be useful. Furthermore, benchmarking could lead to a conclusion that your collection is "diverse enough," which is not a useful conclusion and not necessarily true. A positive finding in comparison to other libraries only means you're outperforming your peers. Rather than comparing your library to peers, it is more likely you'll be identifying areas of weakness or areas where you see improvement within your own collection. Given the lack of an ideal collection to use for comparison, a diversity audit is more likely to be about discovery or measuring progress than meeting a goal.

This book begins with a discussion of questions you should ask before undertaking a project, such as how you will define diversity, which parts of the collection you will assess, and what the goals of your assessment are. Subsequent chapters introduce specific approaches to understanding and measuring the diversity of your collections. Before getting into the specifics of any methods, this book will discuss three lenses, or facets, of collections: subject matter, authorship, and institutional efforts.

The first two lenses are commonly discussed in library diversity assessments. Studies of collections diversity frequently raise the question of whether the goal is to ensure the collection contains works *about* various underrepresented groups or the actual *voices of members* of those groups. Of course, some books are both about and written by a member of a particular population. Whether or not you are concerned with subject matter or authorship will affect which method you use. Chapter 3 briefly introduces three methods—list-checking, metadata searching, and diversity coding—and discusses which of these can be used to study subject matter and which allow for studying authorship. That chapter will present shortcomings of each method, from challenges of the process to limitations in how well each method can capture the identities you are interested in. Each method has advantages as well, despite being imperfect, and can give a greater understanding of your collection.

The third lens this book presents for assessing the diversity of a collection is institutional efforts. Given the shortcomings of any method of measuring the contents of a collection, and the likelihood that no library's collections are as equitable as they ought to be, some people prefer to measure inputs rather than outputs. Examples of inputs could be putting in the work to identify a new vendor, finding minority-owned publishers, or creating a fund designated for a diversity-related acquisitions project. This lens does not have a specific method associated with it, as the inputs can vary greatly. The chapter on this final lens will thus focus more on identifying possible metrics related to staff development, policies, and processes, with suggestions of how to measure progress on different actions.

Chapters detailing specific methods will be followed by spotlight chapters by guest authors, each describing a DEI assessment project or several projects they have conducted at their own library. A concluding chapter proposes next steps for using findings from a DEI assessment to inform collection build-ing and resource promotion. By the end of the book you should feel ready to implement your own project, including choosing a scope and an approach, and finding or creating the tools you'll use to evaluate your collection.

WHAT'S NOT IN THIS BOOK

There are several important pieces of equitable and inclusive collections-building that this book does not cover. Most notably, it does not discuss acces-sibility, which is sometimes included as a fourth letter in the growing initialism DEIA. While important as an aspect of inclusion, accessibility is more about the format and presentation of materials, whereas this book focuses on content and authorship of works.

Another important piece of diversity and inclusion outside this book's scope is whether materials in the collection constitute good representation of minoritized groups. Good representation requires accuracy and not reli-ance on stereotypes or overused tropes. Evaluating this aspect of DEI requires fairly extensive knowledge of the work itself and can be subjective. Most of the methods in this book would not involve looking at individual works closely enough to make a judgment call. Quality representation is nevertheless an important issue to keep in mind when collecting new works or weeding.

There are some topics this book does not cover which a more general collection assessment would cover. Most DEI assessments focus on books rather than journals, as the authorship and subject matter within each journal varies from year to year. It is worth keeping in mind that efforts to diversify a collection may involve adding subscriptions to journals that have an explicit focus on a certain racial or ethnic group, geographic area, LGBTQ identity, or other topics.

As noted earlier, this book does not include methods for analyzing the usage of your collection and has only minimal mention of comparison to peers. Both of these methods rely on and validate existing structures of dominance. Relatedly, the book does not discuss weeding, as this is typically done with a heavy emphasis on circulation data. Weeding with a DEI focus would not rely on circulation but rather would consider the quality of representation as well as whether the library's mission involves retaining potentially offensive books in order to preserve the scholarly record.

This book will also not describe any assessment software except in one of the guest chapters, as the vast majority of diversity assessments described in the literature do not rely on any special software. Lastly, it focuses on general collections rather than archives or special collections.

While there are pieces of the collection and aspects of inclusion that are not addressed by the methods here, and while the methods have their limitations, nevertheless this book should give you a place to start. A diversity audit will never be able to give a complete picture of the contents of a collection, and in fact the desire to get such a picture could hold you back from beginning a project. With the guidance in this book, you should be able to choose one or more methods to review your collection and begin the process of understanding your current collecting practices with regard to DEI.

NOTES

1. Sara Ahmed, *On Being Included: Racism and Diversity in Institutional Life* (Durham, NC: Duke University Press, 2012), 69.
2. Moriah Caruso, Faye Christenberry, Anne Davis, Leslie Gascon, Judith A. N. Henchy, Claire Kenny, Sarah Schroeder, Zhijia Shen, and Madison Sullivan, *UW Libraries Task Force on Diversity, Equity, Inclusion, and Anti-racism in Collections Final Report* (The University of Washington Libraries, 2022), 31, https://digital.lib.washington.edu/researchworks/handle/1773/49181.
3. Susan V. Iverson, "Troubling Diversity: An Intersectional Analysis of Diversity Action Plans at U.S. Flagship Universities," in *Intersectionality and Higher Education: Identity and Inequality on College Campuses*, ed. W. Carson Byrd, Rachelle J. Brunn-Bevel, and Sarah M. Ovink (New Brunswick, NJ: Rutgers University Press, 2019), 250.
4. S. R. Ranganathan, "Library Science and Scientific Method," *Annals of Library and Information Studies* 4, no. 1 (1957): 19–32.
5. American Library Association, "Library Bill of Rights. Advocacy, Legislation & Issues," June 30, 2006b, https://www.ala.org/advocacy/intfreedom/librarybill.
6. American Library Association, "Diverse Collections: An Interpretation of the Library Bill of Rights. Advocacy, Legislation & Issues," July 26, 2006a, https://www.ala.org/advocacy/intfreedom/librarybill/interpretations/diversecollections.

7. Jonda C. McNair and Patricia A. Edwards, "The Lasting Legacy of Rudine Sims Bishop: Mirrors, Windows, Sliding Glass Doors, and More," *Literary Research: Theory, Method, and Practice* 70, no. 1 (2012): 202–212.

8. Leah Hakkola and Rebecca Ropers-Huilman, "A Critical Exploration of Diversity Discourses in Higher Education: A Focus on Diversity in Student Affairs and Admissions," in *Higher Education: Handbook of Theory and Research*, ed. Michael B. Paulsen (Cham: Springer, 2018), 417–468.

9. Penguin Random House, "Diversity, Equity, & Inclusion U.S. Report," 2022-2023, https://randomhouse.app.box.com/s/gu32fxcyozvdmdz0ryohb2fck8gvolkv.

10. Lee & Low Books, "Where is the Diversity in Publishing? The 2023 Diversity Baseline Survey Results," 2024, https://blog.leeandlow.com/2024/02/28/2023diversitybaselinesurvey/.

11. American Library Association, "Diversity Counts 2012 Tables," 2012, https://www.ala.org/aboutala/sites/ala.org.aboutala/files/content/diversity/diversitycounts/diversitycountstables2012.pdf.

12. Amanda Rybin Koob, Arthur Aguilera, Frederick C. Carey, Xiang Li, Natalia Tingle Dolan, and Alexander Watkins, "Beyond the Diversity Audit: Uncovering Whiteness in Our Collections," in *Antiracist Library and Information Science: Racial Justice and Community*, ed. Kimberly Black and Bharat Mehra (West Yorkshire: Emerald Publishing, 2023), 69.

13. Annabelle Mortensen, "Measuring Diversity in the Collection," *Library Journal* 144, no. 4 (2019): 28–30.

14. Rasha Kardosh, Asael Y. Sklar, Alon Goldstein, Yoni Pertzov, and Ran R. Hassin, "Minority Salience and the Overestimation of Individuals from Minority Groups in Perception and Memory," *Proceedings of the National Academy of Sciences* 119, no. 12 (2022): e2116884119.

15. Ahmed, *On Being Included*, 103.

16. Peggy Johnson, *Fundamentals of Collection Development and Management* (Chicago, IL: ALA Editions, 2018), 289.

2

Defining Diversity

One of the first steps in planning an assessment for diversity, equity, and inclusion (DEI) is thinking about what types of diversity you want to measure. This chapter presents considerations for developing a general definition of diversity in library collections and a working definition specific to your project and its scope.

Several people in the library field have noted the lack of a clear definition of diversity in library collections.[1] David Macaulay, who studied strategic plans of members of the Association of Research Libraries, found that "the authors of these documents are not always drawing on a well-defined understanding of what collection diversification might involve" and often reference a "vaguely defined diverse community."[2] Ithaka S+R's guide *Leading by Diversifying Collections* notes that "a major barrier to developing these strategies [for DEI in collections] is the lack of definitional consensus around what DEI collections building entails."[3] While you do not need to have a definition of diversity written into your library's collection development policy in order to conduct an assessment, you will benefit from creating a definition that can apply to the project.

The broad definitions of diversity offered by library organizations offer a starting point. Macaulay describes how the American Library Association's Interpretation of the Library Bill of Rights describes diversity in collections in a way that "reflects a concern for the effects of structural inequality."[4] This focus is a shift for ALA. Macaulay writes, "Adding specificity to previous commitments to universality of service, this relatively new emphasis on equity moves beyond general professions of neutrality and all-inclusiveness."[5] Ithaka S+R's guide similarly states its focus as "the diversity that comes from building opportunities for equity and inclusion for historically marginalized groups."[6] These definitions of diversity are in line with the intention set in the previous chapter, that diversity should not simply mean difference but should involve special attention to groups that have been excluded.

While Ithaka S+R and the ALA provide broad guidance, the definition of diversity at an individual library or for a particular assessment project should be more specific. Andrea Jamison, who has studied mentions of diversity in collection development policies, advocates naming exactly which groups your diversity efforts will target, as "specificity in policies can serve as a compass to help librarians select books that represent specific populations that have been impacted the most by diversity inequities."[7]

DOMINANT AND NONDOMINANT GROUPS

Though most people have an intuitive sense of which groups in their own society are dominant, conversations about privilege do not always consider the wide range of ways in which people can be marginalized. In her book *Promoting Diversity and Social Justice*, Diane Goodman lists axes of oppression such as race, gender, sexuality, disability, class, age, and religion. She mentions other forms of oppression that exist as well, such as fatphobia.[8] Marginalization can also occur based on immigration status, language, or other traits.

Marginalized or nondominant groups are not necessarily those in the minority in a given setting. For instance, more than half of undergraduates in the United States are female, yet women are still not the privileged group.[9] Sociologists sometimes use the term "minority" to mean a nondominant group, regardless of numbers.[10] This work will avoid that usage, since there are a variety of less ambiguous terms available, such as marginalized, nondominant, or underrepresented, all of which draw attention to the social status of various groups.

Some of what you define as your nondominant groups will depend on context. Morgan Harrington, reviewing the collection of the National Library of Australia for its representation of culturally and linguistically diverse Australians, mentions conducting catalog searches for books about Scottish, Italian, and Polish people, none of whom have been the target of any known diversity assessment in the United States.[11] At the individual book level, books published in countries other than your own, particularly in other languages, may broaden the range of your library's collection but be widely held in the country in which they originated. Such books, and the languages they are written in, would represent nondominant groups in your own setting even if they reflect the dominant group elsewhere.

The ability to clearly name certain aspects of identity as dominant does not mean that people are easily categorized as privileged or marginalized. All people have multiple aspects of their identities, which often contain a mix of dominant and marginalized traits. Furthermore, the boundaries of groups can change, with a prominent example being the ways different ethnic groups have come to be considered white over time. To assess the diversity of your collection, however, you will need to assign people or books to categories, despite the categories being simplistic and specific to the current era. Some of the complexities of this task are discussed in chapter 8.

LABELING BOOKS AS DIVERSE

When talking about books that represent nondominant identities, it is easy to find yourself referring to these books as diverse. While diversity within a collection is the end goal of DEI assessment, opinions differ on whether it makes sense to label individual books as "diverse." Some people talk about diverse books as a type of book, that is, those by or about underrepresented groups, while others use the term "diverse" to describe the range of a collection. Using the most basic definition of diversity as simply variety, it would be nonsensical to call an individual book diverse unless it was a compilation of multiple writings by or about different life experiences. Some people whose definition of diversity prioritizes marginalized or nondominant social categories do classify specific books as diverse. E. E. Lawrence argues that despite the apparent illogic of considering diverse books to be a type of book, it is nevertheless useful to think this way. He writes, "Understanding these books as belonging to a unified class makes visible the ways in which varied inequities arc in some important sense related."[12]

Kelsey Bogan, a high school librarian who has blogged and presented about the diversity audit she conducted, has a contrasting view. She notes that labeling certain books as diverse can be othering and actually centers dominant traits, the opposite of the goal of a diversity assessment. She also sees the term "diverse" used "as coded language" when the speaker actually means something more specific that they are for some reason avoiding saying, such as non-white or non-heterosexual.[13]

This book will not refer to specific books as diverse or to diverse books as a class of book, for the reasons Bogan gives as well as the contradiction between the traditional definition of the term and its application to individual works. It will instead discuss diverse *collections* or refer more precisely to the traits that are being measured by an assessment project, such as books about LGBTQ people or people of color. Lawrence's point stands, however, that certain books are disadvantaged when it comes to their likelihood of being published and then purchased for libraries. It is useful to be aware that when a library doesn't own books about a certain population, this is probably part of a pattern and not solely due to the library's inability to own everything.

CHOOSING TRAITS TO ANALYZE

Though the concept of DEI can encompass many marginalized groups, an assessment can only consider a few without becoming too cumbersome. By far the most common aspect of identity measured in library diversity assessments is race, followed by gender and sexuality. Though specific studies often do not explain why they chose to focus on race, doing so makes intuitive sense given the significant ways race influences American life. Though racial categories are widely accepted to be socially constructed, the ways this construct affects people's lives are real.[14] In 1978, sociologist William Julius Wilson wrote a controversial book called *The Declining Significance of Race*, in which he argued that due to the economic opportunities available to African Americans after World War II, "economic class gradually become more important than race in determining the life chances of individual African Americans."[15] In a follow-up article in 2011, however, Wilson moderated his view to explain that although economic opportunities for Black people in the United States have increased, there are many legacies of past inequality that continue to affect Americans in ways that correlate with race. He mentions differing amounts of family wealth or parental education as conditions that disproportionately negatively affect Black people.[16] Others hold stronger views on the significance of race in the United States. Critical race theory, a school of thought founded in 1980 and still active today, holds that "race is a central structure in society . . . racial inequality permeates every aspect of social life."[17]

In addition to using the social significance of race as a central assumption of an assessment project, another frequent occurrence is that assessment projects are driven by the librarian's organizational role. If you are the Latin American Studies librarian and the person initiating the assessment, counting the number of books your library has related to Latin American Studies would be an obvious goal. At first you might not think about defining dominant groups and choosing which traits to study. However, even for an area studies assessment there are various forms of marginalization you could investigate. You might choose to look at your collection's representation of different ethnicities within Latin America, such as various indigenous peoples or people of African descent. Another approach would be to look at the intersection of Latin American identity with other traits, such as LGBTQ or disability.

If you know from the start which disciplinary area you want to assess, the nature of the discipline might suggest which traits are most important. David Alexander, who works with the Native American Studies program at the University of South Dakota, explained the field, which was previously called American Indian Studies (AIS) as one that "specifically studies American Indians from a perspective that originates inside Indian cultures . . . it is the endogenous perspective that separates AIS from more traditional academic disciplines such as history, religion, politics, sociology, and ethnology."[18] Though Alexander's article is not about an assessment project, the clear takeaway from it is that any assessment of a Native American Studies collection would have the authors' Native American heritage or tribal affiliations as its most important criterion.

Often the curriculum or student needs drive a diversity assessment. A social work program or a psychology department might include courses on children and adolescents or on aging, so someone assessing the collections that support these programs might do an analysis of the ages covered in the library's holdings. Scott Stone, at the University of California Irvine, noticed frequent student requests for plays written by women, LGBTQ people, or African Americans. The assessment inspired by these requests therefore tracked the gender, sexuality, ethnicity, and nationality of playwrights included in the collection.[19]

Many diversity assessments stem from a general sense that the library ought to be doing more to build equitable collections. If this is your situation, you'll need to articulate a clearer motivation before designing your study. If you decide that your primary concern is supporting the curriculum, you could look at what courses are offered and what populations are mentioned in course descriptions and learning objectives. On the other hand, if your main motivation is to enhance a sense of belonging among your students by allowing them to see themselves reflected in the collection, you might start by looking at the demographics of your own institution and structuring your assessment around the traits that your institution tracks.

As you learn more about the methods for evaluating your collection for DEI, you will see whether the method you choose allows you to consider many different races, sexualities, and disabilities or whether you will need to pick one or two. For instance, you might investigate the race or ethnicity of every author in a set of books or solely quantify the size of your collection related to African Americans. Though identifying which aspects of diversity are of interest and choosing an evaluation method are described in separate chapters in this book, these decisions are interrelated.

In addition to analyzing the diversity of content or authors, you may want to include some variables that will help you make changes to your acquisitions processes. Looking at whether books by and about underrepresented groups tend to have independent publishers rather than major academic publishers can help you make changes to your purchases so that you can acquire more of these books. If you have information on whether specific books were acquired through an approval plan or a firm order, this can also help you think about modifying your purchasing.

SETTING TARGET VALUES

Once you know whether you want your assessment to cover race, sexuality, or other traits, you may start to ask what numbers you are aiming for. While it is usually a good idea to have goals, this does not always make sense for a diversity assessment. As noted previously, comparison to your peers might show you are doing similarly in terms of DEI, but it may be that you and your peers all want to do better. One comparison that sometimes makes sense is to the demographics of your own institution. Many diversity assessments compare the prevalence in the collection of books about or by members of a racial or ethnic group to the proportion of their student population that is part of that group. This can be helpful, particularly if you find that the discrepancy is larger for some groups than others.

Comparing the demographics of your collection to the student body may not make sense if your enrollment is not very diverse, or if your goal is to teach your students about people different from themselves. In this case census data might be a reasonable substitute for enrollment data. Data about nationwide college student demographics can also serve as a benchmark. A report from EBSCO provides some statistics compiled from a variety of sources over the last decade, sharing that 21.5 percent of college students identified as non-heterosexual, 2.9 percent identified as Jewish, and 19 percent had a disability.[20]

In some situations, your collection goals might go beyond any demographics that you could compare them to. Using some of the examples above, if you were building a collection to support Native American Studies, you would want as many of the books as possible to be written by Indigenous American authors, regardless of the size of this population at your institution or within the country. If your students are asking for playscripts by African Americans, you would also probably seek to have African Americans represented in your play collection beyond the percentage of your students with this identity. When deciding if you have target numbers for representation, ask what makes sense given your motivations for doing the study and the population you serve. It is okay if you end up without a measurable target. The assessment can still help you learn about and improve your collection.

CHOOSING BETWEEN CONTENT, AUTHORSHIP, OR BOTH

You may have noticed that some of the scenarios mentioned so far involve investigating how many books are *about* a given population, whereas others consist of looking for books *by members* of a particular group. Which lens you choose will be intertwined with your choice of methods, as not every method allows you to analyze author identities. In some cases it will be clear which lens is most relevant to your assessment and in other cases you will need to decide.

There are several rationales for considering a book's content. A project structured around curriculum goals would probably evaluate the subject matter of books. A study motivated by students' sense of belonging could be concerned with subject matter as well, as books about people who share their identity traits could contribute to students seeing themselves reflected in the collection. The fact that students are more likely to notice if there are books about people like themselves than they are to pay attention to authors is also an argument for assessing subject matter.

The reasons for considering authorial identity are various and complicated. Some theorize that membership in a marginalized group inherently affects the perspective an author brings to their work. Critical race theory contends that "because of their different histories and experiences with oppression, Black, Native American, Asian, and Latino writers and thinkers may be able to communicate to their white counterparts matters that the whites are unlikely to know."[21] This could be true even if a book is not explicitly about race, as race is associated with differential health outcomes, interactions with the legal system, poverty or wealth, and understanding of history. One could therefore argue that the voices of people with diverse backgrounds are necessary for creating a library collection that provides a variety of angles for understanding the world.

Author identities are especially important if your assessment project focuses on the portion of your collection that is about a particular group. In other words, if you are evaluating the African American studies collection, you would be especially likely to want to know if the authors were African American. In seeking to build a decolonized collection of works on Pacific Island Studies, Rachel Blume and Allyson Roylance focus on what they call "authentic authorship . . . a term which refers to the correlation between author and subject area, and seeks to share views on history, culture, and experience through a genuine lens."[22]

Having authors from underrepresented groups does not guarantee that your collection will be full of accurate depictions of these groups. Writers are individuals with distinct experiences and combinations of traits. They may share certain aspects of identity with their subjects and not others, so that the risk of misrepresenting those different from them is still present, or they may write books that rely on stereotypes. The risk of misrepresentation is less, however, if your collection includes authors from underrepresented groups than if these authors were excluded.

Even in parts of the collection where the books are not explicitly about any underrepresented group, there are arguments that author identities matter and therefore are worth assessing. Quantifying the presence of authors from marginalized groups, and then deliberately growing this presence, can help counteract the barriers such authors face to publication. Another goal could be to show students that the library values the contributions of people who share important traits with them. You may lean more on some motivations for evaluating author identities than others, depending on what part of the collection you are evaluating and your reasons for doing the assessment.

A NOTE ON #OWNVOICES

Books whose authors share significant aspects of identity with the subjects of the book are sometimes, especially in young adult or children's literature, referred to with the hashtag #ownvoices. The hashtag was coined by young adult author Corinne Duyvis in 2015 as a way to aggregate book recommendations on Twitter and has since become popular in the publishing world.[23] Some people are moving away from the use of this shorthand, however, for a few reasons. One is that when the hashtag is used as a promotional tool, it puts pressure on authors to disclose aspects of their identities when they may not be comfortable doing so. This is less likely to be an issue for collection assessment, but respect for those who have felt this pressure is a reason not to use it.

Another criticism of #ownvoices has been its lack of specificity: an author may share some characteristics with the individuals in their book, whether it is fiction or nonfiction, without belonging to all the same groups. It is possible to use #ownvoices in a way that is more specific. Duyvis gives an example of phrasing that is clear, suggesting that one could say a book "features a Chinese-American trans girl—the trans aspect is #ownvoices!"[24] One can be equally clear without using the hashtag, however. The organization We Need Diverse Books, in their statement about why they have stopped using the hashtag, explains that they will continue to be specific about authors' identities, for instance sharing if a book has a Korean author or a trans author.[25] The move away from using #ownvoices is not due to discounting the value of seeking out sources in which marginalized people can speak about their own experiences and does not preclude noting when an author shares identity traits with the subject of a book. While supporting the inclusion of authors from nondominant groups, especially when these identities are the topic of the works being assessed, this book will avoid using the term #ownvoices.

ASPECTS OF DIVERSITY THAT ARE DIFFICULT TO MEASURE

Having books whose authors' identities align with the topic of the book does not guarantee a perfectly diverse, representative collection. There are several important aspects of DEI that are difficult to measure using the methods in this book. Thinking about these issues and keeping them in mind can help, as the assessment will probably leave you with a deeper knowledge of the collection than what is strictly measurable. The collection development strategies that you adopt or modify after conducting the evaluation can include awareness of issues of nuanced representation, using what you have learned from doing the assessment.

Quality of Representation

One consideration is the overall quality of representation. Lawrence observes an approach to diversity that he names *evaluative inclusionism*, which requires that the descriptions in a book meet some standard. One such standard is accuracy, and another might be that "a narrative must in some way depict a character's experiences as a member of the social group(s) to which they belong rather than merely announcing or implying social identifications."[26] The requirements of accuracy and meaningful portrayal of experiences, while important concerns, are subjective and cannot be evaluated without an in-depth knowledge of each book.

Variety of Stories

Even when a book portrays a group accurately and genuinely, there is a danger that a collection of works about that group could be skewed. Nigerian author Chimamanda Ngozi Adichie gave a TED Talk titled "The Danger of a Single Story," in which she talked about how the stories British and American people hear about Africa tend to always be those of poverty and tragedy. She says, "Of course, Africa is a continent full of catastrophes . . . But there are other stories that are not about catastrophe, and it is very important, it is just as important, to talk about them . . . to insist on only these negative stories is to flatten my experience and to overlook the many other stories that formed me."[27] Timothy Morton observed this exact phenomenon when assessing the University of Virginia's African Studies collection. "There is a perceptible bias toward both tragedy and American national interest in our collection. For instance, . . . most of our materials on Rwanda or Somalia are about the genocide and U.S. intervention in the Somali civil war, respectively. Those are important stories to tell, but at present they are being told to the exclusion of the rest of those countries' stories."[28] Other "single stories" that tend to occur are LGBTQ books always revolving around coming out, or Jewish books always being about the Holocaust. This might be something that you notice while looking at books for your assessment, but you probably cannot formally use the single story as a component of your assessment unless you have a narrow enough scope that you are able to look at each book closely.

Intersectionality

Another important aspect of diversity that most assessment methods don't measure is intersectionality. The theory of intersectionality, introduced by Kimberlé Crenshaw, explains that many people belong to multiple disadvantaged groups, and the discrimination they face cannot be understood as simply the sum of the discrimination each group faces. Using Black women as an example, Crenshaw explains that the gender discrimination they face is different from what white women face, and their experiences of racial discrimination differ from Black men's. Multiple axes of discrimination interact to affect Black women in a distinct way. Furthermore, when discrimination is analyzed along any single axis, this "erases Black women . . . by limiting inquiry to the experiences of otherwise-privileged members of the group."[29] In other words, a study of sexism alone will usually focus on white women, and a study of racism alone would focus on Black men. There is a danger that without explicit attention to the intersections of multiple marginalized identities, there would be no consideration of Black women.

Though Crenshaw's focus is on legal situations, applying her observations to library collections might mean that a gender studies collection would often be comprised mostly of books about white, straight women and an African American studies collection would mostly focus on straight men. Black lesbians, bisexual women, or nonbinary people would be nearly invisible.

To some extent it is possible to measure the presence of intersectional identities in a library collection by looking at multiple aspects of an author's identity or the combination of different subject terms and call numbers. Most diversity evaluation methods do not easily lend themselves to doing this, however. Furthermore, theorists of intersectionality point out that attempts to understand complex identities by breaking groups down into ever-narrower categories is always an inadequate approach. Any individual's identity is made up of more than a list of two or three demographic traits, and methods that simply count the number of books by or about people who share these traits is necessarily simplifying.[30] As tends to be the case with library assessments, measurement is imperfect but worth attempting when possible. This book will note when a method allows for intersectional analysis, most prominently in chapter 8 on diversity coding.

Once you have clarified your motivations for conducting a diversity assessment and thought about whether you are interested in race, gender, sexuality, or other traits, you will be in a better position to plan a project. This will involve setting a scope and choosing a method. Despite the structure of this book, the various planning aspects of assessment cannot be separated. Your method will influence what scope is feasible, and your motivations will influence what method you choose. The next chapters will discuss methods and scope.

NOTES

1. See Andrea Jamison, "What Does Diversity Mean?" *American Libraries*, May 3, 2021, https://americanlibrariesmagazine.org/?p=123233; David Macaulay, "Applications of Diversity Language to Descriptions of Collection Development Activities at Academic Libraries: An Exploratory Analysis of Strategic Plans and Diversity Information Webpages," *Journal of Academic Librarianship* 49, no. 4 (2023); Margaret Maguire, "From Concept to Practice: Themes of Diversity Within the Strategic Planning of Academic Libraries," Master's Paper, University of North Carolina at Chapel Hill, April 2020, https://cdr.lib.unc.edu/concern/masters_papers/s1784r89b.
2. Macaulay, "Applications of Diversity Language to Descriptions of Collection Development Activities at Academic Libraries," 8.
3. Kara Bledsoe, Danielle Miriam Cooper, Roger C. Schonfeld, and Oya Rieger, "Leading by Diversifying Collections," November 2022, https://sr.ithaka.org/publications/leading-by-diversifying-collections/.

4. Macaulay, "Applications of Diversity Language to Descriptions of Collection Development Activities at Academic Libraries," 2.

5. Macaulay, "Applications of Diversity Language to Descriptions of Collection Development Activities at Academic Libraries," 2.

6. Bledsoe et al., "Leading by Diversifying Collections."

7. Andrea Jamison, "The Diversity Stalemate: An Analysis of How the Collection Development Policies of Academic Libraries Address Diversity in Children's Books" (Library Assessment Conference, virtual 2020), 11, https://www.libraryassessment.org/wp-content/uploads/2021/08/237-Jamison-The-Diversity-Stalemate.pdf.

8. Diane Goodman, *Promoting Diversity and Social Justice: Educating People from Privileged Groups* (Thousand Oaks, CA: Sage Publications, 2001), 8.

9. National Center for Education Statistics, "Table 306.10., Total Fall Enrollment in Degree-Granting Postsecondary Institutions, by Level of Enrollment, Sex, Attendance Status, and Race/Ethnicity or Nonresident Status of Student: Selected Years, 1976 through 2021," *Digest of Education Statistics* (2022), https://nces.ed.gov/programs/digest/d22/tables/dt22_306.10.asp.

10. Tonja R. Conerly, Kathleen Holmes, and Asha Lal Tamang, *Introduction to Sociology*, Third edition (Houston, TX: OpenStax, 2021), section 11.1, https://openstax.org/details/books/introduction-sociology-3e.

11. Morgan Harrington, "Rethinking Diversity beyond Catalogue Representation: Lessons from Efforts to Develop a Methodology to Evaluate Diversity within the National Library of Australia," *Journal of the Australian Library and Information Association* 70, no. 1 (2021): 23–43.

12. E. E. Lawrence, "The Trouble with Diverse Books, Part II: An Informational Pragmatic Analysis," *Journal of Documentation* 77, no. 1 (2020): 182.

13. Kelsey Bogan, "Diversity Audit: Final Presentation," *Don't You Shush Me* (blog), December 16, 2020, https://dontyoushushme.com/2020/12/16/diversity-audit-final-presentation/.

14. For more discussion, see Richard Delgado and Jean Stefancic, *Critical Race Theory, Fourth Edition: An Introduction* (New York: NYU Press, 2023), 9. "People with common geographic origins may share certain physical traits, of course, such as skin color, physique, and hair texture. But these constitute only an extremely small portion of their genetic endowment, are dwarfed by what we have in common, and have little or nothing to do with distinctly human, higher-order traits, such as personality, intelligence, and moral behavior. . . . [S]ociety frequently chooses to ignore these scientific truths, creates races, and endows them with pseudo-permanent characteristics."

15. William Julius Wilson, "The Declining Significance of Race: Revisited & Revised," *Daedalus* 140, no. 2 (2011): 56, https://dash.harvard.edu/handle/1/8052151.

16. Wilson, "The Declining Significance of Race: Revisited & Revised."

17. Margaret Zamudio, Christopher Russell, Francisco Rios, and Jacquelyn L. Bridgeman, *Critical Race Theory Matters: Education and Ideology* (New York: Routledge, 2010), 3.

18. David L. Alexander, "American Indian Studies, Multiculturalism, and the Academic Library," *College & Research Libraries* 74, no. 1 (2013): 63.

19. Scott M. Stone, "Whose Play Scripts Are Being Published? A Diversity Audit of One Library's Collection in Conversation with the Broader Play Publishing World," *Collection Management* 45, no. 4 (2020): 304–320.
20. EBSCO, "DEI in Campus Libraries: Key Challenges and Opportunities," November 1, 2023, https://www.ebsco.com/resources/dei-campus-libraries-key-challenges-and-opportunities.
21. Delgado and Stefancic, *Critical Race Theory*, 11.
22. Rachel Blume and Allyson Roylance, "Decolonization in Collection Development: Developing an Authentic Authorship Workflow," *The Journal of Academic Librarianship* 46, no. 5 (2020): 102175.
23. Corinne Duyvis, "#OwnVoices," Corinne Duyvis, accessed January 16, 2024, https://www.corinneduyvis.net/ownvoices/.
24. Duyvis, "#OwnVoices."
25. We Need Diverse Books, "Why We Need Diverse Books Is No Longer Using the Term #OwnVoices," June 6, 2021, https://diversebooks.org/why-we-need-diverse-books-is-no-longer-using-the-term-ownvoices/.
26. E. E. Lawrence, "The Trouble with Diverse Books, Part I: On the Limits of Conceptual Analysis for Political Negotiation in Library & Information Science," *Journal of Documentation* 76, no. 6 (2020): 1482.
27. Chimamanda Ngozi Adichie, "The Danger of a Single Story," July 2009, TED Talks, video, 12:45–13:33, https://www.ted.com/talks/chimamanda_ngozi_adichie_the_danger_of_a_single_story.
28. Roxanne Marie Backowski and Timothy Ryan Morton, "Something to Talk About: the Intersection of Library Assessment and Collection Diversity," in *Proceedings of the Charleston Library Conference,* ed. Beth R. Bernhardt, Leah Hinds, and Lars Meyer (Lafeyette, IN: Purdue University Press, 2019), 175, https://docs.lib.purdue.edu/charleston/2019/collectiondevelopment/2/.
29. Kimberlé Crenshaw, "Demarginalizing the Intersection of Race And Sex: A Black Feminist Critique of Antidiscrimination Doctrine, Feminist Theory and Antiracist Politics," *University of Chicago Legal Forum* 139, no. 1 (1989): 140.
30. Leslie McCall, "The Complexity of Intersectionality," *Signs* 30, no. 3 (Spring 2005): 1771–1800.

3

Choosing an Approach

After thinking about how you want to define diversity and what your motivations are for assessing it, you will be in a good position to choose an appropriate method. This chapter provides an overview of four different assessment methods, noting advantages and disadvantages of each. These brief descriptions should help you choose which method(s) to use, while later chapters provide more detailed guidance on carrying out each type of assessment.

LENSES FOR VIEWING COLLECTION DIVERSITY

A major influence on your choice of method is whether you want to evaluate diversity in your collections through the lens of subject matter, author identities, or institutional efforts. An assessment can include more than one lens, especially if it also relies on multiple methods. Though previous chapters have already discussed these lenses to some extent, this chapter provides a review to help you prepare to choose a method. Table 3.1 summarizes the rationale for using each lens, as well as its limitations.

Assessing your collection through the lens of subject matter could be appealing for many reasons. Since your patrons will usually notice what a book is about before they learn about the person who wrote it, content can play more of a role than authorship in their perceptions of the collection. If your goal is to see how well the library can support courses about specific populations, the topics of books are in some cases more relevant than their authorship. Because library catalogs already contain metadata related to the subject of books, you can assess the collection relatively quickly, without having to make your own judgments of whether a book covers a topic extensively enough to count. There are methods that let you assess the entire collection by subject rather than needing to narrow your assessment to only a portion of the collection. The largest caveat with assessing subject matter is that you won't

Table 3.1 Lenses for Understanding Collection Diversity

Assessing Subject Matter

Reasons to Use This Lens	Limitations
As subject matter is visible to your patrons, whereas author identities may not be, it may be more significant in their experiences of the collection. Curricular needs relate to the content of books more often than to their authors. Assessment can be done using existing data. There are methods for reviewing the entire book collection.	A book may be about a particular population without necessarily providing positive or accurate representation.

Assessing Author Identities

Reasons to Use This Lens	Limitations
Identity can affect an author's perspective. Books by diverse authors let students see themselves reflected. If a collection is about a particular marginalized group, it should include the voices of members of the group. Assessment can spur librarians to seek out more works by authors from marginalized groups, who are often underrepresented due to the barriers they face to publication.	Collecting data is time-consuming, as it requires many sources outside the catalog. Personal information may be unavailable, particularly for authors of older books. Author identities can only be assessed through sampling. Identities can be flexible, changing, or exist outside common categories. Staff may feel uncomfortable assigning categories to authors.

Assessing Organizational Efforts

Reasons to Use This Lens	Limitations
Taking action to improve the collection may feel more urgent than assessing its current state. A focus on actions allows for a broader view of the work of your library, including all types of materials and all parts of the collections workflow. Institutional actions can help create a mindset of valuing DEI, which can infuse future work.	You won't necessarily learn about the content or your collection or the effects of your efforts.

Source: Author.

always know if the books about a population portray that group positively or accurately.

While author identities are less visible to your patrons, there are several reasons why they matter. The previous chapter mentioned the unique perspective that comes from being part of a marginalized group, the message you are sending to students about valuing the work of those who share aspects of their identities, the value that ethnic studies programs place on endogenous writing, and the ways that the publishing world disadvantages marginalized authors. Assessing author identities is complicated, however. As information about authors' demographic characteristics is not usually included in the catalog, finding this information requires additional searching, and the information is not always available, especially for authors of older works. Often projects to assess author identities limit themselves to recently published books for this reason. The need to research each author means that you can't assess the whole collection but would need to investigate either a sample or a small section. Classifying authors by identity is complicated, as categories of identity change over time, as do some aspects of individuals' identities. Difficulties can arise when someone's identity changes after their work is published, for instance coming out as gay or transgender, or when someone lived in an era in which identity categories were defined differently than they are today. Staff are not always comfortable assigning real people to categories, even when they are relying primarily on each person's self-description. There is also the question of what constitutes a reliable source of information on a person's identity, particularly if that information comes from a third party. Chapter 8 describes at greater length some ethical considerations related to analyzing authors' identities.

The third lens could be called institutional efforts, actions, or inputs. Some libraries that focus on assessing their own actions explicitly eschew assessing the collection, though assessing your collection does not mean you can't also assess your work in changing it. This lens could appeal if you want to start by taking action, as most libraries know before doing an assessment that there is room to improve the diversity of their collections. A focus on actions lets you reflect on all your library's activities that affect your users' experience of the collection and even those that affect the scholarly communications marketplace. A report from the University of Nevada Las Vegas (UNLV) states, "It is our collecting practices—the vendors, publishers, and selection methods we use [—] that enable or limit our ability to develop inclusive collections. Understanding how our current practices do, or do not facilitate our inclusive collecting goals will allow us to identify and implement necessary changes."[1] The efforts that you assess can involve changes to how your library selects books, purchases, catalogs, and creates displays. This lens can be tailored to your institution, as you will set goals based on what next steps seem most feasible and necessary. The downside of focusing entirely on your efforts is that you may miss out on being able to quantify the effect they have had on the collection.

Because this lens involves regularly setting goals and reflecting, it has the potential to influence the culture of the institution so that DEI is a constant consideration, which could then spur even more positive changes. The UNLV report recommends that selectors set individual goals and believes these "will facilitate forward momentum and advance a culture that prioritizes thoughtful collection development practices."[2]

METHODS

The lens you choose will influence your choice of assessment method but will not always dictate it. Multiple methods can be used for assessing subject matter, though only one method is appropriate for investigating author identities. There is no specific method associated with assessing organizational efforts, though there are some common approaches, which are described in more detail in chapter 10.

Another factor influencing your choice of method will be your motivations and goals for assessing diversity. Different methods will provide different types of information about your collection. For instance, if you are interested in how the diversity of your collection compares to the composition of your student body, you would want a method that will tell you what percentage of books in the collection are about or by members of various groups so you can compare that percentage to the demographics of your institution. If you are trying to see how well your collection supports a particular program, you may want to use list-checking, which lets you check for the presence of specific significant works.

Table 3.2 summarizes what is feasible using each assessment method. As with the lenses above, all methods have shortcomings but could also be useful. The table and this section are intended to not only help you choose but make you aware from the beginning of your project of what your chosen method can measure and what it cannot.

List-Checking

List-checking involves finding or creating a list of significant books and checking your library catalog to see how many of them you have. This method has also been called the checklist method, comparison to standard bibliographies, or a reverse audit.[3] The word "reverse" refers to the fact that rather than starting with your own collection and examining what is in it, this method starts with a list of books that it would be desirable to have.

The lists used for this method usually contain books about one or more marginalized groups, rather than works by members of those groups. In theory,

Table 3.2 Benefits and Limitations of Each Assessment Method

Method: List-checking

Applicable Lenses: Subject Matter

Benefits	*Limitations*
The process is simple. Lists can capture interdisciplinary topics that are hard to isolate using call numbers or subject terms. The list provides clear next steps for improving the collection.	It can be time-consuming to create a list. When generating a list based on awards, some disciplines are not well covered (sciences, business), nor some populations (disability, Native Americans). You can't use a list for evaluation if you've already been using it as a selection tool. Any lists you use will be small compared to the overall size of your collection and compared to the number of books you ought to have representing marginalized people. An emphasis on lists of recommended books can send a message of having a higher standard for acquiring books about marginalized people than about the dominant group. The results will not put the list in the context of your full collection and will not produce numbers you can compare to external targets, such as the composition of the student body or the census. The list will not help you identify titles to weed.

Method: Metadata Searching

Applicable Lens: Subject Matter

Benefits	*Limitations*
The results can be turned into a percentage, allowing for comparisons to the full collection and to other targets such as student population. You can evaluate the entire collection rather than a sample. Searches can be done relatively quickly. It is easy to repeat the searches annually once you have constructed them.	Searches usually need to focus on one or two populations. Books might not be positive or accurate portrayals. Topics or populations of interest are not always clearly described by existing metadata. Terminology used in the catalog could be outdated or offensive.

(Continued)

Method: Diversity Coding

Applicable Lenses: Subject Matter or Author Identity

Benefits	*Limitations*
Collecting data from external sources allows for more detail than is in the catalog. Creating codes offers the flexibility to define your own categories. The coding process can include many traits, such as race, gender, and sexuality. Projects often look at multiple population groups, i.e., multiple racial groups rather than one or two. Analysis can account for intersectionality. Inspection of books may help identify candidates for future weeding.	It is only feasible to code a small subset or sample of the collection. Seeking external sources of information is time-consuming. You will need to develop customized guidelines for staff doing the coding.

Method: Various

Applicable Lens: Organizational Efforts

Benefits	*Limitations*
The assessment process is flexible and can encompass whatever projects feel most important or achievable at your library. You can set goals based on what is possible for you to achieve. The process can help identify barriers to building a more inclusive collection. Assessment of your own work will be more accurate than assessments of subject matter or authorship of the collection.	May need to make a special effort to identify your library's shortcomings, as the assessment will not necessarily do this.

Source: Author.

you could use list-checking to assess author identities as well as subject matter by creating a bibliography of books whose authors were members of the same marginalized group. In practice, however, list-checking is rarely used to assess the collection through the lens of author identities. One of the common ways that librarians create lists of desired books is by looking at winners of awards, and few awards include the author's identity as a criterion.[4] Though some reverse audits build their bibliography using a mix of awards with subject-based criteria and those with author-based criteria, the former tend to dominate the list.

The basic process of list-checking is simple, as it involves searching your library catalog for titles. The more complicated piece is finding or developing a list that targets the populations or subjects relevant to your analysis. Some reverse audits have relied on existing lists, making the preparation for the audit relatively easy. Melissa Gonzalez describes in chapter 6 how she compared her library's collection to the core titles in Bowker Book Analysis System. A much more extensive process was required for Glyneva Bradley-Ridout, Kaushar Mahetaji, and Mikaela Mitchell's assessment of dermatology books depicting diverse skin tones. To create a list of such books, the authors conducted a literature review, solicited recommendations from faculty, and looked at other libraries' online guides.[5] Laurel Kristick's project falls between these two in terms of the complexity involved in creating the list. Kristick's assessment primarily relied on winners of diversity-related book awards but, given the scarcity of awards relating to disability studies, relevant reference works became a source of additional titles to add to the list. Kristick notes what is true for most projects of this type, "the longest part of the process was creating the bibliography."[6]

The need to correct some sort of imbalance is common when relying on existing lists. Temple University Libraries' initiative to purchase winners of awards honoring diverse experiences found very few related to disability or to Native Americans.[7] Imbalances occur between disciplines as well. When comparing a list of past award-winners to her own collection, Gonzalez noted that there were many more awards for books in the humanities and social sciences than in science, health, or business.[8] It may take some extra effort to ensure your assessment includes the populations or disciplines that you want.

This author's previous work on collection evaluation noted that list-checking is useful for evaluating an interdisciplinary area that is not well defined by call numbers or subject headings. List-checking can also be a good place to start if you are trying to build a retrospective collection in an area where you haven't previously focused, since a list can help you check if you have significant older works.[9] DEI assessment often resembles both scenarios, as ethnic or area studies collections do not fit neatly into a call number range, and a focus on diversity is new for many libraries.

Part of the usefulness of list-checking for retrospective collection-building is that the analysis doubles as a selection aid, automatically telling you how to fill in gaps. Bradley-Ridout, Mahetaji, and Mitchell say that comparison to a list "not only checks the existing collection for representation, but simultaneously identifies missing resources."[10] If the creators of the list are known to have a relationship with the group in question that you and your colleagues don't have—for instance Ibram X. Kendi's Antiracist Reading List—checking the list and later using it to fill gaps is a way to rely on others' expertise in building your collection. The one caveat is that if you have used a list in the past as a selection tool, you can't use it for assessment, as you already know you'll have almost everything.

The largest problem with the list-checking method is the fact that a diverse collection should include more than the limited number of books that have won awards or are listed in a bibliography. María Evelia Emerson and Lauryn Grace Lehman take issue with using lists of award winners for assessment, saying, "If only award-winning books are considered the 'must-haves' to include in a library collection, it further implies to underrepresented students that they only belong if they meet a certain threshold."[11] The relatively small size of your list could also overestimate how well you are doing at diversifying your collection. In Bradley-Ridout, Mahetaji, and Mitchell's study of dermatology books illustrated with darker skin tones, they found that their library already held more than three-quarters of the books on the list they had created. Yet despite their extensive efforts to create an authoritative list of diverse dermatology texts, they were only able to find fifty-five such works.[12] While they rightly concluded that they were doing a good job collecting what was available, this finding does not mean their collection of dermatology books sufficiently represents darker skin. It means they are doing the best they can given what has been published. Even for topics on which more than fifty-five books exist, any list of award-winners or recommended books will be small compared to the number of books you'd ideally have in your collection. It is important to keep in mind that, while list-checking can tell you if you have certain significant books, your goal ultimately should be to have more books by or about marginalized people than those on the list.

Another limitation to note is that a list-checking assessment will show you the number or percentage of books on the list that your library has, but it will not tell you how these holdings compare to the rest of your collection. Even if you have most of the books on the list, the materials you have are probably vastly outnumbered by books about straight white men. Because the assessment won't involve calculating your holdings as a percentage of the full collection, you also won't be able to compare the composition of your collection to target values, such as the percentage of your student population with a particular identity.

Another shortcoming of list-checking is that it won't help you discover inappropriate books that your library owns that you want to remove. As Gonzalez says, "Checklists can tell you what a library 'should' own, but don't address the quality of what you 'do' own."[13]

Metadata Searching

While list-checking hones in on a small number of desirable books, the next method provides more of a bird's-eye view of the collection. This book calls this method metadata searching, though William Walters calls it the catalog search method.[14] Metadata searching involves creating a list of subject headings or call numbers related to a specific population and searching your catalog to obtain counts of how many books your library has about this group. Since library catalogs have not traditionally included demographic information about authors, catalog searching can only assess the subject matter of a collection.

The process of metadata searching is substantially the same as for the assessment method sometimes called benchmarking. This author's previous work on collection evaluation "uses the term [benchmarking] to refer to all kinds of evaluation that focus on numbers of books or other materials rather than what particular titles are owned or used."[15] Though the metadata searches described in this book fit this definition of benchmarking, the term is not appropriate here because it implies a comparison to other libraries' collections. As explained in chapter 1, diversity assessments do not generally compare one library's collection to that of other libraries, since there is no example of a perfectly equitable, inclusive library that can be used as a point of comparison.

For diversity assessment, you are more likely to want to compare your holdings to the demographics of your institution or community, and catalog searches can facilitate this. After doing the searches, you would calculate what percentage of the books in your collection are about a given population and compare this to your student population or to census data.

The main advantage to the metadata search method is scale: a catalog search can cover the entire collection, and since the process doesn't involve reviewing individual titles it is relatively quick. Another advantage of catalog searching is its repeatability. You could easily repeat the same searches in your own catalog each year to track progress.

As with list-checking, the most time-consuming aspect of the assessment is the preparation for conducting searches. Thorough assessment requires making a list of all subject headings or call numbers relevant to the population of interest, which can be tricky. Though there are some studies that rely on keywords, this can lead to inaccurate results. Morgan Harrington provides an example of a search for the word "Scottish," which "turned up books about the terriers" in addition to people from Scotland.[16] Because of the care involved in creating a list tailored to a specific demographic, metadata search projects usually only assess one or two populations.

There are a few disadvantages to using metadata to evaluate your collection for diversity, equity, and inclusion (DEI). The most significant is that the metadata usually won't indicate whether the material is describing a given marginalized group in a respectful and informed way. A book disapproving of interracial marriage might have the seemingly innocuous subject headings "Black people" and "Race relations," and an anti-trans book could have the subject heading "Transgender people." Such books do not contribute to building an inclusive collection, but they would still be counted in the total. The opposite could also be true, that a book appears to not contribute to the diversity of the collection, even though the author's perspective means you'd want to count it. Amanda Rybin Koob and colleagues ask, "What if the authors were actually using anti-colonial theoretical frameworks to critically engage Western-centric content?"[17]

In addition to not indicating what stance an author has taken on a book's topic, metadata are not always able to adequately or appropriately name what the topic is. Walters cautions that "users of this method must have confidence in the available search mechanisms" and goes on to observe that Library of Congress subject headings "do not encompass all relevant aspects of diversity."[18] There might be no existing subject terms that capture the population you are trying to assess. The terms used in the catalog are at times outdated and may be offensive to you and the people they describe. Conducting searches using offensive terminology can be jarring and upsetting to the staff who do the searches. Even when the subject terms are appropriate, there are inherent limitations to describing people using a controlled vocabulary or set of call numbers, which simplify multifaceted identities.

Diversity Coding

A method that allows more consideration of complex identities is diversity coding, which is the process of looking closely at a selection of books from a collection and recording whether they have characteristics related to your diversity goals. This is often called a diversity audit. In contrast to a "reverse audit," or a list-checking assessment, which starts with a list of desirable books and compares it to your holdings, this method uses existing holdings as a starting point and evaluates them. The coding process involves creating your own categories and assigning them to books or authors, rather than relying on how someone else has classified the work. Codes can be applied to either the subject matter of the book or the author, or both. Coding projects do not involve inspecting the entire book collection but usually rely on sampling. You can take a random sample from the full collection, making the findings descriptive of the collection as a whole, sample from a portion of the collection, such as the fiction section, or focus on a section that is small enough to code in its entirety. Some coding projects limit by date to review only recent purchases. This is particularly common when investigating author identities, as information is much less likely to be available for authors from earlier eras.

Compared to list-checking or metadata-based searches, this method offers more flexibility. Not only can you easily choose an area of the collection to focus on or take a representative sample, but you can also define your own categories of diversity. For instance, you could code for LGBTQ content in general or record each letter of the initialism distinctly. Rather than relying on existing metadata that could contain outdated terminology, you can define and name your own groupings that are meaningful to your institution, for instance matching the ways the university classifies students. This is especially useful if you want to compare the composition of your sample to your student body. Coding is well suited to such comparisons, as it allows you to calculate what percentage of the selected books represent a particular identity.

Since coding generally involves noting whichever identities appear in the sample, the resulting analysis will often include many different races, whereas a metadata search usually focuses on just a few. In addition, because you will have information on multiple characteristics of each book, for instance the author's gender, race, and sexuality, you can quantify the presence of intersectional identities, such as Black LGBTQ women. Coding is the only assessment method that lets you consider intersectionality.

The flexibility of diversity coding has a corresponding downside, which is that it involves a lot of decision-making about how you will structure your categories and apply them to books or authors. While several coding projects for author identities have used Emerson and Lehman's work as a model, each project will have its own distinct set of guidelines and codes.[19]

Walters' term for this method, "book inspection," highlights that it is the only method that involves looking closely at individual books.[20] This close inspection offers an advantage, which is that it may help you identify books that should be weeded. Inspection is also time-consuming, however, which is why diversity coding never takes the entire collection as its scope. The assessment project must be limited to a number of books that the staff can reasonably inspect and code.

Methods for Assessing Institutional Efforts

How you assess your organization's efforts toward building more diverse and equitable collections depends on what those efforts are. Your activities could be focused on learning, changing policy, making changes to processes, or advocating for changes to systems beyond your library. For a goal that is concrete and easily measurable, such as creating a guide to African American literature, the assessment might simply involve noting that you had achieved the goal. For more complicated projects, the assessment would occur at a few different points. At the beginning of a project, assessment would involve taking stock of the current situation, for instance confirming what your current policies say about DEI or checking which publishers are on your approval plans. The next step is to set a goal of what to change, so that you can later note that you've accomplished your goal. The final step is reflection. This could involve some type of measurement, such as how many books you ordered from a new BIPOC-owned vendor or how many headings from alternate thesauri you added to your catalog. It could also be more subjective, such as thinking about whether the continuing education you pursued was helpful or whether the effort of making additional displays is one you can continue annually.

A major advantage to assessing your actions rather than the collection itself is flexibility. You can assess any action that is relevant to collections and diversity, whether it is educating staff, changing workflows or spending patterns, buying from new vendors, modifying your catalog, or increasing promotional activities. This not only leaves room for thinking more broadly about collections beyond what materials you acquire but lets you focus on what is most important and appropriate for your library. If finding ways to acquire books from BIPOC-owned bookstores matters more to you than studying the books you have been acquiring through your current vendor, you can set a goal of investigating new vendors and setting up a purchasing relationship, then evaluate whether the new purchasing is creating extra work or costs.

The one downside to assessing institutional efforts is it doesn't necessarily help you identify shortcomings, whether in your work or in the collection. Because you'll be setting your own goals and tracking whether you've achieved them, your assessment will almost always show positive momentum, without necessarily highlighting where you could still improve. The other assessment methods, in contrast, might paint a more accurate picture of overwhelmingly white male collections, which could spur change and give ideas of where to begin.

The strategy of assessing organizational efforts does not need to be an alternative to assessing the collection but could be a supplement to any of the methods above. In fact, you may want to mix methods no matter what your approach. Julia Proctor, whose study of LGBTQ materials mixed catalog searches and list checking, writes "using multiple methods is the only way to address the shortcomings that individual methods may have."[21] All methods present their challenges and have limits to what they can teach you about your collection. Nevertheless, all will teach you something.

NOTES

1. Annette Day, Sarah R. Jones, Amy Tureen, Susan B. Wainscott, Amanda Melilli, Thomas Padilla, and Aidy Weeks, *Inclusive and Anti-Racist Collecting at UNLV: Draft Report and Recommendations* (University of Nevada Las Vegas, September, 2022), 6, https://digitalscholarship.unlv.edu/lib_articles/748.
2. Day et al., *Inclusive and Anti-Racist Collecting at UNLV*, 2022, 5.
3. William Walters, "Assessing Diversity in Academic Library Book Collections: Diversity Audit Principles and Methods," *Open Information Science* 7, no. 1 (2023): 8, https://www.degruyter.com/document/doi/10.1515/opis-2022-0148/html.
4. See Melissa Gonzalez, "Methods," Diversity Collection Audit & Assessment, 2023, https://libguides.uwf.edu/divassess/methods; Amalia Monroe-Gulick and Sara E. Morris, "Diversity in Monographs: Selectors, Acquisitions, Publishers, and Vendors," *Collection Management* 48, no. 3 (2023): 210–233. A project at this author's institution to purchase winners of book awards also found significantly more awards with criteria related to subject matter than to author identity.
5. Glyneva Bradley-Ridout, Kaushar Mahetaji, and Mikaela Mitchell, "Using a Reverse Diversity Audit Approach to Evaluate a Dermatology Collection in an Academic Health Sciences Library: A Case Presentation," *The Journal of Academic Librarianship* 49, no. 6 (2023): 102650.
6. Laurel Kristick, "Diversity Literary Awards: A Tool for Assessing an Academic Library's Collection," *Collection Management* 45, no. 2 (2020): 157.
7. Karen Kohn, Emily Crawford, Noa Kaumeheiwa, and Jenny Pierce, "Inclusive Collecting, Inclusive Cataloging – Acquiring and Describing Award-Winning Books Honoring Diverse Experiences," *Library Resources and Technical Services* 68, no. 4 (2024), https://journals.ala.org/index.php/lrts/article/view/8325.
8. Gonzalez, "Methods."
9. Karen Kohn, *Collection Evaluation in Academic Libraries: A Practical Guide for Librarians* (Lanham, MD: Rowman & Littlefield, 2015), 73.
10. Bradley-Ridout, Mahetaji, and Mitchell, "Using a Reverse Diversity Audit Approach To Evaluate a Dermatology Collection in an Academic Health Sciences Library."
11. María Evelia Emerson and Lauryn Grace Lehman, "Who Are We Missing? Conducting a Diversity Audit in a Liberal Arts College Library," *The Journal of Academic Librarianship* 48, no. 3 (2022): 2.
12. Bradley-Ridout, Mahetaji, and Mitchell, "Using a Reverse Diversity Audit Approach To Evaluate a Dermatology Collection in an Academic Health Sciences Library."
13. Gonzalez, "Methods."
14. Walters, "Assessing Diversity in Academic Library Book Collections," 8.
15. Kohn, *Collection Evaluation in Academic Libraries*, 42.
16. Morgan Harrington, "Rethinking Diversity beyond Catalogue Representation: Lessons from Efforts to Develop a Methodology to Evaluate Diversity within the National Library of Australia," *Journal of the Australian Library and Information Association* 70, no. 1 (2021): 32.
17. Amanda Rybin Koob, Arthur Aguilera, Frederick C. Carey, Xiang Li, Natalia Tingle Dolan, and Alexander Watkins, "Beyond the Diversity Audit: Uncovering Whiteness in Our Collections," in *Antiracist Library and Information Science: Racial Justice*

and Community, ed. Kimberly Black and Bharat Mehra (West Yorkshire: Emerald Publishing, 2023), 73.

18. Walters, "Assessing Diversity in Academic Library Book Collections," 9.

19. María Evelia Emerson and Lauryn Grace Lehman, "Filling in the Gaps: A Diversity Audit Toolkit from Tredway Library, *Library and Information Science: Faculty Scholarship & Creative Works,* 2021, https://digitalcommons.augustana.edu/libscifaculty/14.

20. Walters, "Assessing Diversity in Academic Library Book Collections," 14.

21. Julia Proctor, "Representation in the Collection: Assessing Coverage of LGBTQ Content in an Academic Library Collection," *Collection Management* 45, no. 3 (2020): 228.

4

Project Planning

Before you dive into your assessment project, it will be helpful to plan, to the best of your ability, how the project will proceed. In addition to the broader questions of method and aspects of diversity mentioned in the previous chapters, project planning should involve a desired timeline, an idea of how many staff will participate, and an estimate of how much of the collection you will assess. These details of project planning are intertwined. Your resources affect how much assessment you can do and how quickly you can do it, and the amount you hope to assess will influence how long you expect the project to take and how many staff you need. Assessment projects vary in which parameters are known at the outset and which are decided later. You might know that you want to look at author identities using diversity coding, but before you decide how many books to code you need to find out how many staff will be doing the work. Alternately, you might intend to work alone and use metadata searching as your approach, but you need to try constructing a search before you really know how many populations you'll be able to search for. There is no required order for going through the planning process, and you might even adjust some of the parameters after you've started the assessment. Try to plan as much as you can ahead of time so that your goals are clear, and be intentional about making changes if you need to.

TIME FRAME

One of the first questions to consider is how quickly you want or need to complete your assessment. Most often there is no external constraint on when an assessment needs to be finished, so you don't necessarily need to design a project based on what you can complete in a semester or a summer. Meghan Kwast's audit at California Lutheran University stands out in part for its long timeline. The work was expected to take two years due to its broad scope and small staff.[1] A more typical time frame is one semester to six months. You may want to plan your assessment project for a similar length of time, whether due to the expense of hiring student workers, the desire to repeat the assessment annually, or the wish to see some data sooner rather than later.

STAFFING

A significant factor affecting how long a project will take is how many people are working on it. Many DEI assessments are the work of a single librarian. The projects with a larger scope often involve multiple librarians, other staff, and/or student workers. The audit at University of the Pacific, which relied on eight student interns, stands at the upper end of the staffing spectrum. In addition to their coding responsibilities, interns completed assigned readings and attended twice-monthly meetings. Together with four library staff members and three additional student workers, the team was able to code 4,391 books and music scores over the course of a semester.[2] In contrast, Kwast's project, which was expected to take two years, involved coding almost exactly the same number of titles (4,383) but divided the work among a smaller staff of four people total.[3]

If your assessment is an initiative of a DEI committee, you may already have a small group that can divide the work. If you are launching the project as an individual, you may be able to ask for volunteers from among your coworkers, though there is no guarantee you will get a positive response. You can also check whether there is funding to hire designated student workers.

There is also the possibility of a hybrid approach in which a committee serves in a consulting role while an individual or smaller group carries out the assessment work. In early 2024, the DEI in Collections committee at Temple University Libraries solicited volunteers to conduct small, focused assessments, and three subject specialists expressed interest. Each of the three volunteers completed a separate assessment, but the committee provided feedback and suggested readings or resources as the projects progressed. The relevant committee member also provided support when a particular technical skill was helpful, such as running reports in the integrated library system or working with Excel.

In addition to the staff who are conducting or designing the assessment, you might also need support from people who are not part of the main project team. For instance, if there is a specific person in the library in charge of running reports you might request some from that person. Someone comfortable in Excel could help you create a random sample or set up a worksheet for coding, though the instructions in chapter 8 may suffice. Since none of the assessment methods described in this book involve specialized tools other than your own integrated library system and Excel, you shouldn't need extensive technical support but may want to think through who can help with specific tasks.

Though your team's composition will depend on who initiated the project, who volunteered to participate, or people's organizational roles, you should be aware that there is a pattern of DEI work being assigned to staff from non-dominant groups, creating the burden of an extra responsibility. Silvia Vong, Allan Cho, and Elaina Norlin, who studied equity, diversity, inclusion, and anti-racism work in academic libraries, note that "this work tends to fall on racialized people. . . . This can be a heavy workload unfairly distributed and absolves nonracialized people from doing the important work to engage with important topics related to equity, diversity, inclusion, or anti-racism."[4] Gilbert Singletary, Kenneth Royal, and Kathy Goodridge-Purnell, writing about diversity committees in universities, concur that "advancing diversity, equity, and inclusion must not rest solely on the shoulders of marginalized committee members."[5] You may not have control over whether the staff of your assessment project is comprised of marginalized people. What you will probably have somewhat more control over is ensuring that team members receive credit for their work. Vong, Cho, and Norlin observe that DEI work is not always given adequate weight when it is counted toward the service requirement for a promotion and tenure review.[6] Working within whatever your organization's processes are, you can be conscious of drawing attention to the work in appropriate ways, such as by writing to team members' supervisors or to a promotion committee. Student workers who contribute to an assessment project might appreciate an opportunity to co-present or publish about the work and should be thanked by name if librarians present or publish.

In addition to adding to the workload of members of nondominant groups, a DEI assessment can be uncomfortable for these staff, as it increases the frequency with which they encounter offensive descriptors in the catalog or books that stereotype or denigrate their identities. María Emerson and Lauryn Lehman recommend checking in with the staff involved in the audit to provide opportunities for them to share their emotions. They noted that during their audit, "there were several participants who identif[ied] with groups that were underrepresented or absent from the collections that were being audited. Checking in with these participants became essential to helping preserve their emotional and mental health as they processed their own lack of representation within the library space."[7]

One final consideration for staffing is that if the project involves more than you alone, you will need to provide some training and a means of ensuring that employees are consistent in their processes.

CHOOSING A SCOPE

Kara Bledsoe and colleagues advise, "Rather than seeking perfection in terms of comprehensiveness, many library leaders and their partners on this work may instead wish to find a tangible place to begin."[8] What constitutes a "tangible place to begin" depends on the capacity of your institution, which is influenced by the number of staff involved in the assessment and your desired timeline. Your choice of method is relevant as well. Some methods work better with a targeted subject area or a focus on just one or two populations, while others allow you to assess the full collection or include many demographics.

There is no analysis that looks at every book in a library's collection. Both large and small libraries typically need to limit the scope of their assessments in some way. Catalog searches and list-checking would take the same amount of time at a larger library as at a smaller one, and any library would need to select a focus when using these assessment methods. Diversity coding always involves some selection of which books to code, as no academic library could apply diversity codes to its entire collection. None of the methods described here are inapplicable to large libraries, though Emerson and Lehman observe that larger libraries have a greater need to limit the scope of their assessments.[9] Scott Stone of the University of California Irvine looked only at play scripts, while Julia Proctor at Penn State University focused on LGBTQ-related terms in the catalog of a thirty-six-library system.[10] Morgan Harrington wanted to survey the National Library of Australia's overall representation of cultural and linguistic diversity within the country, but as the Australian Census includes "1,260 countries of origin, ancestries, religions and languages," a full assessment was not feasible. Harrington decided to focus on only two populations when conducting catalog searches.[11]

Limiting to a Part of the Collection

There are a variety of ways to carve out a segment of the collection to assess. An assessment project can investigate a single subject area, books acquired within a specific date range, or works in a particular genre or location. David Cox at the University of Alaska Southeast undertook an initial audit of only the call number range PS3600-PS3626, "American authors 2001 to present." A second round covered PS3551–3576, "American Authors 1960–2000."[12] Melissa Gonzalez coded new acquisitions at the University of West Florida in fiscal year 2020, then repeated the process in FY21 and FY22.[13] Limiting to recent purchases is a good option if you are gathering information on author identities, as you are more likely to find information on recent authors than on those who published years ago. Another option for subdividing your collection is to assess a section that is already treated as distinct, such as fiction or graphic novels.

Coding projects often use random sampling to create a reasonably sized list of books to inspect, though sampling is not an option for the other assessment methods. Two examples illustrate how sampling can make a project feasible without narrowing its focus. Michele Gibney, Mickel Paris, and Veronica Wells's audit of the entire print and ebook collections at the University of the

Pacific was based on selecting titles from each discipline using "a randomized sample size of either 10% or 1,000, whichever was fewer."[14] Kwast created a sample for the audit at California Lutheran University by dividing the collection into eight subject areas, then selecting from each area a sample that was large enough to achieve a 99 percent confidence interval, meaning there was a 99 percent chance that the patterns observed in the sample would reflect the overall collection.[15]

Sampling is a possibility even if you have already limited the analysis to a specific subject area within your collection. One of the aforementioned focused assessments at Temple University included only books related to World War II, with the intention of seeing which countries and populations were most heavily represented. As there are twenty-two thousand print and electronic books in the catalog with a subject heading or call number related to World War II, the librarian conducting the audit took a sample from the full title list.

Limiting Your Demographic Focus

Another way that you might limit the scope of your assessment is by studying only select demographic groups. The assessment method you use strongly influences the number of groups it is possible to assess. William Walters's review of the literature on diversity assessment found that coding projects were the most likely to cover multiple aspects of diversity.[16] These assessments not only observe multiple traits, such as race, gender, and LGBTQ identities, but also allow coders to note any race, gender, or sexuality that appears in the books they are inspecting. In fact, even though you'll have an idea at the outset of which identities are of interest, throughout the coding process you are likely to encounter identities that you hadn't thought about before you began, and you can modify your process to record these.

List-checking assessments can also involve multiple populations, though unlike diversity coding projects they might also focus on one or two. Laurel Kristick's study included eight populations represented by the seven resource centers at Oregon State University, plus the disability services office.[17] Melissa Gonzalez, author of chapter 6, checked her library for recommended titles from more than ten groups. Of the list-checking assessments that Walters included in his review, however, more than half measured the representation of only one group.[18]

Metadata searches often involve only a small number of population groups, due to the time involved in putting together an appropriate search strategy for each population. As noted earlier, Harrington, at the National Library of Australia, decided to search for only two populations, Polish-Australian and Asian, as this allowed for more time to review the search results for accuracy.[19]

If the methodology you are using requires you to limit your focus to just a few demographic groups, your motivation for conducting the audit should help you choose. As explained in chapter 2, depending on whether your goal is to support the curriculum or to allow students to see their own identities reflected, you might focus on populations that are the subject of class assignments or those that are present in significant numbers at your school.

OTHER CONSIDERATIONS FOR SCOPE

In addition to choosing what section of the collection you want to assess and which populations are of interest, there will be a few smaller details to figure out that relate to the scope of your assessment. These details include specifics of format, acquisition method, location, and date of acquisition. Table 4.1 lists some questions to ask yourself when clarifying your scope and what to consider when answering them.

Table 4.1   Questions Related to Scope

Question	Considerations
Will you include lost or missing books?	Are you evaluating what is available to your students or what your selection methods allow you to discover?
Will you include unowned ebooks?	How did these books come to be in your catalog (e.g., a subscription collection or demand-driven acquisitions), and will you be comparing the performance of various selection methods? How will you exclude these if you choose to?
Which locations will you include?	Do some locations contain books with different selection criteria than the general collection, e.g., leisure reading, juvenile literature, government documents, or rare books? Do you only want to include locations where you'd be able to influence selection going forward, or all locations whose books are accessible to your users?
How will you limit the assessment so that it only includes books acquired before the start of any data collection?	Can you take all your samples on the same date, even if analysis will occur over a longer time period? Can you conduct all catalog searches on the same date, even if preparation takes place over a longer time period? Can you limit catalog searches to resources acquired before a certain date?

Source: Author.

You will probably include both print and electronic books in your assessment, though you may have a reason for including only one or the other. It is advisable to include purchases made through all selection methods, such as firm orders, approvals, and demand-driven acquisitions (DDA). As noted in chapter 2, you may want to include information about selection methods (e.g., firm orders, approval plans, demand-driven acquisitions) as part of your assessment, so that you can see whether one method is yielding more diverse books than another.

When assessing print books, you will need to decide whether to count lost and missing books as part of the collection. This will depend on whether you are trying to assess what is available to your students or the ability of your current selection tools to identify diverse books for purchase. If you expect part of your analysis to involve questioning how well your approval plans are catching books by or about marginalized people or from BIPOC-owned publishers, books you had acquired and lost would still be relevant to this analysis.

When assessing ebooks, there is a question of whether you should include books that are in the catalog but that your library does not own. These could be books available for DDAs, those in subscription collections, or open-access books. When considering which ebooks to include, you can again return to the motivations discussed in chapter 2. Including unpurchased books in the catalog helps make them accessible to your students and sends a message that the library values these books. Furthermore, if part of the goal of the assessment is to understand what your own selection methods are potentially excluding, the criteria you use to select your pool of DDAs titles, decide which packages to subscribe to, or choose open-access books to catalog are among these selection methods. A practical reason for keeping unowned ebooks in your search might be the difficulty of separating them from owned ebooks.

It is likely you'll want to exclude some books from your analysis based on location. Almost all libraries have many different catalog locations, and there could be reasons not to include all of them. If you are part of a multi-campus library system, there is a question of whether you are only assessing your own library or the entire system. Considerations could be whether purchasing is done collectively or separately, and whether your own students have access to materials at the other libraries. Temple University has a branch campus in Japan, and as that library's print materials are not accessible to users in the United States, they are almost always excluded from analyses conducted on the main campus. A nearby campus in the suburbs of Philadelphia, however, is always included, as books from that campus are regularly delivered to the main library at patrons' request.

There are also probably locations within your library that you would want to exclude. Leisure reading and juvenile books are selected according to different criteria and through different processes than the main collection, so these might not make sense to include in a general assessment. There are situations, though, where you might be interested in these locations. For instance, award-winning recent literature about marginalized people might be more likely to appear in the leisure collection than the main collection, since new novels are usually a focus of leisure collections. Rare books and government documents are other items selected and acquired very differently from general collections, so you might also exclude these from your DEI assessment. Think about what makes sense for your situation.

A final consideration is the date the books were acquired. Even if you aren't limiting your assessment to acquisitions from a specific fiscal year, there are reasons to put some date limits on the analysis. Ebooks could be removed from the collection or added while you are in the process of doing the assessment, and print books are usually added continuously. If your assessment takes months to complete, you don't want to be evaluating the education books you had in January and the science books you had in May. Also, if you plan to repeat the assessment in future years, you want the first round to have a cutoff so that future assessments can include books acquired after that date.

Luckily there are relatively easy ways to ensure that you are consistently assessing the holdings of your library as of a set date. If you are doing catalog searches, for either a list-checking or a metadata searching project, you might be able to do the searches within a narrow time span, even if the preparation for these searches takes longer. Alternately, you may be able to filter catalog searches to include only the holdings acquired before the date you started the assessment. If you are working with an export from your catalog to Excel, as you would for a coding project, try to do all the exports close together as well, or limit to books you acquired before the start of the assessment.

EXAMPLE SCOPES

Table 4.2 gives examples of project scopes, arranged from narrow to broad. The projects vary in the methods they used for assessment. The table does not include the number of books assessed, since the quantity of books that it is feasible to evaluate depends on the assessment method and thus isn't comparable between projects that use different methods. Projects that list their scope as the full collection or full book collection usually rely on a method that does not require closely inspecting books.

PROJECT TRACKING

As you prepare to begin your project, remember that you will need some mechanism for tracking progress and making sure work is proceeding on schedule. It could be useful to set intermediate goals, such as asking everyone to code a set number of books by a certain date or planning when to finish compiling your list of recommended books so you can move on to checking

Table 4.2   Example Scopes of Assessment Projects

Citation	Institution	Staff	Traits/Population	Portion of Collection
Glyneva Bradley-Ridout, Kaushar Mahetaji, and Mikaela Mitchell, "Using a Reverse Diversity Audit Approach to Evaluate a Dermatology Collection in an Academic Health Sciences Library: A Case Presentation," *The Journal of Academic Librarianship* 49, no. 6 (2023): 102650.	Gerstein Science Information Centre at the University of Toronto	3 librarians	Skin color	Dermatology books
Scott M. Stone, "Whose Play Scripts Are Being Published? A Diversity Audit of One Library's Collection in Conversation with the Broader Play Publishing World," *Collection Management* 45, no. 4 (2020): 304–320.	University of California, Irvine	1 librarian	Gender, Nationality, Sexual Orientation, Race (6 categories)	Plays acquired in FY11 and FY19
Janet Calderon, "Acquisitions for the Sciences—Using a Diversity Assessment to Serve BIPOC Students in STEM," presented at the Acquisitions Institute at Timberline Lodge, May 22, 2023, https://acquisitionsinstitute.org/wp-content/uploads/2023/05/Monday_Calderon_s-Presentation_final.pptx.	California Polytechnic University, Humboldt	1 librarian	Race (9 categories)	Physical books, published 2000–2022, with the subject heading "natural resources"

(Continued)

Table 4.2   (Continued)

Citation	Institution	Staff	Traits/Population	Portion of Collection
María Evelia Emerson and Lauryn Grace Lehman, "Who Are We Missing? Conducting a Diversity Audit in a Liberal Arts College Library," *The Journal of Academic Librarianship* 48, no. 3 (2022): 102517.	Augustana College	7 librarians, 1 staff member, 4 student workers	Gender, sexuality, or current relationship, race (6 categories)	Physical book, single-author, published 2000 or later, some locations excluded
Laurel Kristick, "Diversity Literary Awards: A Tool for Assessing an Academic Library's Collection," *Collection Management* 45, no. 2 (2020): 151–161.	Oregon State University	1 librarian	LGBTQ, women, Arab American, Asian American, Asian, Native American, Black, Latino or Hispanic, disability,	Full book collection
Julia Proctor, "Representation in the Collection: Assessing Coverage of LGBTQ Content in an Academic Library Collection," *Collection Management* 45, no. 3 (2020): 223–234.	Penn State University	1 librarian	LGBTQ identities (separate counts for Lesbian, Gay, Bisexual, Transgender, Queer, and Gender Nonconforming)	Full collection
Meghan Kwast, "California Lutheran University's Diversity Audit: A Project in Progress," Presented at SCELCapalooza, March 2, 2023, https://docs.google.com/presentation/d/1y8ksacioG429UArHHBDK3OQr6715pGSN.	California Lutheran University	3 staff members, 1 student worker	Race (7 categories), gender identity, sexual orientation, disability, nationality, first generation American	Print books, random samples from all disciplines
Michele Gibney, Mickel Paris, and Veronica Wells, "A Diversity, Equity, and Inclusion (DEI) Approach to Collection Development in a University Library," Scholarly Commons. (Pre-print), 2022, http://scholarlycommons.pacific.edu/libraries-articles/121.	University of the Pacific	4 staff members, 8 interns, 3 student workers	Race (7 categories), gender (with transgender counted separately), disability	Print and electronic books and music scores, random samples from all disciplines

Source: Author.

holdings. If you plan to repeat the analysis at intervals, you should also plan when you will do these later assessments, though you don't necessarily need to decide on a cycle until the first assessment is completed and you've seen whether it took the amount of time you expected. Emerson and Lehman recommend planning how you will monitor your progress, such as with spreadsheets and meetings.[20]

One obstacle to staying on track to meet your goals may be the temptation to pursue new ideas that arise throughout the project. It is quite likely that you will come up with some ideas for action steps while the assessment is still underway. Cox's presentation about assessment at the University of Alaska Southeast noted that the work "[g]enerat[ed] far more collection development ideas than our budget or users can likely handle" including "many [books] to purchase and to weed."[21] You might realize missing subject headings that you'd like to add to LCSH and want to get in touch with librarians who can help make a proposal. Your assessment might also produce observations about aspects of diversity that cannot be formally assessed, such as the quality of representation or the prevalence of particular common stories. Though these findings are useful and can lead to constructive action, you don't want to lose momentum on your assessment by switching your focus to weeding, new acquisitions, or cataloging changes in the middle of it.

The concept of a "parking lot" could help in this situation. A parking lot is a tool for capturing out-of-scope ideas that arise so that the team can discuss them at another time. Having a place to record these ideas can help keep you focused so that the project can move forward, while also ensuring that you don't lose the insights you gain along the way. Parking lots are sometimes created using a structured template, although this is not necessary.[22] The intention is that any participant can add an idea that the team can address later. Sarah Gibbons notes that an ideas parking lot can be especially useful for people who tend to go off-topic or for projects that are complex and can easily expand into larger projects.[23] In both situations the parking lot helps the team maintain its focus on the original goals. Especially with a project related to DEI, it is important to have a plan to revisit the parking lot when you can address the ideas or actions in it. Vong, Cho, and Norlin note that diversity work can often be performative, whereas real change requires follow through.[24]

Returning to the parking lot when you are ready to act on the ideas in it lets you maximize what you will gain from the assessment. Your assessment work will most likely spark many ideas, and you will learn even more about your collection than the concrete measurements the assessment will produce. The following chapters will help you move from planning to doing the work.

NOTES

1. Meghan Kwast, "California Lutheran University's Diversity Audit: A Project in Progress" (presented at SCELCapalooza, March 2, 2023), https://docs.google.com/presentation/d/1y8ksacioG429UArHHBDK3OQr6715pGSN.

2. Michele Gibney, Mickel Paris, and Veronica Wells, "A Diversity, Equity, and Inclusion (DEI) Approach to Collection Development in a University Library," *Scholarly Commons*. (Pre-print), 2022, http://scholarlycommons.pacific.edu/libraries-articles/121.

3. Kwast, "California Lutheran University's Diversity Audit: A Project in Progress," 2023.

4. Silvia Vong, Allan Cho, and Elaina Norlin, "The Five Labours of Equity, Diversity, Inclusion, and Anti-racism Work by Racialized Academic Librarians," *The International Journal of Information, Diversity, & Inclusion* 7, no. 3/4 (2023): 13, https://jps.library.utoronto.ca/index.php/ijidi/article/view/41002. As explained in the article, "racialized people" is a category similar to Black, Indigenous, People of Color, but the terminology emphasizes processes by which a society ascribes racial meaning to social phenomena or people.

5. Gilbert Singletary, Kenneth Royal, and Kathy Goodridge-Purnell, "Diversity Committees During The Era of Social Justice: Where Do We Go From Here?" *The International Journal of Information, Diversity, & Inclusion* 5, no. 5 (2021): 50.

6. Vong, Cho, and Norlin, "The Five Labours of Equity, Diversity, Inclusion, and Anti-Racism Work by Racialized Academic Librarians," 2023.

7. Emerson and Lehman, "Filling in the Gaps," 2021, part 3.

8. Kara Bledsoe, Danielle Miriam Cooper, Roger C. Schonfeld, and Oya Rieger, *Leading by Diversifying Collections* (New York: Ithaka S+R, November 9, 2022), https://sr.ithaka.org/publications/leading-by-diversifying-collections/.

9. María Evelia Emerson and Lauryn Grace Lehman, "Who Are We Missing? Conducting a Diversity Audit in a Liberal Arts College Library," *The Journal of Academic Librarianship* 48, no. 3 (2022): 102517.

10. Scott M. Stone, "Whose Play Scripts Are Being Published? A Diversity Audit of One Library's Collection in Conversation with the Broader Play Publishing World," *Collection Management* 45, no. 4 (2020): 304–320; Julia Proctor, "Representation in the Collection: Assessing Coverage of LGBTQ Content in an Academic Library Collection," *Collection Management* 45, no. 3 (2020): 223–234.

11. Morgan Harrington, "Rethinking Diversity beyond Catalogue Representation: Lessons from Efforts to Develop a Methodology to Evaluate Diversity within the National Library of Australia," *Journal of the Australian Library and Information Association* 70, no. 1 (2021): 23–43.

12. David B. Cox, "Introductory Diversity Audits," poster presented at Alaska Library Association Conference; March 18–20, 2021, https://scholarworks.alaska.edu/handle/11122/12642.

13. Melissa Gonzalez, "Methods," Diversity Collection Audit & Assessment, 2023, https://libguides.uwf.edu/divassess/methods.

14. Gibney, Paris, and Wells, "A Diversity, Equity, and Inclusion (DEI) Approach to Collection Development in a University Library," 2022, 7.

15. Kwast, "California Lutheran University's Diversity Audit," 2023.

16. William Walters, "Assessing Diversity in Academic Library Book Collections: Diversity Audit Principles and Methods," *Open Information Science* 7, no. 1 (2023): 20220148, https://www.degruyter.com/document/doi/10.1515/opis-2022-0148 /html.
17. Laurel Kristick, "Diversity Literary Awards: A Tool for Assessing an Academic Library's Collection," *Collection Management* 45, no. 2 (2020): 151–161.
18. Walters, "Assessing Diversity in Academic Library Book Collections," 2023.
19. Harrington, "Rethinking Diversity beyond Catalogue Representation," 2021.
20. María Evelia Emerson and Lauryn Grace Lehman, "Filling in the Gaps: A Diversity Audit Toolkit from Tredway Library," *Library and Information Science: Faculty Scholarship & Creative Works*, 2021, https://digitalcommons.augustana.edu/libscifaculty /14, part 3.
21. Cox, "Introductory Diversity Audits," 2021, slide 15.
22. "Parking Lot Matrix Template," Miro, accessed April 12, 2024, https://miro.com/ templates/ideas-parking-lot-matrix/.
23. Sarah Gibbons, "Parking Lots in UX Meetings and Workshops," Nielsen Norman Group, https://www.nngroup.com/articles/parking-lots/, September 8, 2019.
24. Vong, Cho, and Norlin, "The Five Labours of Equity, Diversity, Inclusion, and Anti-Racism Work by Racialized Academic Librarians," 2023, 18.

5

List-Checking

This chapter will help you plan and carry out a list-checking project, from comparing different options for lists to checking your holdings and then understanding your findings.

CHOOSING A LIST

The first step in conducting a list-checking assessment is finding a list to use. There are several types of lists that you can compare against your holdings, and you will probably start preparing for your project by seeking existing lists of recommended books. Table 5.1 summarizes common sources of book lists, along with the pros and cons of each type of list. Though there are a variety of possible lists to use, there may not be one perfectly tailored to what you are trying to find out about your collection. It is likely, therefore, that your project will involve supplementing an existing list with your own additions or adjustments. This is the case in most published studies that rely on list-checking.

AWARD-WINNERS

When it comes to diversity, equity, and inclusion (DEI), the most common book lists that librarians use are those made up of award-winners. There are many benefits to using lists of award-winners. The sheer number of awards that exist means you can compile a list that covers a wide range of identities, including some intersectional identities. For instance, the Darlene Clark Hine Award, offered by the Organization of American Historians, recognizes books related to African American women's history. The Fatema Mernissi Award is given by the Middle East Studies Association and recognizes works about women, gender, and sexuality. Awards can also cover a wide range of disciplines: you can find awards honoring African Americans in film and media studies, literature,

Table 5.1   Comparison of Types of Lists

Type	Advantages	Disadvantages
Awards	Several lists of awards are available online. You can evaluate coverage of many populations at once. Awards will have clear criteria for winners. You will be able to evaluate awards based on the composition of the committee. If a population or discipline has very few awards, you can expand your list by including finalists as well as winners.	Your collection shouldn't have only award-winning books by or about marginalized people, as you don't have this high a standard for books by or about other groups. Some populations and disciplines have more awards than others.
Bibliographies	You can create your own and rely on multiple sources. They may have a more targeted focus than awards lists.	Not many exist. They may be dated and/or not regularly updated.
Vendor-curated lists or collections	These may cover a variety of populations in one list. Lists are readily available on many topics.	It is unclear whether the people creating the lists have topical expertise. Some lists will only include titles available electronically.

Source: Author.

history, and sociology. A great place to start is the guide created by Melissa Gonzalez at the University of West Florida, which she describes in the next chapter. It can be found at https://libguides.uwf.edu/diversebkawds.

You can be flexible in how you use award winners to create your own customized list of books to check against your holdings. Since most DEI-related awards target a specific population, you can choose which awards you want to include based on which groups you are trying to cover in your analysis. An assessment focused on race would include a smaller set of awards than a project that aimed to also look at gender, sexuality, and disability. You can also decide whether you want to consider finalists to be part of your list and how far back you want to go in looking at past winners. A project at Temple

University to purchase winners of awards focused on diverse experiences used finalists and runners-up to balance out some disparities in coverage. As there were very few awards related to disability or to North American Indigenous people, Temple's DEI in Collections committee decided to treat the finalists of these awards as must-haves in addition to the winners.[1] Almost every audit that relies on award-winners observes some kind of imbalance in the populations or disciplines covered. You can combine awards with other sources of recommended books to create a more balanced list.

While some populations seem to have few dedicated book awards, other populations have so many awards that they may dominate the list. The Lambda Literary Awards, which recognize LGBTQ books and authors, include awards specific to gay fiction, lesbian fiction, bisexual fiction, and transgender fiction, as well as genre-specific awards for mystery, romance, and speculative fiction. There are nonfiction, poetry, drama, and biography awards as well. The sheer number of distinct awards means a large portion of any awards list might be comprised of books focused on various LGBTQ identities. While you can add or subtract from your list of awards to try to create balance, the list is still likely to have some amount of skew.

If your goal is to do an evaluation based on subject matter, make sure that the awards you are including explicitly mention subject matter as one of their criteria. For example, the Ernest J. Gaines Literary Award for Literary Excellence is given to works of fiction authored by African American U.S. citizens.[2] It does not require the books it recognizes to be about African American experiences, although they usually are. Other awards are primarily concerned with content or may be less explicit about whether their focus is on authorship or subject matter. You may decide to only use awards in your analysis whose criteria refer to the subject matter of the works, or you may want to also include those that consider either subject matter or authorship as a qualification.

Some librarians have also considered the composition of the selection committee when choosing which awards to use. Amalia Monroe-Gulick and Sara Morris expressed a concern that awards granted by scholarly associations without a requirement for author identity would create "a potential bias toward academic titles which are not always representative of those with non-majority identities."[3] Librarians at Temple University had a different concern, which was the danger of inaccurate representation or othering of minority populations. If the members of the committee granting the award were not members or scholars of the population group in question, and the award did not contain a requirement for author identity, then fictional works that told a good story but were based on only superficial knowledge of the populations in the story might be granted awards by a committee that was not concerned with authentic representation. Temple's initiative to purchase winners of diversity-related awards categorized all awards according to "whether the award criteria specified that the book should be about or by a member of the population in question and . . .

the organization granting the award."[4] If an award did not require the book's author to be a member of a specific demographic group, *and* the organization granting the award did not have any apparent connection to that group, the default decision would be to not purchase the book.

When creating your own list of award-winners to use in an assessment, you can focus on those given by organizations whose members have either scholarly or personal knowledge of the population. For instance, while the Association for the Study of American Indian Literatures (ASAIL), which grants several book awards, does not require that its members be Native American, it does state that its membership "includes leading scholars, writers, and activists committed to the interdisciplinary study and continuance of Native American and Indigenous languages, cultures, and aesthetic traditions."[5] It seems likely that this group would pick books that didn't other or stereotype North American Indigenous people, so the books they choose as award-winners would be appropriate for your library, provided they meet other collections criteria.

BIBLIOGRAPHIES

Another type of list that is sometimes used to evaluate a collection for DEI is a topical bibliography. These can be created by a professional organization, librarian, or a single expert. These can have the advantage of being more targeted than awards lists—for example, multiple bibliographies exist related to race in medicine or to reproductive rights. Several bibliographies are noted in text box 5.1.

TEXT BOX 5.1 SOME BIBLIOGRAPHIES RELEVANT TO DEI

ACRL Women and Gender Studies Section: Core Books https://acrl.ala.org/wgss/core-books/
Maintained by academic librarians, this list includes books currently in print that are considered essential to supporting a women's or gender studies program. It contains many subcategories, including intersectional identities.

The Anti-Racist Reading List, by Ibram X. Kendi https://www.theatlantic.com/ideas/archive/2019/02/antiracist-syllabus-governor-ralph-northam/582580/
Published in 2019 and not updated, this list by the author of *How to Be an Antiracist* describes "38 books for those open to changing themselves, and their world."

Bibliographies in Gender and Women's Studies https://www.library.wisc
.edu/gwslibrarian/bibliographies/
Curated by the Office of the Gender and Women's Studies Librarian at the
University of Wisconsin – Madison and written by librarians, faculty, and
graduate students, this is a series of many lengthy bibliographies on topics
within gender and women's studies, such as sex work, infertility, or queer
pulp fiction. The first list was created in 1977, and new lists are added each
year.

Book list from the First Nations Development Institute https://www.firstna-
tions.org/knowledge-center/books/
Created by the staff of the First Nations Development Institute, a nonprofit
with a mission to "strengthen American Indian economics," this list contains
"essential reading for anyone interested in the Native American experience."

Charleston Syllabus https://www.aaihs.org/resources/charlestonsyllabus/
Initially crowdsourced, then compiled into a list by a professor affiliated with
the African American Intellectual History Society, this list aims to "provide
valuable information about the history of racial violence in this country and
contextualize the history of race relations in South Carolina and the United
States in general."

Source: Author.

As with awards, when choosing a bibliography you will need to pay attention to who is responsible for deciding what goes on the list. One type of list
that is easy to find but should not be used as a stand-alone evaluation tool is
that found on library guides. These lists usually include only the holdings of the
library that created the guide. Such a list could form a piece of a larger bibliography that you create yourself, but since the other library probably doesn't
have every highly recommended book on any given population, a bibliography
limited to a single library's holdings won't be useful on its own. Another type
of list to avoid is one that is crowdsourced with no control over the contributions, such as the many lists that exist on the popular book review website
Goodreads. The bibliography should rely on the contributions of identifiable
people who have a connection to the population being represented and enough
expertise to say which books are significant.

It's also important to pay attention to the date that a bibliography was
created and whether it is currently updated. A desirable, though not essential,
feature of bibliographies is that they clearly indicate whether each resource
is a book, article, website, or something else. Though it is usually possible to

differentiate resource types based on how the citations are formatted, it will be easier to use a list that is already sorted or labeled.

There is a tool that can provide bibliographies on many subjects, and that is *Resources for College Libraries (RCL)*. It is a database of over 90,000 reviews of books considered desirable for undergraduate research and teaching. Reviews are written by subject editors, who are librarians and academic faculty. There are editors for African American Studies, Asian American Studies, Gender Studies, Latino Studies, LGBTQ Studies, and Native American Studies, among many other subject areas. Melissa Gonzalez's audit, described in the next chapter, involved title lists from *RCL* that she compared to her university's holdings. This allowed for an evaluation of many identities at once. The primary downside is that *RCL* is a subscription database to which many libraries don't have access. Its undergraduate focus may also make it insufficient for research libraries.

Creating your own bibliography is also an option. While this is more work than using an existing bibliography, you might appreciate the flexibility to design your reverse audit to cover the specific topics or populations relevant to you. When Glyneva Bradley-Ridout, Kaushar Mahetaji, and Mikaela Mitchell evaluated their collection of dermatology books illustrating non-white skin tones, the scarcity of such books required combining many strategies to find enough titles to compile a bibliography. They started with a literature search in databases such as Google Scholar, PubMed, Web of Science. These searches returned articles, which the authors mined for citations. They also looked for articles that cited the ones they had found. Other medical librarians and faculty served as additional sources of suggested titles. Lastly, the authors did a web search for LibGuides on "Skin of Color." The resulting list is published in an appendix to their article.[6]

Other ways to create your own bibliography could be pulling together citations from your students' dissertations, titles mentioned in reference books, or faculty recommendations. If you are building a list from disparate sources, make sure you set a guideline for how significant something needs to be to make it on the list. It would not make sense to be checking for award-winning books by and about Black people but have your list of books by or about Native Americans be based on the works cited in one person's dissertation. It would be more comparable to have a list of books recommended in a reference work or frequently cited.

VENDOR LISTS

A third type of list that could be the basis of a reverse DEI audit is a list or a collection created by a vendor. These have the advantages of easy availability (if you are a customer of that vendor) and breadth.

ProQuest, a Clarivate company, maintains "Curated Topics" lists on their OASIS ordering platform as well as their newer acquisitions tool Rialto. The lists cover many topics that would be relevant to a DEI audit, such as Asian Studies, Black History, Indigenous Studies, Autism, Disability Studies. Created by ProQuest's collection development librarians, the lists include recent, highly requested books and prioritize reputable academic publishers and books that have been reviewed or won awards. Books on curated lists are available in both electronic and print forms.[7]

GOBI Library Solutions, part of EBSCO, similarly offers Spotlight Lists devoted to DEI. These cover a number of populations, with lists for African American, Global Black Studies, Indigenous United States, Indigenous Canada, Indigenous Australia and New Zealand, Islamic Studies, and LGBTQIA Studies, among others. The lists, selected by GOBI Senior Collection Development Managers, contain top sellers and award winners. Staff make an effort to seek out smaller publishers and may include nonacademic titles.[8] They appear to be limited to ebooks and primarily consist of books published in the last decade, though some are older.

Both ProQuest and GOBI offer DEI-focused ebook collections as well. While these are intended as packages for purchase, rather than lists to use for assessment, some people have used them as a point of comparison against their existing collections. ProQuest's collection includes books that have won awards from *Resources for College Libraries* or *Choice*. This list could be an alternative assessment tool for libraries that do not have access to *RCL*. The main drawback is that by nature the list only includes books that are available as ebooks. Rather than one overarching collection, GOBI has several collections on topics such as African American Studies, African Voices on Africa, Latin American Studies, LGBTQIA+ Studies, Worldwide Topics in Antiracism. These would have the same drawback as the ProQuest collection.

COMPILING AND FINALIZING YOUR LIST

As stated earlier, you might mix several types of lists together to create your own or make slight revisions to whichever list you've decided to use. As noted above, you could use winners-only of some awards and winners plus finalists of other awards to balance out the representation of different populations or disciplines. You may want to check if there are books you want to eliminate from the list as well. If you don't collect books in languages other than English, for instance, you would remove these. Decide if you want to include children's books in your list or exclude them. You might also want to stratify your list in some way. For example, if your list is based on awards that have been granted annually for many years, you might separate the analysis of books that won awards before 2000 from those that won later.

PREPARING TO CONDUCT THE EVALUATION

The process of doing an assessment based on a list is not technologically complicated. Most likely you will simply look up the titles one by one. Start by putting all the titles in a spreadsheet. It would be useful to include the publisher, as your analysis of the results might include noting whether you are more likely to be missing the titles issued by smaller publishers. You should also include the year, as you might find you're more likely to have the newer titles. Author is also helpful so that you can verify a match in cases where the title is made up solely of common words or a single word. You can include the ISBN, but most likely you won't be using it to search. If you are counting something as a match that is a later edition or an ebook, it won't have the same ISBN that is on your spreadsheet. If your audit will involve making comparisons by population, it would help to note the population in its own column. This will make it easier later on to check if, for example, you have a greater percentage of the books on the list about LGBTQ people than those about Asian Americans. It is likely some books will relate to multiple groups, however. The book *Shadow Life* by Hiromi Goto won the 2022 Asian/Pacific American Literature Award for Adult Fiction and was a 2021 finalist for the Lambda Literary Awards in the category of LGBTQ Comics. In this case you would list both Asian/Pacific and LGBTQ as the population. The spreadsheet should also have a column for recording holdings. You may want to have multiple holdings columns, such as one for print and one for online, or columns based on different library locations.

Another preparatory step is deciding what counts as a match. Some considerations are listed in text box 5.2. If multiple staff members will be doing the lookup, it is important to have clear instructions written out, especially if there are student workers who might be working at times that full-time staff are not available to answer questions.

**TEXT BOX 5.2 DECIDING WHAT TO COUNT AS HELD
BY YOUR LIBRARY**

- Will ebook holdings count, or only print?
- Will books that are not allowed to circulate count?
- Will books from a rental collection (i.e., McNaughton Leisure books) count?
- Will lost or missing items count?
- Will you count open-access ebooks that are not yet in your catalog?
- Will you count titles that are in your catalog but not yet purchased, such as demand-driven acquisitions?
- Will you count different editions than the one mentioned in your list?

Source: Author.

Table 5.2   Example Tracking Sheet for List-Checking

Author	Title	Publisher	Year	Population	Print	Electronic
Swan	Pauulu's Diaspora: Black Internationalism and Environmental Justice	University Press of Florida	2020	Black/African diaspora	1	1
So	Afterparties	Ecco	2021	Asian/Asian American; LGBTQ	1	1
Wong	Disability Visibility: First Person Stories from the 21st Century	Vintage Books	2020	Disability		1
Total					2	3

Source: Author.

CONDUCTING THE EVALUATION

The process will involve verifying your holdings by looking for title and author matches in the catalog. You may want to instruct student workers or other staff on techniques for searching, such as whether they should include the author's name in the search, or how far down in the results list they should scan looking for a match.

The most straightforward way to indicate findings is to put a number 1 in the appropriate cell of the spreadsheet if your library has the title. Using numbers rather than an X or the word "yes" allows you to tally the total number of matches using the SUM formula in Excel. Be aware, however, that if you have a tally of print holdings and a tally of electronic, you can't add them together to get the total number of books that you own. You may have access to some books in both formats, and you don't want to double-count them.

While it may be tempting, don't start purchasing books off the list while the evaluation is underway! Doing so will give you a false sense of what a great job you are doing collecting books about the underrepresented groups you are targeting in the evaluation. The list can be a useful selection tool once you are done with the audit.

LOOKING AT RESULTS

The basic outcome of a list-checking analysis will be a percentage, or several percentages. Depending on whether you have divided your list by year or identity and whether you have noted the holdings separately by format, you might find numbers such as: how many of the titles you hold in print and how many electronically, how many of the books about each population you have, how many of the newer books and how many of the older. You then want to convert these to percentages. Having both raw numbers and percentages generally makes it easier to understand the significance of a number, and it also means that if you want to make comparisons across different sections of the list, you can compare like to like. For instance, you could find you have 75 percent of the books on your list related to African American Studies but only 50 percent of the books related to Jewish Studies. This could help your library target future collection development efforts, using the relative percentages of titles owned about different populations to decide where to initially focus.

As noted earlier, list-checking is the only evaluation method that shows you what you are missing, and therefore it is especially likely to lead to changes in purchasing. Some libraries simply note what percentage of the books they have and then buy the rest. This turns the project into less of an audit and more of a collection development activity, where the audit replicates your usual process of checking existing holdings before ordering. In this case, finding or creating a list and searching your catalog may still teach you about the field or population of focus and about your collection, so the process itself may be more valuable than the number you calculate at the end. If the list is long, you might select titles from it to purchase rather than ordering them all. If certain smaller publishers recur on your lists, you might research them and decide to add them to your approval profiles or request their catalogs. Some additional steps will be discussed in chapter 12.

NOTES

1. Karen Kohn, Emily Crawford, Noa Kaumeheiwa, and Jenny Pierce, "Inclusive Collecting, Inclusive Cataloging – Acquiring and Describing Award-Winning Books Honoring Diverse Experiences," *Library Resources and Technical Services* 68, no. 4 (2024), https://journals.ala.org/index.php/lrts/article/view/8325.
2. Baton Rouge Area Foundation, "Criteria & Submission," The Ernest J. Gaines Award for Literary Excellence, 2023, https://ernestjgainesaward.org/criteria.
3. Amalia Monroe-Gulick and Sara E. Morris, "Diversity in Monographs: Selectors, Acquisitions, Publishers, and Vendors," *Collection Management* 48, no. 3 (2023): 215.
4. Kohn et al., "Inclusive Collecting, Inclusive Cataloging."
5. "Aanii / Boozhoo / Osiyo / Halito / Ya'at'eeh / Greetings!" Association for the Study of American Indian Literatures, 2022, https://www.asail.org/.
6. Glyneva Bradley-Ridout, Kaushar Mahetaji, and Mikaela Mitchell, "Using a Reverse Diversity Audit Approach to Evaluate a Dermatology Collection in an Academic Health Sciences Library: A Case Presentation," *The Journal of Academic Librarianship* 49, no. 6 (2023): 102650.

7. Ex Libris, Part of Clarivate, "Working with Curated Lists," Knowledge Center, viewed on July 25, 2023, https://knowledge.exlibrisgroup.com/Rialto/Product_Documentation/020Rialto_Selector_Guide/Working_with_Curated_Lists; ProQuest, Part of Clarivate, "Curated Topics," viewed on December 8, 2023, https://about.proquest.com/en/customer-care/curated-topics/.

8. EBSCO, "Building a Diverse and Inclusive Collection Using GOBI Spotlight Lists," October 6, 2022, https://www.ebsco.com/blogs/ebscopost/2158243/building-diverse-and-inclusive-collection-using-gobi-spotlight-lists.

6

Two Strategies for List-Checking at the University of West Florida

Melissa Gonzalez

I began thinking about conducting a diversity audit at my library in 2019 with increasing awareness of various social movements in the public consciousness, like Black Lives Matter, #MeToo, gay rights, and Indigenous land rights. Cognizant of my own evolving collection development practices, I was curious as to how well the University of West Florida (UWF) Libraries' overall monograph acquisitions and holdings supported these areas. UWF is a mid-sized regional comprehensive research university located in Pensacola, Florida, serving students, faculty, staff, and community members across three physical facilities. Enrollment is almost 15,000 students, of which 57.5 percent self-report as white and approximately 51 percent reside in the local tri-county area. UWF offers more than seventy-five undergraduate degree programs, thirty-four master's programs, two specialist degrees, and three doctoral degrees. The libraries shelve over 750,000 print volumes and electronic resources include more than 390,000 e-books and access to approximately 150,000 journal and other serial titles.

I started preparing for my audit by reviewing the literature related to diversity collection assessment and methodologies and found more about public and school libraries than academic, particularly with emphases on children's and YA literature. Most of what I found about academic libraries described assessments focused on a particular identity group and/or library subcollection, like a project at University of California Irvine that studied the diversity of authors of the play scripts the library had purchased over nine fiscal years,[1] or a 2016 study of the availability of LGBTQ materials across ten Protestant College Libraries.[2] However, a 2010 article by Ciszek and Young at the Pennsylvania

State University about assessing diversity in academic libraries discussed more holistic approaches and multiple methodologies.[3] This article laid the framework for my project as it aligned with my original vision of a more comprehensive diversity collection audit. I began the assessment in March 2020, roughly a week before the Covid-19 pandemic shutdown, which fortuitously provided me with larger blocks of uninterrupted time to devote to the endeavor.

The goal of the audit was to evaluate UWF's monograph collection through a diversity lens in order to learn what percentage reflected something other than the experiences of white, heteronormative, and non-disabled males, as articulated by Jensen.[4] I made the ambitious (and now admittedly naive) decision to assess as much content as I could with the idea of establishing a baseline for moving forward. My first step was to review the list of federally protected classes at UWF, using it as a starting point for deciding what themes to include in the overall assessment.[5] Taking some classes from this list and adding a few others, I chose areas of interest based on themes of race, ethnicity, immigration, gender, sexual identity, socioeconomic status, ability/neurodiversity, and general diversity, intersectionality, and social justice. I intentionally excluded topics related to political and religious diversity, largely because 2020 was a contentious election year, particularly in the state of Florida. I also did not include an author identity component in the audit. I firmly believe that authentic voices and lived experiences are essential to a truly diverse collection, but I am not willing to make any assumptions about author's identities in cases where they have not self-identified. I then compiled student enrollment data and demographic statistics for the local region for guidance about what I should be looking for in the results.

Knowing that no single method would tell me everything I wanted to know, I decided to take a multi-method approach that included list-checking, reviewing circulation data, and diversity coding. This case study will highlight the list-checking phases of the project. The list-checking method has been in practice for a long time and as you read in the preceding chapter, it is one of the simpler approaches you can take to assessing a collection. Since I was conducting this audit solo and had not previously done anything similar, I concluded that list-checking was a logical place to start.

BOWKER BOOK ANALYSIS SYSTEM

My initial step was to make use of UWF's access to the Bowker Book Analysis System (BBAS), a collection analysis tool, which allows libraries to upload their holdings and compare them to *Resources for College Libraries'* (*RCL*) core bibliography.[6] UWF had already been using BBAS for several years, so I was already familiar with the interface and functionality. One of the main advantages of BBAS is the automation, as the data collection and counting are done for you. The turnaround time is also pretty quick, which is useful if you have a tight

                                                   Melissa Gonzalez

deadline or are working solo. In my first iteration of this collection evaluation, it took less than an hour to run twenty-two reports and export them into Excel, plus an additional few hours spent on compilation and analysis.

Another notable advantage of BBAS is that you can compare holdings by either *RCL* subjects or Library of Congress (LC) classification ranges. The *RCL* taxonomy is built on sixty-one curriculum-specific subjects,[7] including traditional disciplines such as anthropology, biology, and visual arts, yet significant value comes in the form of its interdisciplinary subjects, like African American studies, urban studies, and Victorian studies. The established *RCL* categories I used in my assessment were African American Studies; African History, Languages, & Literatures; Asian American Studies; Asian History, Languages, & Literatures; Gender Studies; Latin American History; Latino Studies; LGBTQ Studies; Middle Eastern History, Languages, & Literatures; Native American Studies; and Spanish History, Languages, & Literatures.

I also ran reports using LC call ranges covering similar topics to those in the *RCL* interdisciplinary categories, but also for those areas not covered by the interdisciplinary categories. For example, there are no *RCL* subjects for disability/neurodiversity, immigration, or Jewish studies, so LC classification was the only avenue for collecting that data. I initially used eleven LC ranges: Afro-Americans; Class; Elements of the Population (includes racial, ethnic, and religious groups that have significance in the history of the United States);[8] Emigration and Immigration; Ethnology, Social/Cultural Anthropology; Indians of North America; Latin America; People with Disabilities; Race; Sexual Life; Women, Feminism. After analyzing the results, I recognized how much diversity I was missing from within other LC classes and added an additional twenty LC ranges in the subsequent assessment. For instance, I did not include Judaism (BM) as part of the Jewish category in my first evaluation because I had intentionally excluded religious diversity from the assessment. However, upon closer investigation, I ascertained that significant coverage of Jewish history and culture appears in this subclass, with fewer titles included within the Elements of the Population (E184-184.4) range. Adding the Hebrew Languages & Literature (PJ4501-5192) and History of Asia—Israel (DS101-151) ranges further fleshed out holdings related to the Jewish theme. See text box 6.1 for a complete list of LC ranges used.

TEXT BOX 6.1 LC CLASSIFICATION RANGES

African Languages & Literatures PL8000-8844	Judaism BM1-990
*Afro-Americans E184.5-185.98	*Latin America F1202-3799

Arabic Languages & Literatures
PJ6001-8517

Asian Languages & Literatures
PL1-4890

*Class
HT601-1445

*Elements of the Population
E184-184.4

*Emigration and Immigration
JV6001-9489

*Ethnology, Social/Cultural Anthropology
GN301-674

Hebrew Languages & Literatures
PJ4501-5192

History of Africa
DT1-3415

History of Asia
DS331-349.9; DS401-937

History of Asia (Israel)
DS101-151

History of Asia (Middle East)
DS35.3-99; DS153-329.4; DS350-396.9

*Indians of North America
E51-99

Indo-Iranian Languages & Literatures
PK1-9601

Islam
BP1-610

Neurosciences
RC321-571

*People with Disabilities
HV1551-3025

*Race
HT1501-1595

Sex Role
HQ1075-1090.7

*Sexual Life
HQ12-449

Social/Public Welfare—Refugee Problems
HV640-645

Spanish & Portuguese Languages
PC4001-5498

Spanish & Portuguese Literatures
PQ6001-9699

Special Classes—Gay, Lesbian
HV1449

Special Classes—Poor, Homelessness
HV4023-4630

Special Classes—Race, Ethnic Group
HV3176-3199

Special Classes—Women
HV1442-1448

*Women, Feminism
HQ1101-2030.7

Note: Starred ranges are those included in the initial set of reports.

Source: Chapter author.

                                                                              Melissa Gonzalez

For each subject or call number range, BBAS reports show the total number and percentage of core titles held by your library and the number of core titles not held. Figure 6.1 shows an example of the numerical results. The numbers provide links to title lists and the percentages provide a benchmark to work from and a basis for comparison year to year. Additionally, the list of titles not held serves as a recommended list for further collection development. Figure 6.2 shows one such list of titles not held.

Using both *RCL* categories and LC classification has the benefit of flexibility. LC ranges are necessary for gathering data on identities and themes with no corresponding *RCL* subject, yet any analysis that relies solely on the

RCL Classification	Core Titles in Library	Core Titles NOT in Library	Total # of Core Titles	% of Core Titles Held
GRAND TOTALS:	18,473	75,794	94,267	19.60%
• - MIDDLE EASTERN HISTORY, LANGUAGES, AND LITERATURES	520	3,067	3,587	14.50%
General and Reference	15	144	159	9.43%
+ History of Specific Countries	255	1,215	1,470	17.35%
+ Islamic Middle East	96	597	693	13.85%
+ Middle Eastern Languages and Literatures	130	1,168	1,298	10.02%
Pre-Islamic Middle East to 622	4	23	27	14.81%
+ Special Topics	156	876	1,032	15.12%

Figure 6.1   BBAS: Middle Eastern History, Languages, and Literatures. **©2024 Clarivate. Certain data included herein are derived from the Bowker Book Analysis System ©2024 of Clarivate.** All rights reserved. You may not copy or re-distribute this material in whole or in part without the prior written consent of Clarivate.

Core Titles NOT in Library: UWFALL

Enter criteria and Click Go to jump to the closest match within the current sort view

Go To Title : [GO]

Core Lists: Resources for College Libraries   Subject: GENDER STUDIES   0 titles selected   [Copy List]   [Clear List]   [DOWNLOAD ALL RESULTS]
1-50 of 1420 rows

* indicates a title with a different format or edition at your library.   (Click on any header to sort this report)   MORE OPTIONS ⚙

Add to List	Title ▲	Author	Publisher	LC Class	Library (ISBN13)	Matched ISBN13	Price	Format	Pub Year	Status
☐	100 Years of the Nineteenth Amendment: An Appraisal of Women's Political Activism	McCammon, Holly J	OXFORD UNIVERSITY PRESS, INCORPORATED	HQ1236.S UBA16 2018		978-0-19-026516-1	USD 53.00	Trade Paper	2018	In Print
☐	25 Women: Essays on Their Art	Hickey, Dave	UNIVERSITY OF CHICAGO PRESS	N8354 H53 2015		978-0-226-33315-1	USD 31.00	Trade Cloth	2016	In Print
☐	37 Words: Title IX and Fifty Years of Fighting Sex Discrimination	Boucher, Sherry	NEW PRESS, THE	KF4155 B67 2022		978-1-62097-563-1	USD 29.99	Trade Cloth	2022	In Print
☐	4000 Years of Women in Science		SYNDETICS REBUILD FAKE CO NAME	Q130						In Print
☐	50 Key Concepts in Gender Studies	Pilcher, Jane	CREDO REFERENCE			978-1-84972-424-1		E-Book	2009	In Print
☐	50 Women Artists You Should Know	Weidemann, Christiane	PRESTEL VERLAG GMBH & CO KG	N8354		978-3-7913-6761-3	USD 19.96	Trade Paper	2017	In Print
☐	A Biographical Dictionary of Women Healers: Midwives, Nurses, and Physicians	Scrivener, Laurie	BLOOMSBURY PUBLISHING PLC	R692		978-1-57356-219-5	USD 98.00	Trade Cloth	2002	In Print
☐	A Biographical Dictionary of Women's Movements and Feminisms: Central, Eastern, and South Eastern Europe, 19th and 20th Centuries	Daskalova, Krassimira	CENTRAL EUROPEAN UNIVERSITY PRESS	HQ1590.7 .Z75A336		978-963-7326-39-4	USD 121.00	Trade Cloth	2006	In Print
☐	A Celebration of Women Writers		SYNDETICS REBUILD FAKE CO NAME	TK5105.5						In Print
☐	A Cheerful and Comfortable Faith: Anglican Religious Practice in the Elite Households of Eighteenth-Century Virginia	Winner, Lauren F	YALE UNIVERSITY PRESS	BX5917.V8W56 2010		978-0-300-12466-9	USD 81.00	Trade Cloth	2010	In Print

Figure 6.2   BBAS: Gender Studies—Titles Not Held. ©2024 Clarivate. Certain data included herein are derived from the Bowker Book Analysis System ©2024 of Clarivate. All rights reserved. You may not copy or re-distribute this material in whole or in part without the prior written consent of Clarivate.

LC classification scheme may miss multi- and interdisciplinary titles as a book can only have one call number no matter the content. For example, the LC call number for *Mouths of Rain: An Anthology of Black Lesbian Thought* begins with PS509, for Collections of American Literature. This title would be missed in a call number range review for E184.5-185.98 (Afro-Americans), HQ75-76.8 (Homosexuality, Lesbianism), or HQ1101-2030.7 (Women, Feminism).[9] However, it does appear in the title list for *RCL*'s African American Studies subject category since it is not restricted by a classification range. To further illustrate, at the time of this writing, *RCL* listed 738 core titles in the E51-73 (Pre-Columbian America. The Indians) and E75-99 (Indians of North America) LC ranges, contrasted with 936 core titles in *RCL*'s Native American Studies subject. While the high-level *RCL* subject categories are quite broad, each is further broken down into subcategories, thus providing options for more granular study. For instance, I can use the overall count for Native American Studies to know how many titles we own that have anything to do with Native American Studies. If I want to know specifically about Native American history holdings, the subdivisions reveal how many titles focus on twentieth century versus Colonial America. See figure 6.3 for some of the subdivisions within Native American Studies.

I ran the first analysis in March 2020 using holdings from 2019, then repeated it each year with updated holdings. If you plan to do annual comparisons, I recommend uploading a current holdings file and running the reports around the same time every year for an accurate snapshot of that moment. The uploaded holdings files are static, while the *RCL* core lists undergo a continuous process of adding and/or removing titles. Thus, comparing an older holdings file against the current *RCL* core list will not deliver an accurate assessment because the *RCL* lists are dynamic and change regularly. For instance, the *RCL* core list for Asian American Studies was 853 titles in 2022 and 1,065 titles in 2023, a difference of 212. As such, comparing a 2022 holdings file in 2022 and again in 2023 would yield different results and percentages for the same list of holdings. I learned this lesson in the second year of my assessment, which explains why there are no BBAS figures for 2020 included in my results. We generally upload a new holdings file in August of each year. Because I ran the reports for 2019 holdings in March 2020, running the 2020 analysis in August 2020 with only five months in between resulted in the core title list not having changed much during that time. Since then I always run reports at the time we upload a new holdings file.

In terms of results, the percentage of core titles owned by UWF unfortunately dropped in all eleven *RCL* subjects between 2019 and 2024. The largest decrease was LGBTQ Studies, which dropped 19.9 percentage points from 44.8 percent to 24.9 percent. The smallest drop was African American Studies, dropping 2.9 percentage points from 37.5 percent to 34.6 percent. Interestingly, despite the drop in percentage owned across all eleven categories, the actual number of titles held increased in five of them.

                                                                                       Melissa Gonzalez

• – NATIVE AMERICAN STUDIES
   + Anthropology and Archeology
   Art
   Education
   Environmental Issues
   General and Reference
   Health and Medicine
   – History
      20th Century
      21st Century
      Colonial Period
      Contact and Exploration
      Early American
      General
      Manifest Destiny
      Removal Period
   + Languages and Linguistics
   + Literature, Music, Dance, and Film
   + Politics and Government
   Religion and Philosophy
   Women and Gender

Figure 6.3   RCL Taxonomy: Native American Studies. ©2024 Clarivate. **Certain data included herein are derived from the Bowker Book Analysis System ©2024 of Clarivate.** All rights reserved. You may not copy or re-distribute this material in whole or in part without the prior written consent of Clarivate.

Likewise, all but two of the thirty-one LC classification ranges experienced percentage declines as well. Both outliers, Special Classes—Race, Ethnic Group (HV3176-3199) and Special Classes—Women (HV1442-1448), increased from 33.3 percent in 2021 to 50 percent in 2024, but when looking at the actual numbers, it was a difference of owning one out of three titles to two out of four and two out of six titles to three out of six, respectively. This scenario precisely illustrates how percentages can be less meaningful when absolute numbers are low. Aside from continuous changes in core title lists, I attribute the primary cause for these percentage decreases to consistently shrinking annual monograph budgets, along with anti-DEI state legislation as a contributing factor. See tables 6.1 and 6.2 for examples of *RCL* and LC results from the BBAS analysis. Full results are available at https://libguides.uwf.edu/divassess/results.

Table 6.1 BBAS Analysis: RCL—Partial Assessment Results

RCL Subject	Year	# Core Titles: Held	# Core Titles: Total	Percentage Held
African American Studies	2024	397	1,149	34.6
	2023	316	1,129	28.0
	2022	319	900	35.4
	2021	302	882	34.2
	2019	321	855	37.5
LGBTQ Studies	2024	214	858	24.9
	2023	262	1,008	26.0
	2022	315	892	35.3
	2021	321	893	36.0
	2019	439	980	44.8

Source: Chapter author.

Table 6.2 BBAS Analysis: LC—Partial Assessment Results

LC Range	Year	# Core Titles: Held	# Core Titles: Total	Percentage Held
Afro-Americans E184.5-185.98	2024	221	513	43.1
	2023	195	503	38.8
	2022	197	441	44.7
	2021	180	433	41.6
	2019	181	406	44.6
Latin America F1202-3799	2024	393	1,430	27.5
	2023	349	1,409	24.8
	2022	352	1,250	28.2
	2021	349	1,231	28.4
	2019	458	1,264	36.2

Source: Chapter author.

While there are many benefits to using BBAS, there are also some limitations. With *RCL*'s focus on the undergraduate curriculum, the core bibliography may exclude some graduate and research-level materials. Furthermore, some of the core titles may be out of your collection scope. As an example, UWF does not have an architecture program, so we do not need to emphasize anything beyond general collecting in that area. There can also be a small margin of error with the title matching comparison, particularly regarding different formats or editions within a collection. This is not a design flaw in BBAS, but more

Melissa Gonzalez

likely the result of inaccurate or incomplete MARC records in the holdings upload, particularly regarding vendor records. Finally, BBAS is a commercial product that requires a subscription. Even if not exorbitant, it is reasonable to assume that it would not be feasible for some libraries to absorb the annual fee.

One of the biggest challenges for analyzing results is defining what indicates a "good" benchmark as there is no obvious goal of what percentage of core titles we should own in each category. For example, we dropped from 21.3 percent *RCL* holdings in Latino Studies in 2019 to 12.6 percent in 2024. Contrast this decline to the three-point increase in our Hispanic enrollment from 9.7 percent in fall 2019 to 12.7 percent in fall 2023. Regardless of any benchmark we may establish for our library, this is a clear trend in the wrong direction. In a 2023 article about diversity audit principles and methods, Walters points out that "no recent study presents a strong, coherent basis for the establishment of specific benchmarks or targets."[10] Similar to the concept of books as mirrors and windows, he further discusses the implications of trying to align collections with the characteristics of a particular community or providing materials that expand a person's knowledge beyond their own experiences. User population demographics are important, but a one-to-one ratio of representation of those community demographics should not be the deciding factor.[11] For instance, if your community includes a large Jewish population, you would want your collection to reflect that. Yet you still want to provide resources reflective of minority groups that may not be heavily represented in your community. As mentioned earlier, I used enrollment and community demographic data for guidance on collection representation, but that data does not translate directly to our collection goals.

DIVERSE BOOK AWARDS

Another list-checking method I utilized was comparing our holdings against winners of diverse book awards, an idea largely informed by several similar studies, including those by Kristick, Proctor, Bosman, and Taler.[12] Similar to my review of the literature on diversity collection assessment, the majority of existing award lists I found focused on children's and YA titles. I did find a few lists and LibGuides through Google that included several adult book awards, and some commercial products, such as BBAS and GOBI, provide search functionality for a number of diversity awards. However, because I had such an ambitious goal for the overall collection assessment, I wanted my analysis to include a wide variety and number of awards, leading me to the decision to develop my own list of awards.[13] There was considerable up-front labor in building the list, and it was arguably the most time-consuming phase of my entire project.

Based on the themes of the overall assessment project, I decided to include ten broad categories: African/African American Studies; Arab/Arab

American/Middle Eastern/Muslim Studies; Asian/Asian American Studies; Disability/Neurodiversity Studies; Hispanic/Latinx/Chicano Studies; Jewish Studies; LGBTQ+ Studies; Native American/Indigenous Studies; Women's/ Gender Studies; and Diversity/Intersectionality/Social Justice. The only original theme not included as an award category was Immigration, as I was not confident I would be able to identify related awards. I spent roughly the equivalent of several dedicated weeks searching Google and professional associations for awards to include in my list, recognizing fairly early on that this task would never be "complete." Again, I conducted these searches when the library was closed during the first few months of the pandemic, so I was able to allocate more time for this research.

My initial investigation yielded an inventory of 138 awards, including 112 awards for nonfiction and 26 for fiction. The longest lists were Diversity/ Intersectionality/Social Justice and LGBTQ+/Sexuality, both with twenty-five awards, followed by Women/Gender at twenty-three and African/African American at twenty-one. Conversely, I only identified two Disability/Neurodiversity and three Native American/Indigenous awards. This wide-ranging sample size between categories does not create a level playing field.

In my effort to keep the project manageable, I compiled only the last three recipients of each award and recorded them in Excel, a process that took approximately two more weeks. In at least two cases I included only two recipients due to the infrequency of awards presented. I also looked solely at the award winners, excluding any finalists or honorable mentions. Assembling the list of winners generated a bibliography of 440 titles. A search of our ILS found that we owned only eighty-seven of these titles, or 19.8 percent. Not surprisingly, the number of titles we owned was highest in the categories with longer award lists and more titles to compare, landing between 21 and 25 percent. Our poorest showings were in Arab/Arab American/Middle Eastern/ Muslim and Disability/Neurodiversity, owning zero of the nineteen and five associated titles, respectively. Here again I struggle with defining appropriate benchmarks. Zero is obviously not enough, but there is no clear target to aim for. Furthermore, I do not deem a comparison of only nine Native American and five disability titles to be a fair or accurate assessment of collection representation in those areas. See table 6.3 for a complete summary of the awards assessment.

It is important to highlight that there exists some intersectionality and crossover between some of the awards, such as the Organization of American Historians' Darlene Clark Hine Award for "the best book in African American women's and gender history," or the Middle East Studies Association's Fatema Mernissi Book Award for "outstanding scholarship in studies of gender, sexuality, and women's lived experience."[14] Trying not to count any title more than once in the assessment so as not to inflate the numbers, I assigned only one category for each award. As a result, the three Hine Award titles were

                                                              Melissa Gonzalez

Table 6.3　Diverse Book Awards—Assessment Results

Category	# Awards	# Titles Compared	# Titles Held	Percentage Held
Diversity/Intersectionality/Social Justice	25	86	22	25.6
African/African American	21	66	17	25.8
Arab/Arab American/Middle Eastern/Muslim	6	19	0	0
Asian/Asian American	9	31	1	3.2
Disability/Neurodiversity	2	5	0	0
Hispanic/Latinx	14	41	10	24.4
Jewish	10	30	2	6.7
LGBTQ+/Sexuality	25	76	16	21.1
Native American/Indigenous	3	9	1	11.1
Women/Gender	23	77	18	23.4
Total	138	440	87	19.8

Soure: Chapter author.

compared in the Women/Gender category but not for African American. If I were to repeat this analysis, I would have less concern for inflated numbers and would count the titles in both categories for more accurate results.

There are also some shortcomings to consider when using the checklist method for award titles. One factor is that the majority of the awards I compiled are for diverse content, whereas only a relative few specifically note diverse authorship and voice in the award's established criteria. If voice representation is something you want to assess, you will probably have to do a substantial amount of investigation on a title-by-title basis as you will not glean much from the award descriptions themselves. Likewise, most of the awards are based in the humanities and social sciences, so business, health, and physical sciences are not well-represented. Expanded research into the professional associations of these underrepresented disciplines would likely yield additional diversity related awards for inclusion in the list.

When analyzing the results, as might be expected in many academic libraries, some awards and titles may fall outside an institution's collection scope for its existing academic programs, providing explanation or justification for why specific award-winning titles are not part of the collection. A somewhat related issue I encountered as I compared our holdings is that many of the titles we own (or have access to) are e-books. Without deeper investigation for confirmation, it is likely that the vast majority of these titles are accessible through subscription packages as opposed to individual purchases, and thus cannot necessarily be attributed to intentional acquisition on our part. In addition, without a "purchased" license, there always remains the potential loss of content access.

Unlike the BBAS analysis that I have conducted annually, I have thus far not repeated the analysis of diverse book award winners. I might reconsider if I could determine how to make it at least a somewhat more equitable endeavor. Ultimately, I do think there is merit in this assessment method, I would recommend pairing it with at least one other approach in an effort to attain more balance.

It should be noted that there are critics of this method who offer several reasons why using checklists of award winners may not be advantageous. Some practitioners posit that a title's presence on an award list itself is an inherent indicator of high quality, including Proctor who reasoned that award titles are "recognized by established organizations as literature with value."[15] Though I do not think many would wholly dispute this line of thought, Emerson and Lehman caution that "it may inadvertently imply that if diverse books are not award winning, then they are lacking in credibility, authority, quality, and value."[16] Monroe-Gulick and Morris remind us that "the criteria used for nominations and final selections is subjective, therefore, all those employing awards list[s] for a diversity audit should question validity of the quality of material included."[17] Walters suggests that checklists of award titles may discount

                                                                 Melissa Gonzalez

the exclusion of "diverse books that have not risen to prominence within the communities" that give out these awards, and further contends that "an over-reliance on award winners and other 'best books' may limit the range of topics and perspectives represented in the collection."[18] Lawrence and Floegel also present a discussion about "library reprizing" and offer suggestions about how librarians and the profession might work to reform "dominant structures of power in print culture."[19] Finally, I believe it a realistic assumption that there are numerous smaller and lesser-known publishers of quality books that may be overlooked by many mainstream awards. However, Kristick found that independent presses accounted for 32 percent of the 2,408 award winners in her study,[20] which could make the case that award titles might also serve as a technique to help discover independently published books that may otherwise be missed through approval plans and other conventional collection development methods.

CONCLUSION

I succeeded in conducting a broad assessment that covered a wide array of topics, yet the dataset itself lacked granularity, which did not always yield the most meaningful data. For example, I may know that UWF holds X number of *RCL* core LGBTQ Studies titles. But because I did not do a deeper content analysis of those holdings, I do not currently know how many of those titles address the different letters of the acronym, such as bisexuality or transgender issues. If the bulk of those books center on the gay male experience, I would argue that while the content is diverse is it not a truly representative LGBTQ+ collection.

Trying to organize humans into categories can be messy because there are no monolith experiences, and the same concept can be applied to books. A collection can be diverse without being inclusive or truly representative. Diverse representation within diversity is fundamental to building an inclusive collection. The breakdown between affirming and non-affirming treatment of the topic is another factor of consideration. Consequently, I now appreciate the importance of starting with a clear focus, and moving forward I am planning smaller, targeted projects that provide more depth than breadth.

I shared the findings with other subject selectors and the library's Collection Development Committee. Based on the data collected thus far, our intent is to define some measurable goals related to collection development of diverse content as part of the UWF Libraries' strategic initiatives, but we have to work carefully to comply with the confines of restrictive state statutes. Nevertheless, even without having anything specific yet set in place, subject selectors are familiar with the data and have been using it informally to influence and guide collection development. Furthermore, the data will also be used to complement the results of a general monograph use assessment we are currently conducting.

As with any collection assessment technique, it is clear there are both benefits and limitations to using the list-checking method. It is a more straight-forward and expedient approach than some other more complex assessment methods and is especially suitable for institutions with less time and fewer staff resources. As has already been mentioned, it is unique in that it can highlight missing items that you "should" own; however, it does fall short in addressing the quality of what you already own. This is one of the reasons I recommend pursuing multiple methods of assessment, if possible. Despite any shortcomings to list-checking, it remains one of the most popular and widely used assessment methods.

NOTES

1. Scott M. Stone, "Whose Play Scripts Are Being Published? A Diversity Audit of One Library's Collection in Conversation with the Broader Play Publishing World," *Collection Management* 45, no. 4 (2020): 304–320, https://doi.org/10.1080/01462679.2020.1715314.
2. Ellen Bosman, "The Availability of Gay and Lesbian Materials in Protestant College Libraries," *Collection Management* 41, no. 2 (2016): 94–106, https://doi.org/10.1080/01462679.2016.1169963.
3. Matthew P. Ciszek and Courtney L. Young, "Diversity Collection Assessment in Large Academic Libraries," *Collection Building* 29, no. 4 (2010): 154–161, https://doi.org/10.1108/01604951011088899.
4. Karen Jensen, "Diversity Auditing 101: How to Evaluate Your Collection," School Library Journal, October 23, 2018, https://www.slj.com/story/diversity-auditing-101-how-to-evaluate-collection.
5. "Prohibition of Discrimination, Harassment and Retaliation," University of West Florida, last modified March 9, 2020, https://confluence.uwf.edu/display/UP/Prohibition+of+Discrimination%2C+Harassment+and+Retaliation.
6. "Bowker Book Analysis System," ProQuest, accessed June 14, 2024, https://about.proquest.com/en/products-services/Bowker-Book-Analysis-System/.
7. "Resources for College Libraries: Frequently Asked Questions," ProQuest, accessed June 14, 2024, https://pq-static-content.proquest.com/collateral/media2/documents/rcl-faqs.pdf.
8. "Schedule E-F," Library of Congress Classification Schedules, Library of Congress, last updated June 27, 2004, https://www.loc.gov/aba/publications/FreeLCC/LCC_E-F2024TEXT.pdf, 36.
9. "Library of Congress Classification Outline," Library of Congress, accessed June 14, 2024, https://www.loc.gov/catdir/cpso/lcco/.
10. William H. Walters, "Assessing Diversity in Academic Library Book Collections: Diversity Audit Principles and Methods," *Open Information Science* 7, no. 1 (2023): 17, https://doi.org/10.1515/opis-2022-0148.
11. Walters, "Assessing Diversity in Academic Library Book Collections," 22.
12. Laurel Kristick, "Diversity Literary Awards: A Tool for Assessing an Academic Library's Collection," *Collection Management* 45, no. 2 (2020): 151–161, https://doi.org/10.1080/01462679.2019.1675209; Julia Proctor, "Representation in the

Collection: Assessing Coverage of LGBTQ Content in an Academic Library Collection," *Collection Management* 45, no. 2 (2020): 223–234, https://doi.org/10 .1080/01462679.2019.1708835; Bosman, "The Availability of Gay and Lesbian Materials in Protestant College Libraries," 2016; Izabella Taler, "The Jewish Studies Book Awards: A Collection Development Strategy for Non-Sectarian Academic Libraries," *Collection Building* 30, no. 1 (2011): 11–38, https://doi.org/10.1108 /01604951111104998.

13. Melissa Gonzalez, "Diverse Book Awards," University of West Florida, May 2020, https://libguides.uwf.edu/DiverseBkAwds.

14. "Darlene Clark Hine Award," Organization of American Historians, accessed June 17, 2024, https://www.oah.org/awards/book-awards-and-prizes/darlene-clark-hine -award; "Fatema Mernissi Book Award," Middle East Studies Association, accessed June 17, 2024, https://mesana.org/awards/category/fatema-mernissi-book-award.

15. Proctor, "Representation in the Collection," 2020, 240; Kristick, "Diversity Literary Awards," 2020, 153.

16. María Evelia Emerson and Lauryn Grace Lehman, "Who Are We Missing? Conducting a Diversity Audit in a Liberal Arts College Library," *The Journal of Academic Librarianship* 48, no. 3 (2022): 2, https://doi.org/10.1016/j.acalib.2022.102517.

17. Amalia Monroe-Gulick and Sara E. Morris, "Diversity in Monographs: Selectors, Acquisitions, Publishers, and Vendors," *Collection Management* 38, no. 3 (2023): 214, https://doi.org/10.1080/01462679.2022.2163019.

18. Walters, "Assessing Diversity in Academic Library Book Collections," 25, 12.

19. E. E. Lawrence and Diana Floegel, "Creating Award Winners in the Library: An Account of 'Reprizing,'" *The Library Quarterly* 92, no. 1one (2022): 39, https://doi .org/10.1086/717235.

20. Kristick, "Diversity Literary Awards," 2020, 157.

7

Metadata Searching

The next assessment method is metadata searching, which involves using the catalog to count how many books you have about a population or topic. There are two types of metadata that provide information about the topic of a work: subject terms and call numbers. Regardless of which type of metadata you use, there will be a large set of applicable search strings, and the most intensive part of the process will be figuring out what these are. Putting the terms or call numbers you've identified into a search interface also requires some care. This chapter will discuss how to create a list of search terms or call numbers and suggest ways of searching your catalog based on the terms or ranges you identify.

UNDERSTANDING SUBJECT TERMS

Catalog searches rely on the metadata that already exists in records. While some assessments rely on keyword searches of catalog records, such searches can result in false matches. A more precise way to search is to use the subject headings, since these are selected from a controlled vocabulary, meaning a governing body authorizes particular terms or phrases for use to ensure consistency and disambiguation.

The majority of subject headings in library catalogs come from the Library of Congress Subject Headings (LCSH). The list of authorized terms has been growing for over a hundred years and currently contains more than 300,000 terms. Controlled vocabularies are also characterized by defined relationships between terms; for instance, the record for an authorized term often contains references to broader or narrower terms. Additional headings can be created by adding an authorized subdivision to a heading, for example "Civil rights—United States," in which the heading of "Civil rights" is subdivided geographically to indicate that the work covers the United States. A work can be assigned up to ten subject terms, but guidance is to only assign headings that are covered by at least 20 percent of the work.[1]

Although there is extensive library literature noting biases or outright offensive language in the Library of Congress Subject Headings, they are still used as a tool for diversity assessments due to their ubiquity and their structure. Headings in a controlled vocabulary are constructed in a way that allows disambiguation between different meanings of the same word or phrase. For instance, LCSH has distinct headings for "Passing (Football)" and "Passing (Identity)." The specificity of LCSH terms means a search using this controlled vocabulary will have fewer irrelevant results than a search done with natural language keywords. A keyword search for accessibility, for instance, brings up many books that use the term in ways that are not necessarily related to disability, for example *Accessibility: The Rural Challenge*, which is about lack of transportation options to rural areas of Britain. In contrast, the official subject heading "Barrier-free design" may be a less familiar term but more reliably offers results related to disabled people's physical access to buildings.

There are other controlled vocabularies used in libraries, though they do not have the breadth of coverage of LCSH. Many academic medical libraries use Medical Subject Headings, or MeSH, which are regulated by the National Library of Medicine. Canadian Subject Headings are produced by Libraries and Archives Canada to describe, in English, subjects related to Canada. Some libraries have begun supplementing LCSH with Homosaurus, a vocabulary of LGBTQ+ search terms initially created in 1997 and updated approximately twice a year. If you know that your library uses one of these vocabularies routinely, you can include headings from it in your searches as well.

SHORTCOMINGS OF SUBJECT TERMS

There are many shortcomings and difficulties to using LCSH. The most straightforward issue is that a catalog record will not always describe a book as completely as it could. Catalog records vary in terms of how extensively they describe a resource, with some records containing more subject terms than others. Fiction is especially likely to have sparse subject headings. The catalog record for *Song of Solomon* by Toni Morrison, for example, includes a summary that mentions "four generations of African American life" but contains no subject headings at all, only the genre term "Fiction." The Afrofuturist novel *The Obelisk Gate* by N. K. Jemisin has only "Mothers and daughters" and several genre terms, including "Apocalyptic fiction" and "Fantasy fiction."

In addition to relevant subject headings simply being missing, a book might not be cataloged with the most relevant subject heading because that heading was not authorized at the time the book was published. In order for a new term to be accepted into a controlled vocabulary, there needs to be a literary warrant. In other words, there must be existing literature to which the new subject headings would be applied before the headings are approved. In practice this means that the earliest materials in any emerging field of study won't have appropriate subject headings, because authorized terms did not yet exist at the times these works were first cataloged. Lori Jahnke, Kyle Tanaka, and Christopher Palozzolo give the example of disability studies, which began to be seen as a field of study in the 1980s but had no subject heading until 2001.[2]

Once terms are added to LCSH, in theory the Library of Congress will change them as language itself changes. However, changes to LCSH do not always keep pace with changes in language, and offensive or outdated terms remain authorized even after people have moved away from using them in speech or writing. The term "Slaves" was changed to "Enslaved persons" in March 2023, despite written articles advocating use of the latter for at least ten years prior. Even when LCSH adapts over time, a term that some members of a group find respectful might feel inappropriate to others. Janis Young notes the evolution of the heading "Cripples" to "Physically handicapped" to the current phrase "People with disabilities," approved in 2001.[3] Though the most recent iteration of the heading is a phrase that is still commonly used in speech, not all people who could be described as people with disabilities like this wording. Some people prefer to describe themselves using disability-first language, such as disabled person or autistic person, though preferences differ between and within disability communities.[4]

Several librarians have noted inherent aspects of the way LCSH is regulated that mean it will always contain some bias or offensive terminology. Steven Knowlton explains that LCSH favors the wording most likely to be used by library patrons searching for materials, and that the hypothetical user is implicitly defined as a white Christian heterosexual male.[5] In addition, getting a revised subject heading accepted requires demonstrating that the new term is considered standard, and encyclopedias or other reference works, which themselves can be slow to change, are often used as authoritative sources on what constitutes standard wording. When Dartmouth College submitted a proposal in 2014 to change the heading "Illegal aliens" to "Undocumented immigrants," it was initially rejected because standard law references were still using the term "illegal aliens."[6] A change was eventually made in 2016 to "Noncitizens" and "Unauthorized immigration."

Subject headings can also be applied in an anachronistic way that imposes contemporary (or slightly outdated) identity categories on people of the past. The term "Transsexualism," which the Trans Metadata Collective says is no longer predominant though still used by some,[7] is an authorized subject heading in LCSH. The term is found in catalog records for several books describing a time before the word would've been in use, books that do not include the word "transsexual" anywhere in the text. Examples are *Debating Sex and Gender in Eighteenth-Century Spain* and *The Intermediate Sex: A Study of Some Transitional Types of Men and Women*, first published in 1908. While using modern terminology can be helpful according to the principle of using vocabulary that the average user might type into a search box, using subject headings to identify these books as ones relating to the LGBTQ community or specifically the trans community will result in imposing contemporary understandings of identity on people of the past who would not have had the same frame of reference.

Using subject headings to count the number of books in your library catalog related to diverse populations has difficulties in terms of practicality, accuracy, and sensitivity. Nevertheless, you might choose this method due to its ability to survey the entire collection relatively quickly. If you are planning to do a search using LCSH terms, be aware that you are very likely to encounter wording that makes you uncomfortable. If you are delegating to others the task of finding appropriate search terms or conducting searches, it is best to warn them as well.

IDENTIFYING SUBJECT TERMS

With the above caveats in mind, you will begin preparing for your search by trying to find all the relevant subject headings on the populations you want to assess. Because of the wide variety of topics that relate to any particular population and the large number of LCSH headings, any search for a demographic group will be very complex. If you are trying to quantify your library's holdings of books about African Americans, for example, a simple search for the phrase "African Americans" would not retrieve a complete list. Many other subject terms relate to African Americans but do not include that exact phrase, for instance "African Methodist Episcopal Church."

Sara Howard and Steven Knowlton, whose work compiling extensive lists of call numbers related to African Americans and LGBTQ people will be discussed later, point out how often a subject term is implicitly about a specific group of people without naming that group. For example, jazz music has its origins among African Americans in Southern states. Therefore, Howard and Knowlton assert that books about jazz should be included in a comprehensive search on African Americans.[8] The names of key individuals would also be useful, as would terms for specific events or movements that centered African Americans, such as the Harlem Renaissance or the Say Her Name movement. A handful of compilations of subject terms related to specific DEI topics or populations exist and are listed in text box 7.1, though due to the small number of compilations you will probably need to make your own list.

TEXT BOX 7.1 COMPILATIONS OF LIBRARY OF CONGRESS SUBJECT HEADINGS

Queer LCSH. https://www.netanelganin.com/projects/QueerLCSH/Queer LCSH.html
Was maintained by Netanel Ganin, no longer updated as of 12/2022. Includes over 1,200 terms. Lists nonauthorized terms with *See* references to the authorized terms. Also notes broader and narrower terms.

Trans and Gender Diverse LCSHs https://zenodo.org/record/6829167
Section 5.2 (page 28) of "Metadata Best Practices for Trans and Gender Diverse Resources," written by The Trans Metadata Collective, July 22, 2022. Includes 130 terms, not including compound headings that can be created with free-floating or geographic subdivisions.

Racism (Researching Racism): Identifying Available Books (print and electronic) https://libguides.asu.edu/racism/LCSH
From Arizona State University. Last updated Sep 9, 2021.
Contains 719 terms related to "race, race relations, racism, multiculturalism, pluralism, ethnic identity, ethnic relations, civil rights, civil rights movements, and diversity." Note that the search terms do not cover all aspects of the experience of nondominant racial groups but are focused on racism.

Source: Author.

There are two strategies you can use to create a list of subject headings. One is to conduct keyword searches of your own catalog, then look at the results and note the headings that appear in the records. For example, a keyword search for the word "Latino" brings up a record for Justice Sonia Sotomayor's memoir *My Beloved World*, which has the subject headings "Hispanic Americans," "Hispanic American women," and "Latinos (U.S.)," among others.[9] If you follow this approach, make sure you check several of the results in each search for relevant subject headings. You can also feed the headings you've discovered back into the search box, as books with these headings will have additional headings that you may not have found yet. Keep going until you are getting no new terms, or the new terms are few and far between. This strategy could uncover some outdated subject headings that are still in your catalog, which is fine. Since you know these terms occur in your catalog, you'd still want to use them in your searches.

The second method is to search the Subject Authority Files directly at https://authorities.loc.gov. The database will tell you whether the term you typed in is an authorized heading or whether a different term is the official one. For instance, a search for "trans women" has a reference to the authorized term "Transgender women." (Again, it is possible that the authorized terms are not preferred by all of the people to whom they refer.) Searches of the LC Authority Files are left-anchored, meaning if you type in a phrase such as "Asian American," you will get results that *begin with* Asian American. It won't return the heading "Older Asian Americans," as this phrase does not begin with your search terms. The results will be listed alphabetically and can be browsed backward and forward. The record for each heading will also show you narrower terms, if there are applicable ones, and you can add these to your list as well if they are appropriate.

Your list of subject headings should contain some key proper names. Names are not included in LCSH, as they are part of the name authority file rather than subject authority file, but if a name is applied to a catalog record as a subject term it can be searched along with LCSH. A specialized encyclopedia or other reference work could be helpful for generating a list of names. Look for one that has entries on individuals, ideally one that provides a list of people so you don't have to find them yourself among a thousand or more entries. For example, the *Encyclopedia of Lesbian and Gay Histories and Cultures* from Routledge is arranged alphabetically but provides a list of biographical entries as part of its index. If you have some familiarity with the population in question, it would not be unreasonable to just pick out the names that you recognize from the list, as these are likely the more famous ones. If you don't feel qualified, see if you can ask a colleague, or look briefly at the encyclopedia entries for people to verify that they are members of the group you are assessing. There will probably always be judgment calls involved in choosing which people to include, particularly if the aspect of their identity that is of interest to you is one they hid or downplayed. If you are looking at coverage of disability, for instance, your library probably contains many books about President Franklin D. Roosevelt that say little about him as a wheelchair user.

Some people prefer to use natural language keywords in conjunction with headings from a controlled vocabulary. Doing so might help retrieve books that were published before a relevant subject heading was created, but it could also result in irrelevant results, as your keywords won't be disambiguated the way that LCSH is. If you want to use keywords, think through whether the words have more than one meaning, and whether your process will allow you to remove irrelevant results.

USING CALL NUMBERS

Besides subject headings, the other standardized data element in library records that indicates the subject matter of materials is the call number. The most commonly used set of call numbers in academic libraries in the United States is the Library of Congress Classification (LCC). This system was created in the first half of the twentieth century as a way of organizing the collection of the Library of Congress. As such, the original schedules had a focus on the United States, and particularly on dominant groups within the United States, though this has changed to some degree as other libraries contribute new classification numbers.[10] The original focus of LCC has left its mark on the classification system. Of the twenty-one main classes, two of them (E and F) are devoted to History of the Americas, with all of E and the first part of F relating to the United States. Meanwhile, the single class D covers Europe, Asia, Africa,

Australia, and New Zealand. Within class B, five subclasses are either explicitly devoted to or dominated by Christianity, while Hinduism is relegated to the relatively small range BL1100-1295 within the subclass BL "Religions. Mythology. Rationalism," and Islam is given the small range BP1-253 within subclass BP "Islam. Bahai Faith. Theosophy, etc." North American Indigenous religions are explicitly excluded from the religion section with a note indicating "For American Indians, see classes E-F" (i.e., history).[11]

As with LCSH, there is extensive literature detailing biases within LCC. The focus on white and Christian people within the United States does not necessarily prohibit an analysis using call numbers, but a close look at the system is going to be uncomfortable in some ways. For instance, if your search includes the call number E185.6, which is designated as "Intermarriage of races. Miscegenation. Mulattoes," viewing these terms will be upsetting to many people. Another example is the classification number BP188.14.H65, which is listed as "Islam. Sins. Vices. Homosexuality." It is important to forewarn anyone who will be preparing lists of call numbers that they will come across offensive or outdated terms. If one person is compiling the set of call numbers and others are conducting the searches, the searchers don't need to see definitions of what each call number represents; they'd only need to know that this was a search for books about, say, Black people in the United States. Similarly, when sharing your findings, you may be able to share only the numbers with a broad description of what concept or population the entire set of call numbers encompasses.

Since call numbers were created as a way of collocating books topically on shelves, each book would only have one in any library catalog. This means that a search for books by call number may return fewer results than a search for subject headings. For example, the book *Inscrutable Belongings: Queer Asian North American Fiction* by Stephen Hong Sohn is classified under PS153.G38, for "American literature by gay authors." A search for call numbers related to Asian or Asian American people would not retrieve this book. Since the subject headings for this book include "Gay people in literature" and "Asian Americans in literature," it would be retrieved in a subject search for books about Asian Americans or about LGBTQ people.

IDENTIFYING CALL NUMBER RANGES

Since books about a population could come from a variety of disciplines, relevant call numbers will be spread out over different areas of the collection, and you will need to use a lengthy list. Knowlton's Library of Congress Classification Numbers Applicable to Materials for African American Studies, available for PDF download at http://muse.jhu.edu/resolve/52 is forty-four pages long, while Howard's Library of Congress Classification Numbers Applicable to Materials for LGBTQIA Studies, included in the same document, fills twenty-six pages!

As very few compilations of population-specific call numbers exist, you will probably have to create your own. The full LCC schedule is available at https://www.loc.gov/aba/publications/FreeLCC/freelcc.html. As with subject headings, you'll want to identify topics closely related to the population you are interested in and also key individuals within that population. Howard and Knowlton include the call number for sickle cell anemia (RA645.S53) on their list pertaining to African American Studies, as this condition is disproportionately found in people of African descent.[12] Similarly, they include several call numbers related to jazz music, due to its origins in the African American community. They include any African American who has a designated call number, for instance PS3552.A45 "Baldwin, James." Again, you may need to check a reference work to find names of key individuals and then check to see if they have a call number.

OTHER PARAMETERS

While using the right metadata for the populations you are including in your assessment is the most important part of the search, there are a few other search parameters you should think about as well. Text box 7.2 has some questions to consider related to defining the scope of your searches. You probably know which locations and formats you want to include, since you would've made these decisions at the beginning of the project. If you are conducting several different searches over the course of a few weeks, it would be good to limit the results to books acquired before a specific date, so that all searches provide a snapshot of the collection at a particular time.

TEXT BOX 7.2 SEARCH PARAMETERS TO CONSIDER

- Are you limiting to only books? Only physical books?
- Are there locations you are including/excluding? (other buildings, juvenile collection)
- Can you limit to books acquired before the date you started your searches?

Source: Author.

Besides confirming the parameters of your search, you should also make sure you understand what will be counted in the search results. Are you counting titles or items? Either is fine, just be consistent and describe your findings accurately. Also, check whether your catalog merges the display if a book exists in print and electronic format. If you are aiming for a title count, this won't be an issue, but if you want an item count and you want to include ebooks in your search, you might need to do separate searches for print books and ebooks so you can add the counts together.

METADATA SEARCH PROCESS AND TECHNIQUE

Once you have a set of subject headings or call numbers, there are two different ways you can search. Most DEI assessment projects that rely on metadata to get counts of holdings do so using the library's online public-access catalog, or OPAC. Because anyone can access the OPAC, whichever staff are leading the project can do the searches themselves or delegate to another staff member. The downside to OPAC searching is you will probably not be able to include hundreds of search terms at once and will need to conduct multiple searches and combine the results.

The second way of conducting a metadata search is using a reporting tool, such as Alma Analytics or EBSCO's Panorama. These tools pull data from an integrated library system and sometimes other sources, to create reports that allow library staff to analyze the library collection and how it is used. If you are able to use a reporting tool, it has several advantages over searching the OPAC. One is that it is intended for analysis of the collection, whereas an OPAC is meant for locating a specific title or item or for discovering books on a topic. A reporting tool can provide aggregated counts broken down by different criteria, such as physical items sorted by material type and location. It also allows for more complex searches than the OPAC does. Reports can be saved and exported, allowing you to document your project and review the results. The one disadvantage of using a reporting tool may be prohibitive, however: not all library staff will be authorized to use it.

If you are hoping to use your OPAC, you will probably need to test out its functionality to figure out how best to construct your search. If you are using LCSH you will want to do a fielded search, which looks for your terms only within a specific field or set of fields, in this case subject fields. Not all catalogs have an option for fielded searching within the call number field. If yours does not, you can do a keyword search with call numbers as the keywords. Build your search slowly—try one search term to make sure you're getting the results you want, then add another term. Pay attention to whether the OPAC is treating your words as a phrase search or whether you need to put quotes around them. To add a second term or call number, you can almost always type OR in the search box, followed by the next term. Again, test by adding one term at a time until you feel confident that the search is working the way you think it should.

Note whether your OPAC gives you the option of specifying whether you want only exact matches for your search term or all strings that contain the term. If you have the option to search for strings containing your term, you will probably want to use this option. Because many subject headings can have subdivisions added at the end, there will be headings that contain the ones you identified but have additional text at the end. For instance if you search for materials about the Oglala Lakota Nation, you'll want your results to include records that have the heading "Oglala Indians—History," not only records with a subject heading exactly equal to "Oglala Indians." (Note also that while the website of the Oglala Lakota Nation does not use the word "Indian," you would still want to search the subject term "Oglala Indians" in addition to the more appropriate "Oglala Sioux Tribe," as the former has been applied more than ten times as often.[13]) When searching for call numbers, it is especially important not to limit your results to exact matches. Since call numbers are meant to be unique for each book, your search for a specific population would only use the beginning classification code, which is common to multiple books. Searching for a call number that contains (rather than equals) E99.O3 will return books with call numbers such as E99.O3 B48 1990, which is what you want.

If the OPAC lets you export results to Excel, you can export each search and combine the results into one large file. If you can't export directly to Excel, a work-around could be to export your results to a citation tool like EndNote or Zotero and then export records from that tool to Excel. The reason for doing this is that it will allow you to comb through your results and remove irrelevant or duplicate titles. Some assessments that rely on searching the catalog involve conducting multiple searches for different terms and adding together the results. This almost definitely results in double-counting (or more) some of the books. Since the same book could have multiple subject headings, for instance "African Americans—Legal status, laws, etc." and "African Americans—Civil rights," it would come up in searches for both of these terms. Getting the results into an Excel spreadsheet is very useful for de-duplication. Exporting also lets you save your files so you have more documentation of your work. If exporting isn't possible, you'll just need to note that your search is over-counting the results and take this into account when interpreting your findings. If you know you're over-counting, and yet you still find a very small percentage of your collection relates to the populations in question, explain this when you present the results, and it will emphasize how striking they are.

Figure 7.1 shows a search of the University of Georgia catalog by call number. It is filtered to show only results from the University of Georgia and not the entire state university system, and it shows only books. Notice that the search field is set to "contains" rather than "equals," as the call number will never be exactly equal to one of the numbers entered. For this type of search, you can't enter a range, like BX6440-6460.9, as the search engine will not know how to interpret that. You would need to list BX6440 OR BX6441 OR BX6442 and so on. Sometimes adding in too many terms will get you fewer or no results, so if a number looks unexpectedly low, scale back to just the first few terms and run the search again. Keep adding terms one or two at a time until you see a problem. Then remove the last call number and record which call numbers you searched and how many results you got. You will need to do several searches

                                                                  Chapter 7

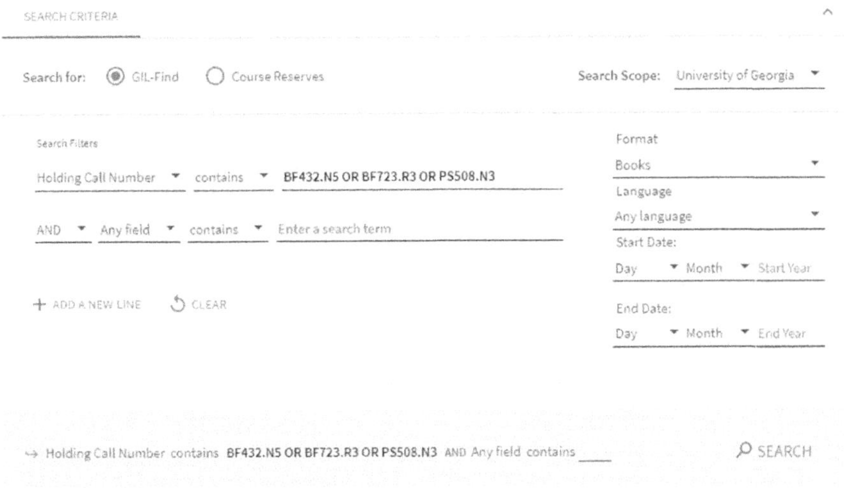

Figure 7.1 A Search for Multiple Call Numbers in the University of Georgia OPAC. Reprinted with permission.

Figure 7.2 Alma Analytics Report for Subject Terms Related to Racism. *Source*: Author.

and add the numbers of results together. The benefit of doing a call number search is that you can do this. There won't be overlap of the same titles showing up in different searches, since each book has only one call number.

If you are using a reporting tool rather than the OPAC, you can fit more terms or call numbers into a search filter at one time, and you can also export the results to Excel. While de-duplicating would not be necessary if you are able to do just one large search for each population or topic, exporting to Excel is still useful for removing inappropriate titles and for documenting your work.

Figure 7.2 shows the setup of an Alma Analytics report of print books related to racism. The largest filter is the one for Subject, which includes

Metadata Searching

several hundred subject headings from the Arizona State University LibGuide mentioned in text box 7.1. This is many more headings that it was possible to include in an OPAC search. Note that the report is filtered to exclude deleted items. These are usually configured not to display in an OPAC search, so you don't have to worry about them there, but most libraries keep these in the catalog. The report also filters out items that are lost or missing, limits to only books and to locations considered to be part of the main circulating collections.

COMPARING TO OTHER NUMBERS

After you've done your searches, and if possible de-duplicated the results and eliminated irrelevant books, your analysis is going to focus on the total numbers rather than any specific books. Most often a metadata analysis will take the numbers of items and divide by the total holdings of the collection to get a percentage. As of fall 2023, Temple University Libraries's main circulating collections contained 4,754 books on LGBTQ topics, compared to a total print collection of 1.8 million physical books (item count). This is 0.26 percent. While it is unclear how many books there should be, especially as there is no count of how many students at Temple University identify as LGBTQ, the ideal percentage is more than 0.26 percent. Many published studies that rely on metadata searches have similar findings: the investigators may be unclear on how many items they should have, but they can tell their numbers are low.

Many studies try to compare the percentages of books about various groups to the prevalence of those groups within their institutions. Others use local census data to create benchmarks. Using your own institution as a point of comparison is not always helpful, because an institution that is not very diverse will still want to teach its students about the broader world and may want books about minority groups to be present in its collection at a larger rate than it is in the institution. Even a majority-minority institution would probably not want its collection to mirror its population. As of 2022, 75 percent of all students in historically Black colleges and universities were Black.[14] Creating a collection that was 75 percent *about* Black experiences would probably involve ignoring historically significant books that focused on dominant groups or on other racial minorities as well as books on basic science that don't deal with race. Nevertheless, having a number to look at and present to others can be illuminating.

When presenting results, you can note the limitations of this method and be clear that the numbers are estimates. The numbers might be somewhat low due to some records not having subject headings that clearly state what demographic group is discussed in the book, or they might be slightly inflated due to subject headings applied anachronistically. When you present findings, be careful to state what you actually found, that is, "Our searches found X number of books with subject descriptors relating to African Americans," rather than describing the results with more certainty than is warranted, that is, "Our library has X number of books about African Americans." You should also avoid using offensive words yourself when sharing information about your assessment project. Few people will need to see the full search strategy unless you are explaining your methodology in detail, so you can note how many books you found on each topic without always listing all the search terms you used.

Metadata searches do not lend themselves to clear action steps. A benefit of having numbers, however, is that they provide an easy way to communicate about your collection to others. Even those who are already committed to building an inclusive and equitable collection might feel spurred on by seeing lower percentages of books about marginalized people than expected. In addition to underscoring the need to find strategies to diversify the collection, the numbers may help you choose an initial focus for your collection-building. Areas where there is the largest discrepancy between the percentage of books in the collection and the prevalence of a group at your institution or in your local population could be targets for special efforts. For identifying specific books, you might turn to some of the lists mentioned in the previous chapter, tags in a vendor database, or other strategies.

NOTES

1. Janis L. Young, "Library of Congress Subject Headings (LCSH)," in *Encyclopedia of Library and Information Sciences* (4th ed.), ed. John D. McDonald and Michael Levine-Clark (Boca Raton, FL: CRC Press, 2018), 2870.
2. Lori M. Jahnke, Kyle Tanaka, and Christopher A. Palozzolo, "Ideology, Policy, and Practice: Structural Barriers to Collections Diversity in Research and College Libraries," *College & Research Libraries* 83, no. 2 (March 2022): 166–183.
3. Young, "Library of Congress Subject Headings (LCSH)," 2871.
4. Cara Liebowitz, "I am Disabled: On Identity-First Versus People-First Language," *The Body is Not an Apology*, March 20, 2015, https://thebodyisnotanapology.com/magazine/i-am-disabled-on-identity-first-versus-people-first-language/.
5. Steven A. Knowlton, "Three Decades Since *Prejudices and Antipathies:* A Study of Changes in the Library of Congress Subject Headings," *Cataloging & Classification Quarterly* 40, no. 2 (2006): 123–145.
6. Library of Congress, *Summary of Decisions, Editorial Meeting Number 12,* December 15, 2014, https://www.loc.gov/aba/pcc/saco/cpsocd/psd-141215.html.
7. The Trans Metadata Collective, Jasmine Burns, Michelle Cronquist, Jackson Huang, Devon Murphy, K. J. Rawson, Beck Schaefer, Jamie Simons, Brian M. Watson, and Adrian Williams, *Metadata Best Practices for Trans and Gender Diverse Resources, Version 1.5,* June 22, 2022, https://doi.org/10.5281/zenodo.6829167.
8. Howard and Knowlton, "Browsing Through Bias," 81.
9. As with the terms "Blacks" and "African Americans," "Latinos" and "Hispanic" are overlapping but not identical groups. See U.S. Census Bureau, "Hispanic or Latino Origin," https://www.census.gov/quickfacts/fact/note/US/RHI725222?. It is common to group them together, as the U.S. Census does. If you do so, make sure

to describe your findings accurately, for instance by presenting a count of books with subject matter relating to Latino and/or Hispanic people.

10. Lois Mai Chan and Theodora L. Hodges, "Library of Congress Classification (LCC)," in *Encyclopedia of Library and Information Sciences, Fourth Edition*, ed. John D. McDonald and Michael Levine-Clark (Boca Raton, FL: CRC Press, 2018), 2847–2855.

11. "Library of Congress Classification Outline. Class B – Philosophy. Psychology. Religion." Library of Congress, accessed October 10, 2024, https://www.loc.gov/aba/cataloging/classification/lcco/lcco_b.pdf.

12. Howard and Knowlton, "Browsing Through Bias," 40.

13. "Oglala Lakota Nation," Oglala Lakota Nation, accessed April 22, 2024, https://oglalalakotanation.org/.

14. National Center for Education Statistics, "Table 313.20 Fall Enrollment in Degree-Granting Historically Black Colleges and Universities, by Sex of Student and Level and Control of Institution: Selected Years, 1976 through 2021," *Digest of Education Statistics*, December 2022, https://nces.ed.gov/programs/digest/d22/tables/dt22_313.20.asp.

8

Diversity Coding

Whereas the methods in the previous chapter require the use of a controlled vocabulary, diversity coding is a much more flexible methodology that allows you to define identity categories according to your goals. Additional benefits are the opportunity to look closely at individual books and investigate authors' identities. Though you can use diversity coding to investigate subject matter as well, this chapter will focus more on authorship for two reasons. One reason is that the ability to explore authors' identities is unique to diversity coding. In addition, categorizing authors by gender, race, sexual orientation, or disability requires careful thought in order to code respectfully and accurately.

CHOOSING A SCOPE

Because diversity coding involves looking closely at specific books, you won't be able to include the whole collection in the audit. Diversity coding projects usually look at 2,000–6,000 books, though some very targeted ones are smaller. Some subsets of collections that have been used for coding audits are: books purchased in the last year, books on a specific topic, a format or genre (e.g., plays, music scores), and books included in displays. If your audit focuses on one of these smaller sections of the collection, you may be able to review every book.

If you want your audit to focus on a larger range of books than you and your coworkers can reasonably code, a good approach is to select a random sample from your desired range. A simple way to obtain a sample is to get a list of everything that is within scope and put it into a spreadsheet. Then add a column titled Random Number. In this column, type =RAND(). This formula works in either Excel or Google sheets to generate a random number between zero and one. Figure 8.1 illustrates the RAND formula. The box at the top of the screenshot shows what the formula looks like, while column G shows the

	A	B	C	D	E	F	G	H	I	J
I2			f_x	=RAND()						
1	Title	Publication Place	Publisher	Subjects	Author	MMS Id	Publication	Location Name	Randomizer	
2	Flatlining : race, work, and health care in the new economy	Oakland, California :	University of California Press	African Americans in medicine	Wingfield, Adia Harvey, 1977- author.	991037293711803811	[2019]	Main Stacks	0.562639437	
3	Trans exploits : trans of color cultures and technologies in movement	Durham :	Duke University Press	Transgender people	Chen, Jian Neo, 1972- author.	991037329403603811	2019.	Automated Storage System	0.139804461	
4	Real life	New York :	Riverhead Books	African American gay men-- Fiction	Taylor, Brandon author. (Brandon L. G.),	991037730513903811	2020.	Main Stacks	0.038949398	
5	Cleft capitalism : the social origins of failed market making in Egypt	Stanford, California :	Stanford University Press	Economic developm ent--Egypt.	Adly, Amr, author.	991038443802903811	[2020]	Main Stacks	0.462535618	

Figure 8.1   Excel Random Number Formula. *Source*: Author.

output. Copy the formula down the entire spreadsheet so that each row has a random number assigned to it. Then sort the spreadsheet by the random number column. The random numbers will change after you sort the spreadsheet. This might feel confusing, as the document will look like it is not sorted in any way at all. You can see in figure 8.1 that the books do not appear to be sorted by the random number column. They were sorted this way, but the numbers re-generated after sorting. Having the numbers change is not a problem, as the sorting process already put the list in random order. You can now select the desired number of items starting at the top of the spreadsheet, and they will be a random sample.

Table 8.1 shows the wide variety of ways that auditors have defined the parameters of their work to achieve a manageable number of books to review. Janet Calderon, working on her audit alone while on a temporary contract, was limited in terms of staffing and timeline.[1] She chose a narrow scope to make her project feasible, as shown in the table. The much larger audit conducted at the University of the Pacific, led by Michele Gibney, Mickel Paris, and Veronica Wells, was also designed with an eye to keeping the project size manageable. They decided to code 10 percent of the titles in each disciplinary area or 1,000 titles, whichever was fewer.[2]

If you are coding author identities, consider how you will handle works with multiple authors. You could exclude them from your analysis, in which case you would go back to your randomly sorted list and select the next titles on the list to analyze instead. Another option is coding the first author only.

CREATING CODES

A significant piece of the preparation for diversity coding is creating the codes themselves. You will need to decide what traits you are looking for and define

Table 8.1 Scopes and Sizes of Diversity Coding Projects

Citation	Parameters	Number of Items	Characteristics Coded
Janet Calderon, "Acquisitions for the Sciences—Using a Diversity Assessment to Serve BIPOC Students in STEM," presented at the Acquisitions Institute at Timberline Lodge, 2023, https://acquisitionsinstitute .org/wp-content/uploads/2023/05/ Monday_Calderon_s-Presentation_final.pptx	• Print books • Published 2000–2022 • Subject heading "natural resources"	508	Authors • Race
David Cox, "Introductory Diversity Audits," poster presented at Alaska Library Association Online Virtual Conference, March 18–20, 2021, https://scholarworks .alaska.edu/handle/11122/12642	Part 1 • PS3600-PS3626, American authors from 2001–present • Print books only	Part 1: 170	AuthorsGender • Race • LGBTQ identity • Disability
	Part 2 • PS3551-3576, American authors 1960–2000 • Print books only	Part 2: 1,500	Works • Genre • Primary or secondary source
María Evelia Emerson and Lauryn Grace Lehman, "Who Are We Missing? Conducting a Diversity Audit in a Liberal Arts College Library," *The Journal of Academic Librarianship* 48, no. 3 (2022): 102517.	• Print books in permanent collection • Published 2000 or later • Single-author	6,465	Authors • Gender • Sexuality • Race/Ethnicity

(Continued)

Table 8.1 (Continued)

Citation	Parameters	Number of Items	Characteristics Coded
Michele Gibney, Mickel Paris, and Veronica Wells, "A Diversity, Equity, and Inclusion (DEI) Approach to Collection Development in a University Library," *Scholarly Commons* (Pre-print), 2022, http://scholarlycommons.pacific.edu/libraries-articles/121	• Print books and music scores • "a randomized sample size of either 10 percent or 1,000, whichever was fewer" from five broad disciplinary categories, plus music scores	3,505 books 839 music scores	Authors • Gender • Race/ethnicity • LGBTQ identity • Disability Works • Decade of publication • Discipline
Melissa Gonzalez, "Diversity Collection Audit & Assessment," 2023, https://libguides.uwf.edu/divassess/methods	New Acquisitions • Three fiscal years • Print and electronic • Monographs Contents of New Books Shelf • Shelflists from two separate dates • Print monographs • Single location	New Acquisitions: 2,841 New Books Shelf: 1,349	Content • Race/ethnicity • Disability • LGBTQ • Socioeconomic disparities • Immigration • Women & Gender

Source	Scope	Sample	Coding
Meghan Kwast, "California Lutheran University's Diversity Audit: A Project in Progress," presented at SCELCapalooza, 2023, https://docs.google.com/presentation/d/1y8ksacioG429UArHHBDK3OQr6715pGSN	• Print monographs • Samples from 8 broad disciplinary areas • Sample sizes varied, calculated to achieve a 99 percent confidence interval	571	Authors • Race • Pronouns used • Opposite-sex or same-sex relationship • Disability • 1st generation Americans • U.S. Territories • International
Kimberly Shotick, "Uncovering Whiteness in Academic Library Collections: a Study of Author Identities in Journalism Monographs," *Collection Management* 49, nos 1-2 (2024): 28-45.	• Print monographs • PN4699-5650 • Published 2013–2023	259	Authors • Race and ethnic identity • Gender
Sanjeet Singh-Mann, "Lessons Learned from Armacost Library's Collections Audit," presented at SCELCapalooza, 2023, https://docs.google.com/presentation/d/18sba5D-cwu2fhA1lWnl1dsLuk-FxxO4O	• Print books • Purchased in previous fiscal year	1,569	Authors • Race • Gender • LGBTQ identity

your coding categories very carefully. As you can see in table 8.1, some projects look only at one trait, such as race, while others look at several traits of the authors or the works. Coding is the only audit method that lets you analyze intersectional identities, for instance comparing gender ratios of Black authors to those of other races. You may want to take advantage of this and code for multiple aspects of authors' identities.

Once you've decided which characteristics are of interest, you'll need to decide what values you'll be coding within these characteristics, that is which races, gender identities, sexual orientations, or disabilities will have distinct codes. For instance, will you have a single category for Asian/Asian American/ Pacific Islander or distinguish between regions or countries within Asia and the Pacific Islands? It can be very helpful to code a small number of books as a pilot to help you think about what categories will be useful and appropriate, given the information that you are able to find. If several people are coding, you can each review a handful and discuss what you found. It is possible the experience of coding just a few books will lead to some changes in your coding scheme. You can retroactively apply these changes to the books you have already coded and then proceed with the audit.

Many projects choose values that correspond with the data that their institution collects. For example, Calderon decided to include Middle Eastern authors in the category of "Asian" because this is how her institution categorizes Middle Eastern students, despite the U.S. Census classifying them as white.[3] Since Calderon wanted to be able to compare the presence in the collection of authors of various races to enrollment at the institution, it made sense to use the same racial categories, even though Middle Eastern students won't always think of themselves as Asian. If you aren't using institutional enrollment to create collection targets, you should generally try to keep the categories granular and based on how people self-identify.

When choosing the values that you'll use for coding, aim to use terminology that reflects the information you expect to find. For instance, you will probably find many authors whose websites offer blurbs about themselves written in the third person using gendered pronouns, but these sites will rarely say "Denise is a woman." As some nonbinary people do use gendered pronouns, it is better to avoid making assumptions. All you know from seeing someone use a particular set of pronouns in their biographical information is that the person uses those pronouns. Therefore, you might code for pronouns used rather than for gender identity. Similarly, many people mention a husband or wife, but they may not provide a label for their sexual orientation. Being in a romantic relationship does not mean someone only experiences attraction to people of the same gender as their current partner, or that they would be comfortable with whatever label others assume applies to them. Rather than imposing a label for sexual orientation, María Emerson and Lauryn Lehman noted whether the person was known to be in an opposite-sex relationship or a same-sex relationship.[4] Some authors will describe themselves as gay, lesbian, or queer without mentioning a specific relationship. For accuracy, you could create a category that includes anyone who uses an identity label such as gay, lesbian, or bisexual *or* who mentions a same-gender relationship.

Some coding projects also include trans and gender diverse people as part of a broader LGBTQ category, which seems intuitive given their inclusion in the initialism. If you are coding for specific identities, however, that is, marking people as bisexual, gay, or lesbian rather than just noting that they belong under the LGBTQ umbrella, you will run into difficulties if your system does not allow you to note when someone identifies as transgender *and* bisexual, gay, or lesbian. Other audits include transgender as an option under gender. This can also be an obstacle to fully recording someone's identity, as it prevents coders from indicating a trans person's specific gender identity, which might be male, female, nonbinary, or something else. The most straightforward way to code for transgender identity is to treat being trans or gender diverse as its own trait. A single person could have a female gender and be bisexual and also transgender. These would be three separate columns in your coding spreadsheet: gender, sexuality, and trans or gender diverse. See the best practices document from The Trans Metadata Collective for an explanation of the varied terminology used by different trans people and distinctions between terms.[5]

In addition to creating diversity codes for the populations or identities of interest to you, you will need to decide whether and how to code for the presence of the dominant group. Some audits don't code for identities such as white and straight, as the goal of the audit is to quantify the presence of nondominant identities. Treating authors who have characteristics of the dominant group the same as those whose identities are unknown is a valid choice, as neither can be said to contribute to the diversity of the collection. Just be careful when you refer to this unlabeled group that you acknowledge that it includes cases in which the author's identity is unknown, and that it is possible these authors belong in another category. In other words, if you are leaving the Lesbian/Gay/Bisexual/Same-Sex Relationship column blank for a particular book, don't assume this means the author is straight.

It is a good idea to create a glossary to explain to your coders, or clarify for yourself, who is included within each category. For instance, you may want to spell out whether coders should mark Middle Eastern people as Asian, white, or as their own category. If you are coding for disability, the glossary can articulate which types of disabilities should be counted. Physical and intellectual disabilities are often what comes to mind, but if your study includes mental illness or neurodiversity the glossary would be the place to state this. Artemis Vex and Ruth Castillo share an excerpt from their glossary in the next chapter.

Text box 8.1 shows two excellent toolkits that can help you plan your coding scheme and process.

> **TEXT BOX 8.1 TOOLKITS FOR DIVERSITY CODING**
>
> María Evelia Emerson and Lauryn Grace Lehman, "Filling in the Gaps: A Diversity Audit Toolkit from Tredway Library," *Library and Information Science: Faculty Scholarship & Creative Works*, 2021, https://digitalcommons.augustana.edu/libscifaculty/14
>
> - Reading List
> - Things to Consider When Designing an Audit
> - Sample Audit Spreadsheet, with codes embedded as dropdown options and a glossary on a separate tab
>
> Artemis D. Vex and Ruth Castillo, "Diversifying the Collection: An Acquisitions Assessment Tool," 2022, bit.ly/acq-dei-toolkit
>
> - Statement of Purpose, with suggested sources of information about books
> - Coding Table, listing all traits that are being coded in the audit and applicable values within these categories
> - Glossary of Codes
>
> Source: Author.

ASSIGNING CODES

In addition to planning out what codes you will use, you will need guidelines on how to apply them. This means defining what is considered an authoritative source of information on a book or its author. If your audit focuses on the content of the books, the sources will be straightforward: you might focus only on the information in your catalog, or if you have the time you might look for a blurb on the publisher's website or reviews. Author identities require a more carefully selected list of sources. Text box 8.2 lists some sources you are likely to encounter, organized by how trustworthy they are. Different coding projects make different decisions about which to accept. Anything that comes directly from the author or has been vetted by the author is preferable to other people's descriptions. Acknowledgments or introductions within a book can be useful, as can an author's personal website. Social media posts are a common source of information, though it might require a fair amount of scrolling to find something useful. Emerson and Lehman offer a guideline for secondary sources, which is that another person's description of the author is acceptable if there is a "reasonable likelihood that the author could have changed the incorrect information."[6] The example they give is biographical information on a university or publisher website. Another common situation is for an interviewer to say something about the author in their presence, in which case presumably the author would have spoken up if the information was inaccurate.

TEXT BOX 8.2 SOURCES OF AUTHOR DATA

Authoritative

- Pronouns listed on a university profile or used on the author's personal webpage
- Author mentions "husband" or "wife" in Acknowledgments or in an interview or mentions "partner" but uses a gendered pronoun. (This establishes same-gender or opposite-gender relationship, provided you know the author's own pronouns, but it is not sufficient for giving a label of gay, straight, or any other sexual orientation.)
- Author mentions own race, ethnicity, or sexual orientation in an interview, Acknowledgments, social media, or elsewhere
- Interviewer mentions author's race, ethnicity, or sexual orientation and author does not provide a correction
- Author's writing is included in an anthology for writers with a common identity

May Be Acceptable

- Statement from the author about the country in which they or their parents were born or raised
- Author's work was nominated for an award that uses author identity as a criterion. (It is unclear if an author would need to agree to be nominated for an award, though if they are announcing their nomination this suggests they believe they meet the criteria. Additionally, many awards use the topic of the work as a criterion rather than author identity, so it is important to confirm award details.)

Not Definitive

- Name (for gender or national origin)
- Photo (for gender, race, or sexual orientation)
- University attended (for instance an HBCU or international institution)
- Name of partner (for sexual orientation)
- Field of scholarship (e.g., Africology or Women's Studies)

Source: Author.

It is not recommended to assign an author to a racial or gender category based on photographs. In an article about cataloging guidelines, Amber Billey, Emily Drabinski, and K. R. Roberto state, "Reading the gender of another person is always subjective, and the harm of getting it wrong outweighs, for us, the cataloger's impulse to fully describe a person."[7] It is easy to imagine the possibility of guessing someone's race incorrectly based on an image as well. While you might feel very confident in your assumption, remember that even if you are correct in one case, there are many situations in which photographs can lead to incorrect assumptions, and therefore they cannot be considered a reliable source of information.

Limiting your descriptions of others to what they have stated about themselves also means not anachronistically assigning authors to identity categories that did not exist in their lifetimes. Novelist Peyton Thomas recently wrote an editorial about the language Louisa May Alcott used to describe her gender identity and the contrasting opinions of scholars on whether it would be appropriate to refer to Alcott as transgender, given that the word was invented long after her death. Thomas concludes, "We must base our understanding of Alcott's identity on her writing[, which says] 'I long to be a man,' [and] 'I was born with a boy's nature.'"[8] While it should be acceptable to describe Alcott using her own words, diversity coding relies on being able to group identities into categories. Given the impossibility of knowing whether Alcott would be comfortable with the label of transgender, it would be better to not code Alcott as trans or gender diverse. This example underscores the point made earlier, that you should not assume that authors left without a diversity code belong to the dominant group. Any number of historical authors might have been transgender, gay, or non-white without readers knowing.

Another complicated situation could arise if an aspect of an author's identity has changed since they wrote the book that you are coding. People regularly come out later in life or become disabled. You may need to decide on a case-by-case basis how to code authors who have publicly changed parts of their identities since publishing the book in question. One example of a book whose author came out after writing it is Glennon Doyle's *Love Warrior*, about her marriage to now-ex-husband Craig Melton. Though she was still married to him at the time the book was written,[9] her author information on Amazon and Goodreads has been updated to say, "Glennon lives in Florida with her wife and three children." Another example is Becky Albertalli, who wrote novels about gay and bisexual teens while publicly identifying as straight, then announced after publishing three such novels that she had come to realize she was bisexual. Albertalli wrote, "I'm pretty sure I've had crushes on boys and girls for most of my life. I just didn't realize the girl crushes were crushes."[10] Do these books count as being written by LGBTQ authors?

To make a judgment call here, it is helpful to recall the varied reasons for caring about author identities discussed in chapter 2. If you value author identities because of the perspective the author brings as a member of a marginalized group, the book Doyle wrote while identifying as straight would not bring that perspective, though Albertalli's books might, given that she mentions being attracted to girls since she was young and says she suspects this was an unconscious motivation for her writing. If you are looking for diverse authors to compensate for the barriers people from marginalized groups face to publication, neither author would have faced the same barriers when their books were accepted for publication. On the other hand, if your goal in collecting and tracking works by authors from underrepresented groups is to let students see authors who are like themselves, you might make the case that since both authors' sexualities are now widely known, any work of theirs counts as being by an LGBTQ author.

Because the internet could contain a myriad of sources, it is a good idea to limit how much time you spend searching for information about each book or author. Ten minutes seems to be a standard guideline. One reason for creating such a limit is practicality, as spending more than ten minutes per author could make your project take so long as to be unfeasible. Another reason is that some of the reasons given above for paying attention to author identities depend on these identities being public. Whether you want your students to see themselves reflected or learn about others who are different from them, they can only do so if relevant aspects of the authors' identities are visible to them. If it takes more than ten minutes of searching to discover that an author who appears white has a Latino parent, or that the author's partner is same-sex, this is not substantially different for your patrons than if these aspects of the author's identity were unknown.

If you are using diversity coding to track subject matter rather than authorship, you will have a different set of issues to consider. The library world has had many conversations about what it means for a book to be "about" something. The guidelines for catalogers assigning subject headings advise only using a heading if it applies to at least 20 percent of the work. Audits of juvenile literature often make a distinction between main characters and secondary characters, counting only the former toward the overall diversity of the collection. There is also a question of how to code a book in which race is named but has no significance. In discussing the possible ways one might consider diversity, E. E. Lawrence suggests but does not necessarily endorse a requirement that "a narrative must in some way depict a character's experiences as a member of the social group(s) to which they belong rather than merely announcing or implying social identifications."[11] As it is not usually possible to judge this when doing an audit, you probably won't use Lawrence's criteria. You will also likely face the question of what to do about books that are racist. Since you won't be able to discern this in all cases without reading the books, it is better to leave issues of quality representation out of your audit but make notes on any books you discover that you want to later weed.

RECORDING DATA AND TRACKING PROGRESS

The final step before you can begin coding is creating a place to record the data. Usually this will be a spreadsheet, either in Excel or Google. In the process of creating a sample, you may have already created a spreadsheet listing the books you want to code. You can add columns to this list for inputting the relevant characteristics of the author or book. Think about whether you want the option of selecting multiple values for a given category, for instance if a book's content covers two races or an author self-identifies as having multiple disabilities. If you are allowing multiple values, your spreadsheet should have a column for each possible value, where coders can put an X if that option applies. If you are not allowing multiple values, you can make a single column for each trait and set up a dropdown menu for coders to select one appropriate value for each trait. In figure 8.2, Race/National Origin is set up as a dropdown, with an option for coding someone as multiracial. Sexual Orientation, on the other hand, is a free text field. The input in this column is a mix of identity terms and relationship statuses. For this trait it was easy to create an aggregated category at the analysis stage, adding together those who were coded as being in a same-sex relationship with those who had used an identity term of gay, lesbian, bisexual, or queer.

Before you and your coders move forward with the project, it is a good idea to start with a brief norming process, in which coders review the same books and compare the decisions they have made about how to categorize them. This is less necessary the more detailed your instructions are, though it could still be helpful. A norming process can involve just a small number of titles.

Once you and the coders feel comfortable that everyone has had enough training and practice to make reliable decisions on how to code, you can split up the workload and assign titles to coders. It might be easiest to create a separate spreadsheet for each person, or you might assign each person specific rows in one common spreadsheet. Although coders should be able to

Title	Publication Place	Publisher	Publication	Gender/Pronouns	Race/National Origin	Sexual Orientation	Trans or Non-Binary
Flatlining : race, work, and health care in the new economy	Oakland, California :	University of California Press	[2019]	she/her	Black	opposite-gender relationship	
Trans exploits : trans of color cultures and technologies in movement	Durham :	Duke University Press	2019.		Black Latino or Hispanic East Asian South Asian Southeast Asian Indigenous or Native American Pacific Islander Middle Eastern two or more races		
Real life	New York :	Riverhead Books	2020.				
Cleft capitalism : the social origins of failed market making in Egypt	Stanford, California :	Stanford University Press	[2020]	he/him	Middle Eastern		

Figure 8.2   Example Coding Spreadsheet. *Source*: Author.

work independently after the norming process, you may still want to check in regularly.

ANALYZING AND PRESENTING THE DATA

Once your team has coded the full sample, you will do some calculations. The most common calculations are simple percentages, such as what percentage of the sample was written by women or people within the LGBTQ umbrella. Diversity coding allows for some analysis of intersectionality, which can be done with fairly simple tables. As chapter 2 explains, the theory of intersectionality recognizes that people who are marginalized in multiple ways experience discrimination in ways that are not equal to the sum of their identities. A Black woman is not going to find her experience reflected in your collection just because you have books about Black people and books about women. It would therefore be faulty to assume that a collection was sufficiently diverse when you've only analyzed one trait at a time. A collection with 50 percent of its books written by women and 13 percent by African Americans might still not have books by African American women. With diversity coding, you can check how well your collection represents identities at the intersection of multiple marginalized groups. Keeping in mind that any attempt to categorize books or people according to a list of demographic traits is necessarily simplifying the complexity of human experience, it is still preferable to look at the intersections of multiple traits than to analyze only one at a time.

Table 8.2 provides an example of how to present and discuss the results of a diversity coding project, particularly with an eye to intersectionality. It shows author identities from one hundred books purchased as part of Temple University Libraries's Award Winners Honoring Diverse Experiences collection. It is logical that this collection includes a much larger proportion of books from authors of color or LGBTQ authors than would be found in the collections as a whole, and the collection does well in including intersectional identities as well. While one might expect most of the Black authors to be male and straight, this is in fact not the case. Of the twenty-three confirmed Black authors coded, seventeen (74 percent) use she/her pronouns. Three of the Black authors using she/her pronouns identify as gay, lesbian, or queer (one person used each label). The table also highlights, however, that there are no Black trans authors, so this identity is missing from this admittedly small sample.

The example also illustrates one way to describe authors who have an uncoded value for a particular trait. In this example, anyone not known to be a person of color was marked as "Unconfirmed." Since no author mentioned their own whiteness, the "Unconfirmed" category includes all the white authors. It also includes some who are probably not white but who did not share enough definitive information to assign to them a different value. While it was tempting to make assumptions about race, for instance if an author was a professor

Table 8.2 Authors' Pronouns, Race/National Origin, and Transgender Identity among Winners of Diversity-Related Awards

	Black	East Asian	Native American	Latino or Hispanic	Middle Eastern	South Asian	Southeast Asian	Two or more races	Unconfirmed	Total
He/him	6		1	4	2	3	1	2	12	31
She/her	17	4		2	3	5	1	2	25	59
They/them				1		1			5	7
He/they					1					1
She/they							2			2
Trans and gender diverse*				1	1	2	2		6	12
Total	23	4	1	7	6	9	4	4	42	100

*includes anyone who uses the pronoun "they" or who has self-identified as trans. These numbers are not included in column totals, as the individuals are counted by their pronouns.
Source: Author.

of African American Studies who had attended a historically Black college or university, the coding did not take this type of clue into account. Therefore, calling the category "Unconfirmed" is more accurate than unmarked, unknown, or presumed white.

SHARING FINDINGS

As with the other types of data mentioned in this book, you will be presenting your data in the aggregate, not sharing information about specific books. This is especially important when discussing authors' identities. Even though the information you will use to code is all publicly available, authors may have a different audience in mind depending on what platform they are using. For instance, one of the authors in the example in table 8.2 was coded as being in a same-gender relationship based on a humorous tweet about her "very gay" partner. While this was both definitive and public, the audit found nothing the author had said in a professional context about her relationship or identity, and it is not clear if she would want her sexuality discussed in relation to scholarly writing.

The guidelines in this chapter are not intended to apply to situations where you would be adding information to the catalog. Adding author data to bibliographic records requires its own set of ethical considerations that others have written about.[12] In particular, the literature on cataloging has much to say about the importance of considering privacy when associating individuals with demographic information. A task force report on adding gender to name authority records recommends considering whether sharing certain information would harm the person in question and whether they have consented to make this information public.[13] Several catalogers provide examples of authors not wanting to be identified by a particular demographic term despite it being applicable. Violet Fox was once contacted by an author who did not want her transgender identity included in her name authority record.[14] Amber Billey, Emily Drabinski, and K. R. Roberto describe an experience with a cisgender woman who did not want her gender mentioned because "gender was simply not an important aspect of the work in question."[15] These concerns are not as relevant when conducting a diversity audit, as you will only share aggregate information about the authors you coded. Stating that almost 60 percent of the authors in the sample used she/her pronouns is very different from sharing a list that names specific authors as female. Nevertheless, these examples underscore why it is important to present your findings in an aggregated way. If you are hoping to undertake a project involving adding demographic information to the catalog, remember to consult literature specific to cataloging rather than applying the guidelines described here.

In order to aggregate your findings, you will need to name the categories. You may have already done this when creating your coding scheme. If not, remember to use the same terminology that you used in your coding and keep in mind what you know for sure. If you coded for mentions of a same-sex relationship, don't present your findings in terms of the number of gay or lesbian authors you discovered. These people could be bisexual and have simply not publicized that label. Similarly, if you recorded what pronouns people use, don't present a total number of women, but rather a number of people using she/her pronouns.

GOING FORWARD

The action steps resulting from a diversity coding audit will usually be similar to those resulting from any other type of diversity assessment: sharing the findings and looking for ways to improve. One next step that is unique to this strategy is the possibility of using your codes to categorize new purchases going forward. Look for an internal note field that you will be able to access later for analysis. Coding titles as they are ordered would make sense if a large portion of your collection is purchased through title-by-title selection rather than packages or approval plans, and if you feel confident you can train all your library's selectors to use the codes accurately. Both of these conditions are more common in smaller libraries. For any size library, there is the option of repeating the audit in a year with a focus on titles acquired since the initial round. It is possible that simply focusing on the characteristics of authors or the range of representation in the works in your collection will lead you to make different decisions in future selection, and as the next chapter illustrates, a repeat audit can help keep diversity, equity, and inclusion at the forefront of your thoughts and also help you measure progress.

NOTES

1. Janet Calderon, "Acquisitions for the Sciences—Using a Diversity Assessment to Serve BIPOC Students in STEM," presented at the Acquisitions Institute at Timberline Lodge, May 22, 2023, https://acquisitionsinstitute.org/wp-content/uploads/2023/05/Monday_Calderon_s-Presentation_final.pptx.
2. Michele Gibney, Mickel Paris, and Veronica Wells, "A Diversity, Equity, and Inclusion (DEI) Approach to Collection Development in a University Library," *Scholarly Commons* (Pre-print), 2022, http://scholarlycommons.pacific.edu/libraries-articles/121.
3. Calderon, "Acquisitions for the Sciences—Using a Diversity Assessment to Serve BIPOC Students in STEM;" Office of Management and Budget, "Revisions to the Standards for the Classification of Federal Data on Race and Ethnicity," *Federal Register* 62, no. 210 (October 30, 1997): 58782-58790, https://www.govinfo.gov/content/pkg/FR-1997-10-30/pdf/97-28653.pdf.
4. María Evelia Emerson and Lauryn Grace Lehman, "Who are We Missing? Conducting a Diversity Audit in a Liberal Arts College Library," *The Journal of Academic Librarianship* , no. 3 (2022): 102517.

5. The Trans Metadata Collective, Jasmine Burns, Michelle Cronquist, Jackson Huang, Devon Murphy, K. J. Rawson, Beck Schaefer, Jamie Simons, Brian M. Watson, and Adrian Williams, *Metadata Best Practices for Trans and Gender Diverse Resources, Version 1.5,* June 22, 2022, https://doi.org/10.5281/zenodo.6829167.

6. Emerson and Lehman, "Who Are We Missing?."

7. Amber Billey, Emily Drabinski, and K. R. Roberto, "What's Gender Got to Do with It? A Critique of RDA 9.7," *Cataloging & Classification Quarterly* 52, no. 4 (2014): 419.

8. Peyton Thomas, "Did the Mother of Young Adult Literature Identify as a Man?" *New York Times,* December 24, 2022, https://www.nytimes.com/2022/12/24/opinion/did-the-mother-of-young-adult-literature-identify-as-a-man.html.

9. Doyle announced her separation in a blog post just before *Love Warrior* was published. See Glennon Doyle, "I Need to Tell You Something," *Momastery,* August 1, 2016, https://momastery.com/blog/2016/08/01/i-need-to-tell-you-something/.

10. Becky Albertalli, "I Know I'm Late," *Medium,* August 31, 2020, https://medium.com/@rebecca.albertalli/i-know-im-late-9b31de339c62.

11. E. E. Lawrence, "The Trouble with Diverse Books, Part I: On the Limits of Conceptual Analysis for Political Negotiation in Library & Information Science," *Journal of Documentation* 76, no. 6 (2020): 1482.

12. See Amber Billey, Emily Drabinski, and K. R. Roberto, "What's Gender Got to Do with It? A Critique of RDA 9.7," *Cataloging & Classification Quarterly* 52, no. 4 (2014): 412–421; Elizabeth Hobart, "Cataloging Gender Diverse Authors: The MARC Field 386, Gender Identity and Privacy," *Journal of Information Ethics* 31, no. 2 (Fall 2022): 48–46; Violet B. Fox and Kelly Swickard, "'My Zine Life is My Private Life': Reframing Authority Control from Detective Work to an Ethics of Care," in *Ethical Questions in Name Authority Control*, ed. Jane Sandberg (Sacramento, CA: Library Juice Press, 2019), 9–24; Thomas A. Whittaker, "Demographic Characteristics in Personal Name Authority Records and the Ethics of a Person-Centered Approach to Name Authority Control," in *Ethical Questions in Name Authority Control*, ed. Jane Sandberg (Sacramento, CA: Library Juice Press, 2019), 57–69.

13. Amber Billey, Matthew Haugen, John Hostage, Nancy Sack, and Adam Schiff, "Report of the PCC Ad Hoc Task Group on Gender in Name Authority Records," October 4, 2016, https://www.loc.gov/aba/pcc/documents/Gender_375%20field_RecommendationReport.pdf.

14. Fox and Swickard, "My Zine Life is My Private Life."

15. Billey, Drabinski, and Roberto, "What's Gender Got to Do With It?" 413.

9

Coding New Acquisitions for Diversity of Subject Matter and Authorship at a Small College Library

Artemis D. Vex and Ruth Castillo

In the fall of 2021, librarians at Emory & Henry University—a small, rural academic library—began having discussions concerning diversity and the current state of their library's collections. It did not require a retrospective assessment to determine that the collection's present narrative was lacking greatly in terms of providing diverse content for library users. A quick browse of the shelves was enough for any library user to recognize that this collection was primarily a reflection of patriarchal White Western culture. Looking to the future of these holdings, the librarians wanted to ensure that, moving forward, the titles selected each year would reflect a greater diversity of ideas, beliefs, worldviews, and opinions. Shaping the library's collections to allow users to see and find themselves on the shelves was an important piece of these initial discussions. A simple solution would have been to incorporate a clause in policy denoting a renewed focus on DEI initiatives to collect specifically diverse materials and call it done. That would not, however, demonstrate if or how we were making progress toward our goal. The authors—Director and Public Services Librarian—wanted to be sure we could actively measure the levels of diverse materials being added to our collections and use this data to determine how well we were doing to improve the library's transition to providing more diverse and inclusive resources for our community of users. Practically, we could not remove enough content to create a diverse and inclusive collection. The amount of content we would need to remove in order to shift the balance of our collection would also decimate it. Instead, our library focused on the evaluation of newly acquired library materials.

    This chapter explores the process librarians at Emory & Henry University took in creating and implementing an assessment tool in our library and how we have continued to use this tool to evaluate purchases and diversify our collections. We also examine the challenges encountered and discuss considerations for what the future of this project will look like. For context, as a small liberal arts focused institution, we acquire approximately 500 individually purchased titles per year. The library does not utilize any approval plans and rarely purchases ebook packages. Monograph titles are recommended by each of the five librarians and then selected for purchase by the collection manager, a responsibility that migrates between the Director of the Library and the Technical Services Librarian based on shifting responsibilities. Most titles the librarians recommend for selection are purchased.

DEFINING DIVERSITY AND INCLUSION

For this project we describe diversity and its relationship with the library as follows: "The focus, when it comes to the use of terms such as diversity and the similar, is to break down the barriers of biases, prejudice, and discrimination and provide resources in the library that cover a wide range of differences."[1] For our library, this has meant addressing the current narratives found in our collection and working to add more diverse themes and voices to the shelves through a revision of our acquisition-selection process. To do this we began compiling categories of diversity descriptors. We also worked alongside the Coordinator of Academic Diversity Initiatives for the College, receiving input and suggestions for the diversity categories we selected as well as for the glossary of terms. This collaborative effort led to the addition of several secondary codes, the creation of an Other category, and additional terms and concepts of importance added to the glossary, such as Cultural Diversity—Refugee/Immigration Status and Other Diversity—Body Diversity/Acceptance.

TOOLS FOR ASSESSING ACQUISITIONS

Library collections, resources meant to reflect a wide array of cultures, perspectives, beliefs, and ideals, have been one area scholars point to as lacking substantially as they relate specifically to diversity,[2] to the detriment of the communities and persons being served, with much of the discourse on making library collections more representative having been limited to the implementation of retrospective diversity audits for collection assessment.[3] Kristick demonstrates how the information collected from diversity audits can be incorporated into a library's acquisition-selection process, specifically through the uncovering of gaps in already existing collections that and in turn, influence any change or new considerations for library acquisitions.[4] While it is true that uncovering gaps can influence new acquisitions, a retrospective diversity audit

          Artemis D. Vex and Ruth Castillo

would not tell us whether or not we were improving our acquisition-selection process.

Though only a few conversations have specifically delved into the matter of acquisition assessment, Ciszek and Young's review of diversity assessments sheds promising light on the feasibility of assessing acquisitions and what that process could look like. Ciszek and Young note how one academic institution developed a series of codes explicitly for acquisition assessment. While this institution's assessment process was discontinued after three years and contained flaws (selector bias being one), it provides a useful explanation of how a set series of codes were created to reflect different areas of diversity and how these codes were assigned as new materials were acquired.[5] In the spring of 2020 one library created a guide documenting a diversity audit and assessment of their collections, drawing obvious parallels from the same diversity coding scheme Cizsek and Young explored a decade prior.[6] It was through this guide, specifically, that we were able to draw inspiration for what our coding table would look like, adopting the two-character code format to represent the different types of diversity.

METHODOLOGY

The first step toward creating Emory & Henry Library's own coding tool was to create the governing framework for what we imagined this tool to look like. Defining our purpose (to measure, then increase, diversity in acquisitions) and what success would entail (data reflecting growth among the various types and levels of diversity in acquisitions), in turn, assisted us in deciding what types of acquisitions we would be coding. While a library collection can consist of many different types of sources (newspapers, journals, books, DVDs, electronic resources), we would concentrate our efforts on coding physical and electronic books.

Here we also selected the characteristics (author, content, purpose, visual representation) we would use when determining whether a library acquisition is diverse or not. While examining content, purpose, and visual representation would certainly provide ample information to code each item, we felt we needed to code for the author as well. As much as diversity can be found in content matter, we must recognize that diversity can also be found in the voices, experiences, and perspectives of the individuals creating the work. What may not be considered diverse content can still be created by diverse individuals, and accounting for the voices they bring to the discussion is valuable. As well, having set the intention to re-create our collections in such a way that users would be able to find themselves among the shelves, it would have felt counterintuitive to not code for diverse authors.

The first attempts explored the utilization of a five-point Likert scale grading rubric, laying out a set number of questions to ask of each acquisition, such as whether or not it offered a voices, perspectives, stories and/or histories from marginalized societies and non-white communities. However, we quickly discovered that, because the elements that make up diversity are so numerous (i.e., national origin, language, race, color, age, etc.), accurately and thoroughly accounting for each in a single set list of questions would not be possible. Additionally, the amount of time required to "grade" an entire list of acquisitions would be overwhelming and not very practical. Stepping back, our discussions pivoted to creating a list of codes that could be assigned to each book, if it were diverse, which would then represent a specific type of diversity found within.

Before a coding table could be created, we needed to understand what types of diversity exist and decide which types we would code for. Initial exploration into diversity types used a broad approach, starting with a clean slate. Our goal was to be as inclusive as we could with our work, but we were quick to recognize that diversity exists in many different forms. It was important at this point to consider the community of patrons on our college campus and which diversity categories they may belong to. For this, we started exploring online content, from discourse in online communities and organizations to blogs and listicles, making notes of the types of diversity and to what extent they were being discussed. Examples of these online discourses included information from organizations such as American Association of University Women,[7] American Association on Intellectual and Developmental Disabilities,[8] and Immigrants Rising;[9] academic library guides;[10] and in a few instances, information being created and shared by different academic departments at various institutions.[11] We then selected the following primary categories of diversity: Age Diversity; Cultural Diversity; Sex/Gender Diversity; Neurodiversity Diversity; Racial Diversity; Religious Diversity; Sexual Orientation Diversity; and Socioeconomic Diversity. After selecting our categories, we created a two or three-letter code to represent each, such as Age Diversity = AGD.

Inspiration for our codes and the coding table came from a library guide documenting one academic library's process of performing a diversity audit of their collection.[12] Additionally, because of the complex nature of diversity, a set of secondary codes was then created for each primary code. While not exhaustive, these secondary codes represent the differences that make up each primary code, that is, Age Diversity–Millennial (AGD–ML), thus allowing librarians to code more specific types of diverse representation. Based on feedback from the Coordinator of Academic Diversity Initiatives and from colleagues in the library, we amended the list of primary code to better reflect the wide expanse of diverse life and experiences represented at Emory & Henry. The most dramatic changes at this point were the renaming of Neurodiversity Diversity to Ability Diversity, and the addition of a category for Other Diversity. Other additions included secondary codes for Appalachian Identity, Body Diversity, Mental Illness, and Immigrant Status. When creating the Other Diversity (OD) primary code, the intention was to ensure space for future growth to happen as more knowledge and discussions about diversity, equity, and inclusion take place. The coding table is shown in the appendix (table 9.1).

          Artemis D. Vex and Ruth Castillo

Simultaneously, as the coding table began to take shape, so too, did a glossary that provides a thorough, but not exhaustive, description of what constitutes "Diverse Content" for each primary code listed. Additional notes and information to assist librarians with the coding process were also provided, including what sources to use when book coding, that is, checking Title and Table of Contents as well as utilizing the library's OPAC (subject heading, keywords, additional labels, and abstract) and professional publications (*Library Journal, Choice, C&RL News*, etc.). Distinctions were also made concerning how many codes an item would be given (up to 3) and what a librarian should do for codes that are broader in scope and don't necessarily fit in a Secondary Category. Attempts were also made to code for author identity only if external confirmation could be found such as the author's website or public statements. Because diversity spans such a large array of different elements and characteristics which often intersect with each other and are not always easily recognizable, creating a glossary that broke down each category and its respective pieces was crucial for the toolkit to work. For an example, see text box 9.2.

TEXT BOX 9.1 EXCERPT FROM TOOLKIT

After selecting a primary code, the librarian will then attach a subcode that further best reflects the content of the book, if possible.

- There are also instances wherein an item's content falls into a broader category of codes. When this occurs, instead of trying to force a more specific DEI code, the approach here is to use a Primary Code only.
- While it is possible that an item could receive multiple codes, it was decided that up to three codes will be assigned to an item.

Source: Artemis Vex and Ruth Castillo, "Collection Assessment Codes Toolkit," Google Docs, 2019, bit.ly/acq-dei-toolkit.

TEXT BOX 9.2 EXCERPT FROM TOOLKIT GLOSSARY

Other Diversities (OD)
****It should be recognized that OD (Other Diversities) is NOT a permanent resting place for new and developing areas of diversity.****

The more time, care, and research that is being spent to understand and define different areas and themes within the DEI Initiative, has already and will continue to witness the growth and development of other such areas of diversity. While these are still in development and expatiating further on them may not, at the time, be possible or appropriate until further information comes out, a category for Other Diversities will be used. It is the intent of this category, to act more as a placeholder for topics, themes, and other issues related to DEI efforts. This section will contain newer and more recent areas that are only just being recognized.

When coding items that fall into the **OD** category, **OD** will act as the primary code, much like the other dominant categories. Additional secondary codes will be used to denote which "other diversity" is being covered. For example, a book that touches on themes of Body Diversity would receive the following: **OD-BD**.

Source: Artemis Vex and Ruth Castillo, "Collection Assessment Codes Toolkit."

TESTING AND EVALUATION

Several test trials were run to determine how consistent the toolkit was when used by multiple librarians, the ease and usability of the toolkit, the time required to code each title, and what the data would look like. Initial testing was performed by the authors, as the coding table creators, and included lists of twenty titles that had been randomly selected from the previous year's acquisitions. We both created codes for the same list of twenty titles before comparing results and addressing any discrepancies in the coding process. Results revealed a 10 percent difference (or two titles) between what was coded "Diverse" (70–80 percent) and what did not receive a code and was considered "Not Diverse" (20–30 percent).

For the second, larger test we provided all five of the librarians in our library with identical lists of a new set of thirty titles as well as the coding table with its glossary and allotted thirty minutes to code. The purpose of this larger test was to see if the tool could be used successfully by someone not involved in the process of development and creation. The question guiding this test was: Could another librarian pick up this tool and get the same results that we were getting? Reviewing the results from five librarians, including the two responsible for creating the toolkit, found a varied, but not drastic, range in what items had been coded as Diverse (37–43 percent) and Not Diverse (57–63 percent). With a 6 percent variance (meaning that differences among librarian's coding tables fluctuated by no more than 1.8 acquisition items), we were able to demonstrate twofold that this toolkit was not only successful in accomplishing an assessment of DEI levels in our purchase of acquisitions but

                                    Artemis D. Vex and Ruth Castillo

could be picked up and used by any librarian wanting to assess their acquisitions and/or collections.

IMPLEMENTATION

Throughout the development of this toolkit, its primary purpose was to assess levels of DEI in the works that Emory & Henry adds to the physical and digital shelves each year. Upon seeing the results from the toolkit trial runs we were confident we were on the right track with an assessment tool that not only would aid our building of more diverse collections, but also assist each of us as we continue building our knowledge and understanding of what DEI is and what it means for all of us. During the initial implementation of this toolkit, primarily as a matter of convenience and time, it was decided that one librarian (one of the creators of the toolkit) would be responsible for the coding process.

Coding began with the acquisition list from the 2019 to 2020 Academic Year (AY) and has since included the 2020-2021 AY, 2021-2022 AY, and the 2022-2023 AY. Originally, the approach was to compile the list of all acquisitions for a single Academic Year and code them at one time; however, this approach became overwhelming. The time required to code each year's list of several hundred acquisitions was roughly ten to fifteen hours, which meant the process required multiple days. As we moved into the 2023-2024 AY the process was amended to now include two librarians that meet and work together each month, coding the acquisitions from the previous month. Working together also allows for multiple perspectives to interact with the toolkit as well as for the building of many discussions around the development of a stronger and more enveloping grasp on DEI within not solely library collections, but the library in its entirety.

RESULTS

Using the toolkit, we have coded five years of library acquisitions totaling 2,269 items. During the 2019-2020 Academic Year (AY) the library added 593 items, of which 43 percent received at least one code denoting diverse themes or creators. From this group, three categories stood out. Twenty percent of acquisitions (117 items) received a code placing them in the Race/Ethnicity Diversity category, wherein 15 percent or ninety items were specifically coded RAD-BK (Race/Ethnic Diversity—Black). Another 20 percent (120 items) coded were placed under the Sex/Gender Diversity category, with 18 percent or 105 items specifically coded GD-FM (Gender Diversity—Female/Women). The category for Cultural Diversity had 14 percent or eighty-four items coded, primarily receiving the broader category code only. A small percentage, 5 percent or twenty-seven items received a more specific code under the Cultural Diversity category—CD-AI (see figure 9.1).

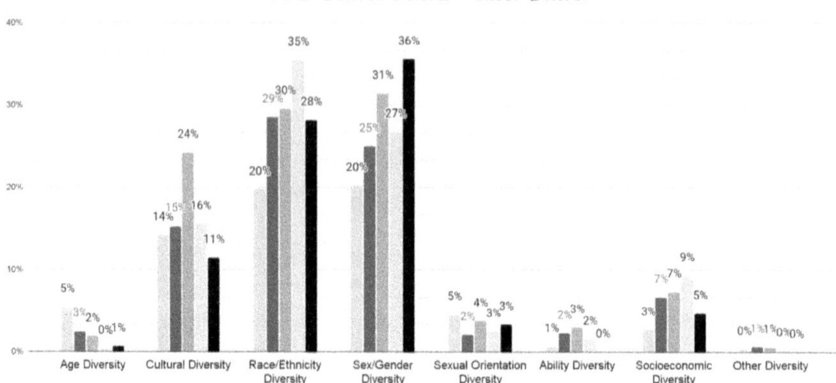

Figure 9.1   Emory & Henry Library Acquisitions AY 2020-2021—AY 2023-2024 Coded by Category. *Source*: Chapter authors.

The following year (2020–2021 AY) 480 items were added to the collections with 50 percent receiving at least one code denoting DEI. Race/Ethnicity Diversity (RAD) continued to demonstrate high numbers with 29 percent of library acquisitions (or 137 items) receiving a primary code of RAD. Specifically, 14 percent were also given the secondary code -BK (Black), 3 percent -LX (Latinx/Hispanic), and 2 percent each for -AF (African) and -IN (Indigenous/Native) (see figure 9.1). The next category was the Sex/Gender Diversity category which held 25 percent or 120 of that year's acquisitions with the secondary code -FM (Female/Women) accounting for 22 percent, with -TR (Transgender) only making up 1 percent or three titles.

Coding for the 2021–2022 AY list of acquisitions, which totaled 530 items, saw an increase of 10 percentage points from the previous year's acquisitions that received coding, amounting to 60 percent of these titles reflecting either content that was DEI or that was created by diverse authors. The category that received the most coded items from this acquisitions list was Sex/Gender Diversity with 32 percent or 167 items receiving a primary code, with 26 percent or 139 of these items being specifically coded with the secondary code -FM (Female/Women) (see figure 9.1). Race/Ethnicity Diversity was the next highest category with 30 percent or 157 items coded; 14 percent received a secondary code of -BK (Black), 3 percent received -LX (Latinx/Hispanic), and 2 percent were given to both -AF (African) and -AP (Asian Pacific).

While the library added 516 acquisitions during the 2022–2023 AY, of this total 53 percent of items had at least one code for diversity attached. The categories with the most coded items for this selection of acquisitions were Racial/Ethnicity Diversity with 35 percent (183 items), of which 17 percent received a secondary code -BK (Black) and 3 percent were each given to -AF (African), -IN (Indigenous/Native), and -LX (Latinx/Hispanic); and Gender

                                    Artemis D. Vex and Ruth Castillo

Diversity with 27 percent (138 items), of which 24 percent (126 of the 138 items) received a secondary code of -FM (Female/Woman) (see figure 9.1). Cultural Diversity was the next largest category with 16 percent or eighty items coded. Few secondary codes were used for the Cultural Diversity category for this set of acquisitions. Of the eighty items that were coded CD (Cultural Diversity), 2 percent (9 items) were given the secondary code -LSp (Language: Spanish), and 1 percent was coded with -JH (Religion: Jewish).

Due to a pause in ordering in AU 2023–2024 for budget reasons, the library added only 150 new titles to its collection with 59 percent being coded for diversity. The categories for Sex/Gender Diversity and Racial/Ethnicity Diversity reflected the highest numbers this year with 36 percent (48 items) and 26 percent (35 items), respectively (see figure 9.1). The secondary codes for Sex/Gender Diversity consisted of 44 of the 48 items (33 percent) receiving -FM (Female/Woman). The Racial/Ethnicity Diversity category was further broken down to reflect secondary coding for -BK (Black) which made up 12 percent of the total items coded for this category, while 3 percent were coded with -AP (Asian Pacific), and 1 percent received either -IN (Indigenous/Native), -LX (Latinx/Hispanic), -MR (Multiracial), or -POC (People of Color). The Cultural Diversity category was next with 11 percent receiving a primary code (CD) and 6 percent receiving a more specific, secondary code of -AI (Appalachian Identity).

DISCUSSION

When we started this project, our primary goal was to track levels of diversity among library acquisitions. With the creation of our toolkit, we have been able to code and run data for the last five years of acquisition purchasing and have been able to chart a steady growth in the number of diverse titles being selected. The 2019–2020 AY was the first year we implemented this toolkit, and we recorded 43 percent diversity for that year's acquisitions. It was also during the 2019–2020 AY that the toolkit was developed, meaning that any acquisitions decisions that were made for this year were done without this framework in mind. Because of this, the data from this year would be our starting baseline for assessment.

The following year there was a 7-percentage point increase in diverse titles and then an additional 10-percentage point increase was experienced during the 2021–2022 year. However, our last two data sets (AYs 2022–2023 and 2023–2024) did show a decrease in diverse items (see figure 9.2). Compared to the 2021–2022 AY numbers (60 percent) the data revealed a 7-percentage point decrease in the number of diverse items being added during the 2022–2023 AY. While the 2023–2024 AY did experience a 6-percentage point increase compared to 2022–2023, there was a 28.9 percent decrease in the number of items purchased which should be taken into consideration when reviewing the data.

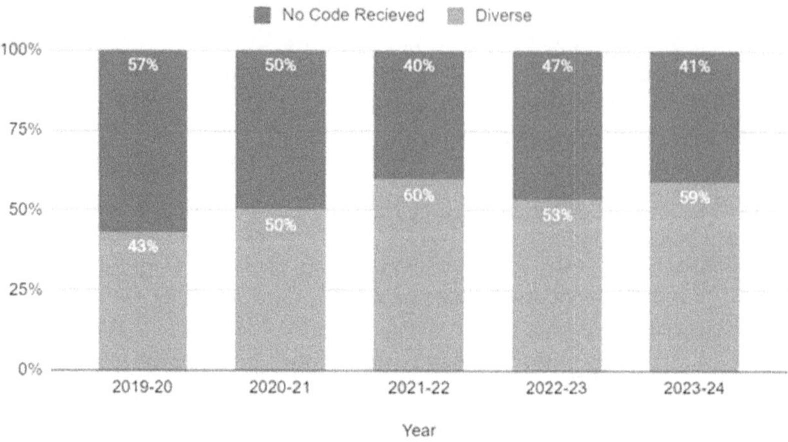

Figure 9.2 Diverse and No Code Received. *Source*: Chapter authors.

It should be noted that during the 2021–2022 AY, the library received a grant toward building a collection of DEI Health Sciences materials and the following year (2022–2023 AY) received a large donation to be used specifically to purchase books on local and state history. Taking into consideration the focus and influencing factors that these additional funds brought to each respective year, it is not unexpected that the levels of acquisition diversity experienced some fluctuations and will presumably continue to do so. Another factor influencing the most recent year (2023–2024) of acquisitions was budget constraints, resulting in a sudden pause of book orders and a decrease in how much content was being added to the shelves.

One challenge that regularly occurred was in assigning codes based on the author(s)'s identity. Identifying the author's identity, or risking misidentifying an author's identity were primary concerns. There were also concerns based on the often-changing nature of identity. Due to these concerns and our cautious approach to author identities, some diversity may be underreported.

Coding for these last five years has shown that the following three categories have consistently led each year's acquisition list: Racial/Ethnicity Diversity, Sex/Gender Diversity, and Cultural Diversity. More specifically, we have been able to observe that for two of these categories, there was one predominant secondary code that was being attached to library acquisitions; for Racial/Ethnicity Diversity it was the secondary code -BK (Black), and for Sex/Gender

 Artemis D. Vex and Ruth Castillo

Diversity it was -FM (Female/Woman). While the Cultural Diversity category continued to receive high numbers, the majority of these items only received a primary code of CD as their scope was broader and didn't necessarily fit into or need a secondary code.

While the category for Sex/Gender Diversity held high numbers, rather than one of the varied identities (Agender, Bigender, Transgender) that would also be included under this primary code, in almost every case the item being coded was receiving a GD-FM, denoting either an item created by or about women. For example, during the 2021–2022 AY, the library added 167 titles that received a primary code of GD, however, a closer look reveals that of those titles 83 percent (139 books) were additionally coded with -FM (see figure 9.3). A similar pattern can be observed for Racial/Ethnicity Diversity. Of the 157 titles with this primary code added during the same year (2021–2022 AY), 48 percent (75 books) received the code RAD-BK (see figure 9.4). For both categories, this pattern is consistent across the five years of data.

While the data has demonstrated we have been successful with both the measurement and increase of diverse content being purchased each year, the data does not specifically address what factors have been responsible for this increase in diversity. As of the creation and implementation of our toolkit, no

Sex/Gender Diversity	GD		167	31%
	Primary Code Only [GD]		20	4%
	Gender fluid	-GF	0	0%
	Bigender	-BR	0	0%
	Third gender	-TG	0	0%
	Two-Spirit	-TT	0	0%
	Genderqueer	-GR	0	0%
	Agender	-AR	0	0%
	Transgender	-TR	6	1%
	Intersex	-IX	1	<1%
	Female/Women	-FM	139	26%
	Gender dysphoria	-GD	0	0%
	Transitioning	-TA	0	0%
	Gender-expansive	-GE	1	<1%
	Bigender	-BG	0	0%

Figure 9.3   GD Acquisitions Coding for 2021–2022 Academic Year. *Source*: Chapter authors.

Race/Ethnicity Diversity	RAD			157	30%
	Primary Code Only [RAD]			30	6%
	African	-AF		13	2%
	Black	-BK		75	14%
	Asian Pacific	-AP		11	2%
	Indigenous/Native	-IN		7	1%
	Latinx/Hispanic	-LX		14	3%
	Alaska Natives	-AN		0	0%
	Hawaiian Natives	-HN		0	0%
	Arab/Middle East	-AE		3	1%
	Multiracial	-MR		3	1%
	People of Color	-POC		1	<1%

Figure 9.4   RAD Acquisitions Coding for 2021–2022 Academic Year. *Source*: Chapter authors.

changes have yet been made in the collection management process to address diversifying the collections. As Mortensen suggested concerning their own work with diversity audits, as gaps in representation are identified, librarians, in turn, become more mindful of what kinds of materials to select to begin "to narrow the[se] gaps."[13] It is this mindfulness, propagated through our regular assessments and coding, that has been a leading influential factor for what materials are and are not selected for acquisition.

At the same time, the results have also offered potential areas where gaps exist in the acquisition process. To revisit the data from 2021 to 2022, a more in-depth look at the secondary codes revealed that while diverse materials were being purchased, the levels of diversity within each category, reflected as the different secondary codes, remained relatively static. While GD-FM was attached to 139 items during this time period, only 6 items (1 percent) were coded GD-TR (Transgender), and two other items received a code of GD-IX (Intersex) or GD-GE (Gender-expansive). This same staticity, reflected in the low numbers of diverse codes given to this list, can be observed in the secondary codes of other categories as well, such as Racial/Ethnicity Diversity and Sexual Orientation Diversity. Reviewing the data for the 2023–2024 AY, the same low, static numbers can be observed, though with some change (and it should be noted this year's purchasing was placed on pause), with what items were receiving coding from Secondary Categories. For example, of the forty-two items coded under the Race/Ethnicity Diversity Category, while 50 percent received a secondary code—BK

　　　　　　　　　　　　　Artemis D. Vex and Ruth Castillo

(Black), only one item was added for each of the following secondary categories: Indigenous/Native (-IN), Arab/Middle East (-AR), and Multiracial (MR). It is specifically the data from these low numbers and areas of staticity that will help in the selection of content created by, for, and about people who identify in these areas where few or no acquisitions had been made in previous years.

CONCLUSION AND NEXT STEPS

Based on initial feedback from colleagues, further development work is focused on how to increase the discoverability of library holdings based on this coding work. Ensuring that patrons see their identities reflected in the collections on the library's shelves is an important step. Improving how those collections are accessed follows as a logical next step. Several issues are under consideration for this next phase such as the limitations of existing controlled vocabulary sets and the need to keep up with evolving language. There are additional local issues influencing this work as well, primarily, being part of a local library consortium in a shared integrated library system that has strict cataloging requirements.

Additional work has begun exploring how to address coding known author identities. While library collections have routinely been classified by subject and content, the identity of the author has not been part of traditional cataloging and metadata classification. However, in recognizing that the perspectives of marginalized communities bring significant contributions to any subject, being able to classify and discover items in collections by author identity will require new cataloging and metadata classification systems. Within our coding system, we plan to begin separate coding based on subject and/or author identity with the next acquisition cycle.

This process for coding new acquisitions based on multiple facets of diversity provides a consistent measure for benchmarking efforts to increase diverse and inclusive library collections. This is a necessary step toward shifting the representation in library collections to be more inclusive. With the data we have collected from the last five years of diversity coding, we can begin to identify and specifically address ongoing collection development gaps in terms of diverse representation.

TOOLKIT AVAILABLE

This toolkit is available under a CC BY-SA 4.0 license at bit.ly/acq-dei-toolkit.

APPENDIX

Table 9.1 Coding Table

Age Diversity	AGD	
Age Groups	Children	**-CN**
	Teens	**-TN**
	Older Adults	**-OA**
Generations	Gen Z	**-GZ**
	Millennial	**-ML**
	Gen X	**-GX**
	Boomer	**-BO**
	Silent	**-ST**
Cultural Diversity	**CD**	
Language	Arabic	**-LAr**
	Bengali	**-LBi**
	Chinese	**-LCh**
	French	**-LFh**
	Hindi	**-LHi**
	Indonesian	**-LIn**
	Japanese	**-LJa**
	Mandarin	**-LMn**
	Portuguese	**-LPo**
	Russian	**-LRu**
	Sign Language	**-LSi**
	Spanish	**-LSp**
Religion	Animism	**-AM**
	Buddhism	**-BM**
	Hinduism	**-HU**
	Indigenous religions	**-IR**
	Islam	**-IM**
	Jewish	**-JH**
	Monotheism	**-MM**
	Non-religious/Atheism	**-NA**
	Paganism	**-PA**
	Polytheism	**-PM**
	Sikh	**-SH**
	Totemism	**-TM**

(Continued)

 Artemis D. Vex and Ruth Castillo

Table 9.1 (Continued)

Refugee/Immigrant Status	Asylum Seeker	**-AY**
	Children of immigrants	**-CI**
	DREAM Act/Dreamer	**-DM**
	Mixed-status family/couple	**-MS**
	Permanent Resident	**-PT**
	Refugee	**-RE**
	Undocumented immigrant/worker	**-UI**
Local	Appalachian Identity	**-AI**
Other	Other	**-OR**
Race/Ethnicity Diversity	**RAD**	
	African	**-AF**
	Alaska Natives	**-AN**
	Arab/Middle East	**-AE**
	Asian Pacific	**-AP**
	Black	**-BK**
	Hawaiian Natives	**-HN**
	Indigenous/Native	**-IN**
	Latinx/Hispanic	**-LX**
	Multiracial	**-MR**
	People of Color	**-POC**
Sex/Gender Diversity	**GD**	
	Agender	**-AR**
	Bigender	**-BR**
	Female/Women	**-FM**
	Gender dysphoria	**-GD**
	Gender-expansive	**-GE**
	Gender fluid	**-GF**
	Genderqueer	**-GR**
	Intersex	**-IX**
	Third gender	**-TG**
	Transgender	**-TR**
	Transitioning	**-TA**
	Two-Spirit	**-TT**

(Continued)

Table 9.1 (Continued)

Sexual Orientation Diversity	SED	
	LGBTQIA	**-LA**
	Asexual	**-AS**
	Bisexual	**-BL**
	Gay	**-GY**
	Lesbian	**-LN**
	Pansexual	**-PS**
	Questioning	**-QU**
	Same-sex	**-SS**
	Transgender	**-TR**
Ability Diversity	**AD**	
	Intellectual abilities	**-IA**
	Mental Illness	**-MI**
	Neurodiversities	**-ND**
	Physical abilities	**-PA**
	Sensory abilities	**-SA**
Socioeconomic Diversity	**SOD**	
Economic	Income inequality	**-II**
	Lower Middle Class	**-LmC**
	Poor	**-PR**
	Restrictions/barriers to access	**-BA**
	Working Class	**-WC**
Limited Educational Attainment	Associates Degree	**-AO**
	High school Diploma	**-HD**
	No degree/dropout	**-NO**
Other Diversity	**OD**	
	Body Diversity/Acceptance	**-BD**

NOTES

1. Artemis Vex and Ruth Castillo, "Collection Assessment Codes Toolkit," Google Docs, 2019, bit.ly/acq-dei-toolkit.
2. Jennifer Bowers, Katherine Crowe, and Peggy Keeran, "'If You Want the History of a White Man, You Go to the Library': Critiquing Our Legacy, Addressing Our Library Collections Gaps," *Collection Management* 42, nos. 3–4 (October 2, 2017): 159–179, https://doi.org/10.1080/01462679.2017.1329104; Hannah Gross, "'Diversity in the Stacks' Initiative Aims to Make All Students Feel at Home in the Library," *Daily Pennsylvanian, The: University of Pennsylvania (Philadelphia, PA)*, October 8, 2019,

  Artemis D. Vex and Ruth Castillo

America's News Magazines; Jeffrey D. Meyers, "The Importance of Linguistically Diverse Collections: Decolonizing the Theological Library," *Theological Librarianship* 14, no. 2 (October 1, 2021): 11–28, https://doi.org/10.31046/tl.v14i2.2889; Kawanna Bright, "The Value of a DEI Audit: What an Assessment Can Show You and Why You Should Care," *American Libraries* 53, no. 11/12 (December 11, 2022): 40–40; Veronica A. Wells, Michele Gibney, and Mickel Paris, "Student Learning and Engagement in a DEI Collection Audit: Applying the ACRL Framework for Information Literacy," *College & Research Libraries News*, September 8, 2022, https://doi.org/10.5860/crln.83.8.335; Heather Howard, David Zwicky, and Danielle Walker, "Put Your Money Where Your Mouth Is: A Values-Based Evaluation Tool for Collections Decisions," *Collection Management*, December 26, 2022, 1–13, https://doi.org/10.1080/01462679.2022.2150733.

3. Karen Jensen, "Diversity Auditing 101: How to Evaluate Your Collection," *School Library Journal*, accessed March 24, 2023, https://www.slj.com/story/diversity-auditing-101-how-to-evaluate-collection; Annabelle Mortensen, "Measuring Diversity in the Collection," *Library Journal* 144, no. 4 (May 2019): 28–30; Julia Proctor, "Representation in the Collection: Assessing Coverage of LGBTQ Content in an Academic Library Collection," *Collection Management* 45, no. 3 (July 2, 2020): 223–234, https://doi.org/10.1080/01462679.2019.1708835.

4. Laurel Kristick, "Diversity Literary Awards: A Tool for Assessing an Academic Library's Collection," *Collection Management*, 2019, https://doi.org/10.1080/01462679.2019.1675209.

5. Matthew P. Ciszek and Courtney L. Young, "Diversity Collection Assessment in Large Academic Libraries," *Collection Building* 29, no. 4 (October 12, 2010): 154–161, https://doi.org/10.1108/01604951011088899.

6. Melissa Gonzalez, "Diversity Collection Audit & Assessment: Introduction," June 25, 2024, https://libguides.uwf.edu/c.php?g=1057279&p=7682341.

7. "DEI Toolkit: Sexual Orientation," AAUW (American Association of University Women), n.d., https://www.aauw.org/resources/member/governance-tools/dei-toolkit/dimensions-of-diversity/sexual-orientation/.

8. "Defining Criteria for Intellectual Disability," American Association on Intellectual and Developmental Disabilities, accessed March 20, 2023, https://www.aaidd.org/intellectual-disability/definition.

9. "Defining Undocumented," *IMMIGRANTS RISING* (blog), August 2023, https://immigrantsrising.org/resource/defining-undocumented/.

10. Marianne Myers, "LibGuides: Ethnography Research: Choosing Your Subculture," accessed July 10, 2024, https://guides.library.tulsacc.edu/c.php?g=1054390&p=7673005; Carmel Henry, "Social Justice: Racial Diversity," Howard University School of Law – Vernon E. Jordan Law Library, accessed July 10, 2024, https://library.law.howard.edu/socialjustice/diversity.

11. Office of Engagement and Inclusion, "What Does Being a First-Generation Student Mean? // First-Generation College Students," Marquette University, accessed July 10, 2024, https://www.marquette.edu/first-generation-students/about.php; International Students and Scholars Office, "What Is a Permanent Resident?," International Students and Scholars Office, accessed July 10, 2024, https://isso.ucsf.edu/permanent-resident; University of Illinois Counseling Center, "Body Size Diversity and Acceptance," University of Illinois at Urbana-Champaign, accessed

July 10, 2024, https://counselingcenter.illinois.edu/brochures/body-size-diversity
-and-acceptance; Center for Disability Sports, Health and Wellness, "Sensory Disabilities," Rutgers University :: Department of Kinesiology and Health, accessed
July 10, 2024, https://kines.rutgers.edu/dshw/disabilities/sensory/1061-sensory
-disabilities.
12. Gonzalez, "Diversity Collection Audit & Assessment: Introduction."
13. Annabelle Mortensen, "Measuring Diversity in the Collection," *Library Journal* 144,
no. 4 (May 2019): 28–30.

                    Artemis D. Vex and Ruth Castillo

10

Assessing Institutional Efforts

The third lens for understanding the diversity of your collections is through a focus on institutional efforts. Rather than assessing the collection itself, this lens involves evaluating the work you've done to build a more diverse collection, or more broadly to instill a DEI mindset in collections work. As institutional efforts can vary greatly, strategies for assessment will also vary and may be more informal. Assessment methods will usually involve tracking what you have done, noting the outcomes of your actions, and deciding whether you need to change course. As methods for assessing institutional efforts are simpler than the techniques described in previous chapters, the main challenge for this lens is not choosing an appropriate method but breaking down a broad vision of DEI into concrete, measurable steps.

This chapter describes different actions you can take to incorporate DEI values into the work of collection development and notes ways you can assess these actions. It suggests projects that aim to influence how staff think about diversity as well as actions that directly target work processes, with the understanding that both are part of making DEI an integral part of your work.

MAKING EFFORTS ASSESSABLE

Incorporating DEI values into collections work can be a large and vague goal. Kara Bledsoe and colleagues recommend giving your library the opportunity for "small wins" that can provide a sense of accomplishment on the way to "big wins."[1] An additional advantage of small wins is that they provide a chance to reflect on your work so that you can continue what has been successful and decide when you need to change course. In other words, turning your aspirations for the collection into a series of smaller goals or projects gives you the opportunity to assess.

You should base your goals, at least in the short term, on what you think you can achieve, rather than on your ideal. Future goals can build on the initial ones. For instance, a goal that involves learning and reflecting might be followed the next year by a goal of taking action. The work of building diverse, equitable, and inclusive collection-building will be ongoing, and you don't need to do everything at once.

In the examples given, you will see that assessment happens in similar ways and at similar points across different projects. Often you will begin a project with a survey of the current situation to identify what you want to change, so assessment will be one of your first steps. In order to assess progress, you'll need to set goals that you want to achieve within a specific time frame. The end of this time frame is the second time you can assess your efforts. The assessment at this point might be as simple as reporting on whether you have achieved the goals you set. It could also involve a quantifiable metric, such as the number of people participating in an activity or number of times you did something. Reflection is another important part of assessment, both at the end of a project and at milestones along the way. You may have found a project harder or less useful than expected, or maybe a new process needs to be adjusted.

A necessary piece of the second and third types of assessment, noting whether you've met your goals and reflecting, is setting a timeline. Without a timeline, you might forget to honor your accomplishments or check in on whether you need to change course. If your goals are integrated into an existing document, such as individuals' performance reviews or a library-wide strategic plan, you can follow your usual process for reviewing goals and noting whether you are on your way to achieving them. If your goals related to DEI in collections are a standalone document, you can include a timeline as part of this document.

BUILDING A SHARED DEI MINDSET

Often the libraries that track and assess collecting practices rather than the collection itself describe an overarching goal of changing culture and ways of thinking. UNLV's report on inclusive collecting practices states an aim to "foster a culture of collecting that prioritizes ongoing, thoughtful collection development with an eye to advancing inclusion of historically excluded groups."[2] MIT Libraries released a report in 2017 titled "Creating a Social Justice Mindset," which provided recommendations on how to "systematically re-envision the daily work of the Collections Directorate through the lens of diversity, inclusion, and social justice."[3] Because projects will influence culture, however, you don't necessarily need to proceed in a linear way of trying to change culture before taking action. Still, efforts to get staff thinking more about diversity and inclusion can be a good place to start trying to incorporate this lens into your work. Designated staff activities that have an explicit goal of asking staff to share thoughts can plant seeds, as can a collaborative project to state institutional values as policy. Text box 10.1 suggests measurable goals for efforts to develop a common DEI mindset.

TEXT BOX 10.1 MEASURABLE GOALS FOR DEVELOPING A DEI MINDSET

Staff Development

Group

- Hold a number of discussions related to DEI topics
- Survey staff on existing strategies for collections-building and share results

Individual
- Attend a certain number of conferences or webinars

Policies

- Review university and library policies for mentions of DEI
- Revise collections policy
- Collect and review feedback on new collections policy

Source: Author.

Staff Development

Staff development events that allow for sharing ideas can help create a more even baseline understanding of DEI considerations by letting staff learn from each other while recognizing the expertise of those who have thought more about these issues. Activities focused on learning or sharing thoughts might naturally generate ideas for new actions or could explicitly solicit such ideas.

One way to encourage staff to share their thoughts about diversity in collections is through open discussions. Both MIT and the University of Minnesota have held series of discussions with staff intended to stimulate thinking and discussion about diversity and inclusion within collections. MIT's Collections Directorate facilitated discussions with different departments related to collections (Acquisitions, Scholarly Communications, and Archives and Special Collections) to generate "specific ideas and strategies for integrating DISJ [diversity, inclusion, and social justice] into that department's work."[4] Kat Nelsen and colleagues at the University of Minnesota hired a consultant to lead twelve focus groups involving over eighty library staff in order to identify elements of anti-racist collection building that were either already happening or needed to happen.[5]

Group discussions can be difficult for people with marginalized identities, however. In describing their efforts to imbue the values of diversity, inclusion, and social justice in their technical services work, Rhonda Kauffman and Martina Anderson note, "Many staff members of color found it emotionally exhausting to be thrust on a regular basis into discussions of painful issues of race and exclusion in the workplace."[6] You might make the discussions or focus groups optional or set expectations at the outset that participants will not invalidate any personal experiences that others share. An outside facilitator, if you can afford one, could also help create a safer environment.

If your focus is on developing the staff as a group, most likely your goal would be to hold a certain number of events or have a certain number of staff participate. The assessment would involve noting that the events happened and how many people had attended, with the organizers or participants reflecting on their usefulness. If participation rates are low, trying to understand why might involve additional assessment.

Knowledge can also be shared among staff asynchronously and even anonymously. The DEI in Collections committee at Temple University surveyed selectors within the library system about their efforts to build diverse and inclusive collections. The survey acted as an initial assessment of the extent to which selectors had incorporated DEI into their work. Because the survey included a question about resources or tools selectors were using to acquire material by or about underrepresented groups, it also allowed the selectors to share information with each other. The DEI committee compiled the resources or strategies mentioned in responses to the survey and used these as the starting point for a guide they later disseminated. The survey was therefore a way to both understand existing levels of engagement and to expand the staff's knowledge of possible ways to build diverse collections.

A third form of staff development is asking individuals to set personalized goals for learning and growth. The MIT mindset report recommends that all staff members in the Archives, Technical Services, Preservation, Scholarly Communication, and Collections Strategy units create personalized performance goals that are specific to the ways diversity, inclusion, and social justice relate to their work.[7] This recommendation was implemented at a library-wide level shortly after the report was published.[8]

Individual goals focused on changing a person's mindset would probably involve learning. A staff member might commit to watching webinars related to diversifying collections or reading about alternative thesauri. Individuals' goals can also include many of the suggested process changes mentioned later in this chapter. Remember to make goals concrete enough to be measurable, for instance by setting a number of webinars to watch. Assessment of individual performance goals would follow whatever process you normally use for performance reviews, which might involve the staff member writing a description of activities they have undertaken.

Policies

Another way to build a common understanding of how collections can reflect DEI values is through writing these values into policy. The process of drafting a policy can raise awareness among the people writing it, and new policies are usually shared and discussed among relevant staff. Like all efforts to incorporate DEI into people's mindset, writing a policy has the potential to lead to changes in workflows or to new initiatives. In the best-case scenario, writing the policy would be a first step toward doing the work your policy says is your intention. If there is difficulty gaining support for DEI initiatives, Sara Ahmed explains that an institutional commitment provides leverage to people trying to change the institution's practices. Having a policy "allows practitioners to indicate when specific actions are inconsistent with the principles the university is meant to be acting upon . . . If organizations are saying what they are doing, then you can show they are not doing what they are saying."[9]

Remember that while writing DEI into your policies can help establish institutional values, saying that you value diversity, equity, and inclusion does not make this statement true. Ahmed observes that diversity policies can sometimes be treated as if the document itself is evidence of the institution's good practices. She says that an institutional "commitment to antiracism . . . could even be used to block the recognition of racism within institutions," allowing an institution to point to official statements of their commitment and ask "how can we be racist if we are committed to equality and diversity?"[10] This is less likely to happen if your library also sets goals related to changing collection development processes, perhaps using some of the examples in this chapter.

A project to revise your collection development policies would start with looking at what relevant documents your organization has already produced, whether at the university level or within the library. Diversity is sometimes mentioned in strategic plans or in a separate diversity statement. Though you can choose to include DEI as a value and aspiration for collection development even if it is not mentioned in the higher-level documents, reviewing institutional documents can give you context and can be a form of assessment. After gathering this information, you would create a timeline with steps for writing the policy and getting it approved. Several parts of the policy-writing process could be considered assessment: the review of the existing collection development policy, gathering feedback from library staff, and reporting on whether the overall goal of revising the policy had been met within the intended time frame.

ACQUISITIONS PROCESSES

Moving from efforts to influence how your library thinks about collections work to changing its actions involves reviewing and revising processes. Diversity work in acquisitions can include adjustments to selection strategies, vendors, and budgets. Suggestions for measurable goals related to acquisitions processes are noted in text box 10.2.

TEXT BOX 10.2 MEASURABLE GOALS RELATED TO ACQUISITIONS PROCESSES

Selection Strategies

Individual

- Find a source for book reviews related to underrepresented groups
- Ask faculty for purchase recommendations related to specific populations
- Invite a student group to make requests or recommendations

Procedural

- Review publishers on approval profiles to see if any have a focus on marginalized populations
- Add DEI awards to approval profiles
- Add independent publishers to approval profiles

Vendors

- Collect information from vendors on their commitment to diversity
- Research possible supplementary sources of purchases, such as local bookstores

Budgets

- Track how much your library spends on books not in English or from international vendors
- Increase use of a DEI fund

Source: Author.

Selection Strategies

The changes you make to your selection strategies will depend to some extent on how your library currently selects books and other materials. Smaller libraries do most of their purchasing by manually selecting titles to order, while larger libraries acquire books through approval plans that tell vendors to automatically ship books that meet predetermined criteria.

For whatever title-by-title ordering your library does, you can commit to expanding your selection strategies so that you will purchase more books by or about underrepresented people in the future. Selectors can set a goal of finding a source for book reviews related to underrepresented groups, such as *QBR The Black Book Review* or *Lambda Literary Review,* and regularly reading these reviews. Other goals could involve working with the campus community to get information about titles to purchase. Selectors might commit to contacting a set number of faculty to ask for purchase recommendations or identifying campus groups to work with, such as a student library advisory committee or an organization for students with a common marginalized identity. Selection strategies that involve soliciting suggestions from your campus community can double as outreach, since they show others your commitment to creating a more diverse collection.

If you use approval plans, there are ways to modify these so that they also contribute to the diversity of your collection. An initial assessment might involve reviewing the publishers that are on your approval profiles, or publishers whose books you have purchased in the last year, to see how many are minority-owned or have a DEI-related focus. A future goal could then be identifying new publishers to add to the profile. Lists of past award-winners can be a source of ideas for smaller publishers to add to an approval profile, or you can also add the award itself, asking the vendor to regularly send you the winners. Your goal would be to gather information about publishers and awards and consider which to add to your approval profiles. The assessment would note that you'd completed the task and what you had learned. The following year's assessment might seek to understand how the changes to your purchasing strategies have affected what you receive.

The large book vendors are often very willing to make changes based on the information customers provide about their needs. GOBI staff have indicated their openness to suggestions from library customers on ways to improve their services with regards to diversity. They note that they appreciate when customers suggest names of publishers for GOBI to profile or awards that they would like the company to track.[11] ProQuest Clarivate has been very helpful to Temple University, the author's own institution, in collecting information on winners of awards related to specific identities, even awards the company had not previously tracked. Representatives have also suggested that if a customer indicates that a publisher is important to them, the company may be able to include it in approval profile coverage.

Vendors

In addition to adjusting what you buy, you might also review the vendors them-selves and consider adding new vendors, particularly those owned by members of marginalized groups. Bledsoe and colleagues suggest an initial step of "[asking] vendors to provide information about their DEI practices, both through staffing, culture, and climate as well as through collections, services, description."[12] Gathering information about vendors that you will use to make decisions is a form of assessment. Elizabeth Speer at the University of North Texas Health Science Center did something similar to this. In 2021, she contacted twenty-one vendors stating her library's "expectation that vendors with which we enter into business will . . . make conscious efforts to broaden their level of diversity by including a broader spectrum of materials which clearly demonstrate the importance of including people of all races, gender identities, socioeconomic backgrounds, and cultures."[13] She then made response to this letter a requirement for renewing contracts with vendors. Speer notes that the letter resulted in improved relationships with existing vendors and more frequent communications.[14]

Another way to incorporate DEI into collections processes is to add new vendors. MIT's mindset document advocates considering how the institution's business decisions affect the marketplace and align with stated values.[15] If it is important to you to support women- or BIPOC-owned businesses, you may decide to do so even if it is somewhat more expensive than relying on your usual vendors. The new sources do not need to completely replace your traditional vendors. Given the extensive services the major companies provide, you will probably keep a relationship with whatever large vendor you currently use but can add a new supplier for some subset of purchasing. A preliminary step might be to gather information on businesses that you might add as vendors, whereas later assessment would confirm whether you had completed your goal of researching new vendors.

Budgets

Considering new vendors raises the issue of the potential cost of building more diverse collections. There will probably be financial limits on how much you can change your purchasing practices, as efficiency and cost-saving are also valid institutional priorities. The report from UNLV "recommends that a feasible percentage of the monograph budget or set dollar amount be dedicated to th[e] effort . . . [of ordering from] publishers and vendors that are owned by and/or support historically excluded communities."[16] After working with new vendors for some time, you'd want to assess how using them has affected your library's expenses, taking into account both book prices and cataloging time. You probably can't keep your diversification efforts cost-neutral, but the added expense may be manageable if it is limited and if staff understand and support the reason for the changes.

Besides designating a portion of your budget for purchasing from new vendors, you might also carve out portions of the budget for buying specific types of materials. Bledsoe and colleagues suggest calculating the percentage of the budget you have recently spent on works not in English.[17] If language diversity is an appropriate goal for your collection, you could set a target for spending on non-English materials, based on an initial calculation of what you have been spending. Later assessment could include reflecting on any difficulties that had come up in trying to increase your ordering of these books, particularly those that were international orders, and considering any feedback you've gotten from patrons.

A somewhat common approach to diversifying library collections is creating a dedicated budget line for DEI purchases. If you have such a fund, there are a variety of ways to assess how you have been using it. Did you end up using it for books you would have purchased anyway, or did the dedicated line allow you to buy items that would have otherwise not had an appropriate funding source? Did you find it hard to fully spend the fund, or would you have made even more purchases if you had more money? If the DEI fund is available to multiple people or if purchasing is based on student requests, you might also count the number of people involved in selecting purchases on this fund and then see if you can increase this number. If you don't have a dedicated DEI budget and think it would be appropriate for your library, you could set a goal to create such a fund and then assess how it affected you to have it.

PRESENTATION OF COLLECTIONS

The goal of incorporating DEI into collecting practices rather than into collections includes thinking about the ways your patrons come into contact with library collections, which could be through the catalog or your promotional efforts. ALA's Interpretation of the Library Bill of Rights says, "Developing a diverse collection requires . . . evaluating how diverse collection resources are cataloged, labeled, and displayed."[18] The ways you describe and display materials about underrepresented groups influences how likely patrons are to find them and sends a message about how the library values these works. This section groups together cataloging and promotional activities, as these both relate to how libraries present materials to patrons. Text box 10.3 lists measurable goals for improving or increasing the ways your library presents materials about marginalized groups to patrons.

TEXT BOX 10.3 MEASURABLE GOALS RELATED TO PRESENTATION OF COLLECTIONS

Cataloging

- Compare processing times for English and non-English materials and aim to bring these closer together
- Plan to add subject headings from alternative thesauri to your catalog
- Measure and increase staff's involvement in efforts to change LCSH

Promotional Activities

- Track how many displays your library has done related to marginalized populations
- Count how many research guides you offer related to marginalized groups, identify gaps, and create new guides
- Survey the ways you have shared your DEI work with the campus community and make a plan to increase communication

Source: Author.

Cataloging

In order for patrons to find and use any material, it needs to be cataloged. It is common for non-English materials to be delayed in getting on the shelves, as the library may not have the language skills in-house and would need to send the books to an external provider for cataloging. Even if you have in-house language expertise to create records, your catalogers' levels of fluency may not be enough to create records with the same amount of detail you would include for English language materials. MIT librarians observed that non-English language materials were delayed in becoming available to patrons and began sending these materials to their outsourced cataloging service more frequently.[19] An assessment could calculate the average time it takes for non-English materials to be cataloged. You would compare this to English materials that require original or copy cataloging, but keep in mind that if most of your books arrive shelf-ready they will become available to your patrons even faster.

Books about marginalized groups may have offensive or inaccurate descriptive terms in your catalog, and viewing this language can be detrimental to students' sense of belonging even if the content of the book is not offensive. One way to address this is to add terms from alternative thesauri to your catalog. The University of Sydney has begun a project to re-catalog items relating to First Nations people using thesauri from the Australian Institute of Aboriginal and Torres Strait Islander Studies. The re-cataloging was part of an extensive review of how the University of Sydney library collected and presented works by and about First Nations people. One of their early steps was to "survey . . . collections to identify materials containing Aboriginal and Torres Strait Islander cultural heritage" to clarify the scope of the work to be done.[20] If you have a goal of adding alternative controlled vocabulary terms to your records, a preliminary assessment step could be to survey how many records contain the terms you want to change. You would then set goals for how many items to re-catalog or how many headings to replace with terms from the alternate vocabulary.

Another way of improving the ways library catalogs describe marginalized people is to advocate for changes to existing controlled vocabularies. Bledsoe and colleagues suggest a goal of "Contributing capacity to a cross-library effort to advocate for DEI-related adjustments to an industry-wide descriptive standard (e.g. LOC [Library of Congress] subject headings)."[21] Two examples of "cross-library effort[s]" are the LAIPA (Latin American and Indigenous Peoples of the Americas) Funnel and African American Funnel. Funnels are "a group of libraries (or catalogers from various libraries) that have joined together to contribute subject authority records for inclusion in the Library of Congress Subject Headings."[22] Assessment of your library's contributions would involve surveying what librarians at your institution are currently doing and how much time they spend on advocacy for changes to subject headings.

Promotional Activities

In addition to discovering items through the catalog or on the shelves, patrons find items that library staff has promoted to them through displays, guides, or social media. One way to assess promotional activities is to track how many exhibits your library has presented that relate to marginalized populations. Morgan Harrington looked at exhibits presented at National Library of Australia over the past thirty-eight years to see which told stories of culturally and linguistically diverse Australians.[23] Another idea is to count how many research guides your library's website offers related to specific populations or DEI considerations and see which populations are not included. Do you offer a guide to resources on dermatology for skin of color? Do you have one on disability? You could also survey your library's various efforts to make the campus aware of any new purchases or changes in purchasing. If you have begun purchasing from a local BIPOC-owned bookstore, for instance, has your library announced this on social media or on its website? Promotion of your own DEI efforts is more than a way of seeking accolades for your work. Making your work visible can increase the feeling among students from nondominant groups that the library is thinking about how to ensure they are represented in the collection.

Another way that libraries try to promote their own materials is by encouraging faculty to use them in courses. Librarians at the University of Minnesota Twin Cities mention a need to initiate conversations with faculty about using antiracist course materials.[24] As Karin Wikoff describes in the next chapter, Ithaca College undertook a project to identify medical textbooks with more diverse representation but determined that none existed. If you've made any attempts to promote more inclusive course materials, even if it has been unsuccessful, recording and reflecting on your efforts can be a form of assessment.

FUTURE STEPS

Unlike some of the other methods in this book, assessing institutional efforts is intertwined with planning future steps. Most of the assessments suggested in this chapter involve pursuing a deeper understanding of current circumstances in the library to understand where you can improve. Your assessments may lead to adding a new vendor, undertaking a new cataloging project, or creating more displays. Like the other methods, however, completing an assessment does not mean the work is done. There will probably always be a need to use organizational structures to help staff think about diversity, particularly as there are inevitable changes in staff. As language use changes and alternative thesauri grow, there will be more opportunities for modifying the catalog. Some goals that are currently difficult to achieve could become easier, such as identifying textbooks with better representation and promoting these to your faculty. Having ways to measure your efforts can allow you to note accomplishments along the way and ensure that you continue to take actions that match your stated values.

There are also cases when a department or group reviews an aspect of collections work through a DEI lens but does not take any action. Sometimes you'll want to do something but be unable to, for instance if the books you wish you could buy haven't been published. There could also be times you investigate an aspect of your library collections to verify whether you are being as inclusive as possible and conclude nothing needs to be changed. Karin Wikoff shares examples of both of these situations in the next chapter. In these cases, going through the process of considering what is possible for you to do still helps build your culture, which should lead you to take actions when appropriate.

NOTES

1. Kara Bledsoe, Danielle Miriam Cooper, Roger C. Schonfeld, and Oya Rieger, *Leading by Diversifying Collections* (New York: Ithaka S+R, November 9, 2022), https://sr.ithaka.org/publications/leading-by-diversifying-collections/.
2. Annette Day, Sarah R. Jones, Amy Tureen, Susan B. Wainscott, Amanda Melilli, Thomas Padilla, and Aidy Weeks, *Inclusive and Anti-Racist Collecting at UNLV: Draft*

Report and Recommendations (University of Nevada Las Vegas, September, 2022), 2, https://digitalscholarship.unlv.edu/lib_articles/748.

3. Michelle Baildon, Dana Hamlin, Czeslaw Jankowski, Rhonda Kauffman, Julie Lanigan, Michelle Miller, Jessica Venlet, and Ann Marie Willer, *Creating a Social Justice Mindset: Diversity, inclusion, and Social Justice in the Collections Directorate of the MIT Libraries* (Cambridge, MA: MIT Libraries, 2017), 18, https://dspace.mit.edu/handle/1721.1/108771.

4. Baildon et al., *Creating a Social Justice Mindset*, 2017, 9.

5. Kat Nelsen, K. L. Clarke, Wanda Marsolek, Sunshine J. Carter, Malaika Grant, Nicole Theis-Mahon, and Pearl McClintock, "Finding Our Way Forward: A Roadmap for Anti-racist Collection Development," Charleston Hub (November 22, 2023), https://www.charleston-hub.com/2023/11/finding-our-way-forward-a-roadmap-for-anti-racist-collection-development/.

6. Rhonda Y. Kauffman and Martina S. Anderson, "Diversity, Inclusion, and Social Justice in Library Technical Services," in *Library Technical Services: Adapting to a Changing Environment*, ed. Stacey Marien (West Lafayette, IN: Purdue University Press, 2020), 231.

7. Baildon et al., *Creating a Social Justice Mindset*, 2017.

8. Frances Botsford, Nina Davis-Millis, Robin Deadrick, Mohamed El Ouirdi, Melissa Feiden, Judith Gallagher, Keith Glavash, Rhonda Kauffman, Grace Mlady, Monica Ruiz, Maria Rodrigues, and Greta Suiter, *Diversity, Inclusion, and Social Justice Resource Manual for MIT Libraries Staff* (Cambridge, MA: MIT Libraries, May 24, 2017), https://libguides.mit.edu/ld.php?content_id=32359042.

9. Sara Ahmed, *On Being Included: Racism and Diversity in Institutional Life* (Durham, NC: Duke University Press, 2012), 121.

10. Ahmed, *On Being Included*, 2012, 116.

11. Ashley Fast, Laura Foss, and Steve Hyndman, "Options and Opportunities for Increased Diversity, Equity, and Inclusion in Collection Development," Presented at SUNYLA conference (virtual), June 16, 2021, https://sunyla.org/sunyla_docs/conferences/presentations/sunyla21/D5_SUNYLA2021.pdf.

12. Bledsoe et al., *Leading by Diversifying Collections*, 2023.

13. Elizabeth Speer, *Letter to Vendors* (Forth Worth, TX: University of North Texas Health Science Center at Forth Worth, January 25, 2021), https://library-apps.hsc.unt.edu/staff/vendor-letter.pdf.

14. Eizabeth Speer, "DEI Collection Evaluation," *Texas Library Journal* 98, no. 4 (Winter 2022): 9–11.

15. Baildon et al., *Creating a Social Justice Mindset*, 2017, 12.

16. Day et al., *Inclusive and Anti-Racist Collecting at UNLV*, 2022, 6.

17. Bledsoe et al., *Leading by Diversifying Collections*, 2023.

18. American Library Association, "Diverse Collections: An Interpretation of the Library Bill of Rights. Advocacy, Legislation & Issues," July 26, 2006, https://www.ala.org/advocacy/intfreedom/librarybill/interpretations/diversecollections.

19. Baildon and Kauffman, "Diversity, Inclusion, and Social Justice Work in the MIT Libraries' Collections Directorate," 2017, 37:57.

20. University of Sydney Libraries, Nathan Sentance, *Aboriginal and Torres Strait Islander Cultural Protocols* (Sydney, Australia: University of Sydney, 2021), 14, https://ses.library.usyd.edu.au/handle/2123/24602.

21. Bledsoe et al., *Leading by Diversifying Collections*, 2023.
22. Library of Congress, "Frequently Asked Questions About Funnel Projects," accessed February 16, 2024, https://www.loc.gov/aba/pcc/saco/funnelfaq.html.
23. Morgan Harrington, "Rethinking Diversity beyond Catalogue Representation: Lessons from Efforts to Develop a Methodology to Evaluate Diversity within the National Library of Australia," *Journal of the Australian Library and Information Association* 70, no. 1 (2021): 23–43.
24. Nelsen et al., *Finding Our Way Forward*, 2023.

Chapter 10

11

Assessing DEIJA Projects at Ithaca College Library

Karin Wikoff

As a middle-aged, middle-class, educated, white woman, I grew up in a bubble of privilege. A few years ago, I became aware of this privilege and felt it was important for me to acknowledge it with humility and work to do better. That work began with learning—workshops, webinars, trainings sessions, readings, discussion groups, and the like. I still have much to learn, but I am now ready to start putting my learning into action.

This chapter will describe a variety of diversity, equity, inclusion, justice, and accessibility (DEIJA) projects initiated and/or tracked at Ithaca College in the 2023–2024 academic year with commentary on assessing their success. Ithaca College is located on South Hill in Ithaca, in the Finger Lakes region of rural, central New York State. Cornell University is our better-known neighbor on East Hill, making Ithaca truly a "college town." Ithaca College began as a music conservatory which evolved over time into a private "comprehensive college" with five schools: Business; Communications; Health Sciences and Human Performance; Humanities and Sciences; and Music, Theater, and Dance. Ithaca College has about 4,600 undergraduate students and 400 graduate students. Ithaca College Library has 236,403 volumes and employs 10 librarians and 10 library staff.

The formal pursuit of these projects began in April 2023 when I attended a Long Island Library Resources Council presentation where three librarians from Colorado State spoke about their project to purchase award-winning books on DEIJA topics.[1] I thought a similar project might be doable at my library if the funds were available. I put together a proposal to reallocate $1,500 of our budget to support such purchasing, and my director approved it. Then our regional library council offered an opportunity for grant-funded consultant support. I applied and was awarded the grant to work with Dr. Kawanna Bright of East Carolina University.

CHOOSING PROJECTS

With our modest funds and our consultant assistance lined up, I wanted to begin with a guiding statement for selecting projects to pursue. It was important that lack of enough resources to do everything did not prevent us from doing something—in other words, that we take the "small wins" approach. Another concept Dr. Bright and I wanted to include was a mindset that brings a DEIJA perspective to all the work we do. She and I devised the following statement:

> Ithaca College Library's commitment to diversity, equity, inclusion, justice, and accessibility (DEIJA) is driven by a belief in the essentialness and value of DEIJA to the work of the library and Ithaca College as a whole. The library strives to focus on what can be done, rather than trying to do everything. An emphasis on small but intentional DEIJA projects, in keeping with the available resources, will allow the library to engage in DEIJA work with the potential for positive impacts. It is through this intentionality that we will be able to create an organization focused on the integration of DEIJA practices into all the work of the library, while supporting and contributing to the success of the college.

Dr. Bright and I next brainstormed small projects we could do within our parameters, then organized them into categories. Our initial list included:

Collections

> Purchase of Award-Winning Books
> Subscription to ProQuest's Black Studies Database

Reclassification of LGBTQIA+ Materials
Policies and Statements

> Guiding Statement
> Collection Development Policy
> Electronic and Technical Services Departmental Mission Statement
> Statement on Potentially Offensive and Harmful Content
> Other policies, as appropriate

I included two recently completed projects in the list because they were so well aligned with our other projects: Subscription to ProQuest's Black Studies Database and Statement on Potentially Offensive and Harmful Content. As our work progressed, at the request of liaison librarians, I added a couple additional projects to our list in the Collections category: Market New DEIJA Resources and Seek Sources for Medical Textbooks with More Diverse Representation.

Collections

Purchase of Award-Winning Books
Subscription to ProQuest's Black Studies Database
Market New DEIJA Resources
Seek Sources for Medical Textbooks with More Diverse Representation

Reclassification of LGBTQIA+ Materials
Policies and Statements

Guiding Statement
Collection Development Policy
Electronic and Technical Services Departmental Mission Statement
Statement on Potentially Offensive and Harmful Content
Other policies, as appropriate

These projects had a built-in timeline based on the end of the consultant's time with us—June 30, 2024. While the projects were underway, I used a Lib-Guide both to track the projects and to communicate with interested parties about them.[2] Each time progress was made on a project, it was recorded on the guide with the date, and "Next Steps" were updated. Using this tool kept us accountable and on track.

Below I will describe each project, how it was initially conceived, how various kinds of interim assessments changed the trajectory of some projects as they progressed, and some ways we plan to assess the projects when they are completed or more data is available for ongoing initiatives.

PURCHASE OF AWARD-WINNING DEIJA BOOKS

The original plan was to follow the lead of Colorado State, using as a starting point their lists of award winners, which they kindly provided for us. Before approving the funding, my director wanted to be sure responsibility for purchasing DEIJA materials was not shifted away from the subject selectors, but rather that the DEIJA-specific purchases were made in addition to theirs. A comparison of the award winners lists against our holdings was the first interim assessment. I manually searched award websites for the titles going back five years, then searched each title in our catalog. I found that we had only purchased 12 percent of these award winners, and almost all of those purchases were from before the post-pandemic budget cuts. That showed that we would not be purchasing items that the selectors would otherwise have been purchasing. Next, knowing that we wanted to focus on indigenous authors or topics, Dr. Bright and I did our second interim assessment of the award winners list. However, only one title was on an indigenous topic, so we realized we would have to scrap the award winners approach for our purchasing. I recruited a colleague in Interlibrary Loan who has an interest in DEIJA work and together with Dr. Bright, we developed the following criteria:

1. DEIJA topics in general
2. Focus on indigenous authors/topics, with a preference for local/regional indigenous peoples (New York State, Northeastern US, and Canada)
3. Intersectionality with other DEIJA topics, including accessibility for differently abled persons and social justice along with the more obvious racial, LGBTQIA+, etc. topics.
4. Award winners
5. Special sub-focus: religious in/tolerance—in particular Jewish and Muslim issues related to the current situation in the Middle East and on college campuses.

We next solicited lists focused on indigenous topics from the vendors whose platforms are supported at Ithaca College. A couple vendors were able to create custom lists while others offered more generic DEIJA title lists. My colleague and I manually reviewed the lists for titles on indigenous topics that also had as much intersectionality as we could find. We selected fourteen titles that came to about $1,500. In the meantime, another $3,000 became available. We expanded our search to include a couple more subject-focused publishers. When we had exhausted the lists for books on indigenous topics, we made a point of selecting titles with the special sub-focus (religious in/tolerance). In this first "pilot" round, we selected twenty-eight titles on indigenous topics and eight on Anti-Semitism and Islamophobia. At this point, funds have been approved to repeat a similar project in the next year and we hope we can eventually establish it permanently.

Post-Project Assessment

Having now purchased these books, we would like to know if they are making an impact. However, it takes time to accumulate usage data before there is anything to assess. After a year has passed, we will look at circulation data. For the coming academic year, I will choose a new focus and continue the basic project with another modest allocation.

SUBSCRIPTION TO PROQUEST'S BLACK STUDIES DATABASE AND MARKETING NEW DEIJA RESOURCES

We have funding for two years' subscription to ProQuest's Black Studies database, which began in March 2023. With a year's worth of usage statistics, this database is not seeing very high usage yet, especially not in relation to the cost. The next step is to launch a marketing campaign to increase awareness and usage of this rich resource. Our Electronic Resources Librarian has taken the lead for this project, partnering with two of our subject specialist librarians. The most important part of this plan is for the subject liaison librarians to do one-on-one outreach to their faculty. Other ideas include librarians using the resource in their work with students, including it in bibliographic instruction, adding it to library guides, and highlighting it on the library webpage and in-house public displays. The marketing effort, which is still in the beginning stages, will be implemented in the fall semester.

Post-Project Assessment

Because the semester was over at the time this chapter was written and databases don't typically see heavy usage over the summer, the marketing efforts will be renewed in the fall. Post-project, the Electronic Resources Librarian and I will investigate whether the marketing plan increased the usage enough to make a case for continuing to fund the subscription.

SEEKING SOURCES FOR MEDICAL TEXTBOOKS WITH MORE DIVERSE REPRESENTATION

In conversation with subject specialist librarians, they requested that we add a project to seek sources for medical textbooks with more diverse representation, in particular for our physician's assistant program. We passed this project to Dr. Bright. She researched the subject deeply, tapping her sources, and found many others also seeking such resources. She even found artists who are trying to interest publishers in their more diverse medical images. However, at this time, despite the demand, no such sources were found. Due to this assessment of the current publishing environment, Dr. Bright and I determined that if we wish to pursue this project at all, we will have to switch to advocating with publishers to provide materials with more diverse representation.

Post-Project Assessment

With no materials currently in existence, our project will take a sharp turn. Our future progress will be measured in efforts made, and success will be measured by the publication of medical texts with more diverse representation in the images used. Specifically, we hope to lobby for the publication of images of more diverse races and genders, including transgender people.

RECLASSIFICATION OF LGBTQIA+ MATERIALS

The cataloger and I had found a source that indicated that, in the Library of Congress Classification, LGBTQIA+ topics were classed as a subdivision of "sexual deviance," along with child abuse, prostitution, human trafficking, fetishism, and sadomasochism. The thought of a student with an LGBTQIA+ identity going to the stacks to find materials on their own identity and finding them shelved with those other topics was disturbing, so we wanted to undertake a project to reclassify the books. Our cataloger researched in the cataloging community to see if any other libraries had reclassed these materials but did not find any that had. I also consulted with the director of the Center for LGBT Education, Outreach, & Services for input from affected folks, and we chatted informally with colleagues with LGBTQIA+ identities. The message from that community was that students seldom go to the stacks for physical books in general, but when they do, they like having these materials together. They did not think there was as much risk of harm as we had imagined. However, Dr. Bright counseled us not to abandon the project because the placement of LGBTQIA+ as a subheading under Sexual Deviance was still philosophically problematic. At that point, the cataloger and I went back to re-research the classification to see if there were a way to rename or shift things that would keep the LGBTQIA+ materials together in the same space but without the offensive classification structure. That was when the cataloger found that the most recent version of the classification from the Library of Congress had been updated.[3] After re-assessing the new structure that places LGBTQIA+ topics under "Sexual Life," we felt that the existing classifications were perfectly acceptable. Instead of considering a reclassification of the entire section, I asked one of the subject librarians to do a careful weeding of older, outdated materials, after which the cataloger checked the remaining items for any offensive headings or classification numbers. There were none. After our interim re-assessment, our project changed completely—no further action was required to achieve our goal.

Post-Project Assessment

To determine if the right choices were made with this project, we are considering focus groups to check in with impacted communities. In the fall, I will reach out to the Center for LGBT Education, Outreach, & Services for their help putting such a plan into action.

COLLECTION DEVELOPMENT POLICY

The most basic purpose of a collection development policy is to provide guidance and a framework for what content a library includes in its collection and why. Ensuring that the materials Ithaca College Library provides meet the needs of all our patrons, and specifically that they are relevant to their curricular, research, and social cultural needs, is of utmost importance. To meet all those needs, the materials need to be equitable, inclusive, and accessible—and the policy needs to say that explicitly. Ours did not. In our guiding statement we pledged to integrate DEIJA practices into all the work of the library and to be driven by a belief in the essentialness and value of DEIJA to the work of the library and Ithaca College as a whole.

I began by searching for other libraries' policies that mention DEI. I reviewed more than a dozen such collection development policies to see how they included a commitment to DEIJA perspectives. I assembled a list of about eight examples and shared it with Dr. Bright. Next, she had us fill out her policy review rubric as a way to deeply consider our existing policy for inclusivity.[4] This assessment, while interesting, didn't turn up any text that specifically needed to change, but it did serve to make us aware of what we had and how it came into being. That focus on the process made me realize that I wanted to be more inclusive in terms of getting input on the policy from everyone in the library. The Web Services Librarian, Electronic Resources Librarian, Electronic Resources Coordinator, the College Librarian, and two reference/subject specialist librarians were all involved in direct editing, and the whole staff was given an opportunity to review the edits and have their feedback taken into consideration before the finished draft went to the College Librarian for formal approval. We reviewed the existing policy, looking for appropriate places to integrate our DEIJA focus. This review showed that many sections unrelated to DEIJA were also outdated and needed revision, so the project expanded both in terms of who was involved and what was revised. With all the revisions complete, the College Librarian approved them, and the newly revised policy was posted on the library's public website.[5]

While working on the Collection Development Policy, I got the idea that we might also want to include a policy and procedures for any book challenges. Some libraries include that information in their collection development policies, while others have it as a separate policy. Book challenges are steeply on the rise in the United States, though they are much less common in private academic libraries. Nonetheless, it is a good idea to be prepared. I researched policies and procedures at other libraries and shared the information I found with our College Librarian for her consideration. I will follow up with the College Librarian to see if she wants to pursue such a policy.

Post-Project Assessment

The most immediate decision will be whether to develop and implement a book challenge policy, after which assessment of the effectiveness of the policy will depend on whether any challenges are submitted. As for the overall collection development policy, we are considering focus groups to help us ascertain the impact of this newly edited policy. It will take some time to have that impact, so I will not likely try to do any assessment for a year or so.

ELECTRONIC AND TECHNICAL SERVICES DEPARTMENTAL MISSION STATEMENT

Another policy I chose for review was the mission statement for the Electronic and Technical Services Department. We were very proud of our policy which the whole department had written as a group effort in 2007 as two stanzas of Haiku:

Team Tech Services
Organizes info for
Resources access.

We, your providers,
Acquire, process, pay; support
the love of learning.

These stanzas describe the work of the department succinctly in terms of what we do in acquisitions, cataloging, invoicing, budget management, and providing access to electronic and other resources, but they lack any mention of the intentional work the department is doing to be more inclusive. At our departmental retreat, we brainstormed the specific concepts we wanted to get across:

- We acknowledge that our work is not neutral.
- We want to include the voices of marginalized people.
- We want our impact to be positive, inclusive, and not harmful.
- We can take small but impactful actions.

Then, consciously choosing to work as a group with each voice heard, we composed two more stanzas of Haiku to express those ideas:

Neutral we are not.
Listen to unheard voices.
Acknowledge bias.

Small, intentional,
Inclusive acts as we seek
Positive impacts.

Post-Project Assessment

At our next annual departmental retreat in the fall, we will reflect on our new statement, and ask ourselves the following questions:

- Is it now easier for us to focus on including a DEIJA perspective in our work?
- How did it feel to be included in the process of developing the policies and statements?
- Have we seen any changes in ourselves and how we conduct our work?
- Did we miss anything?
- Are we helping, hurting, or having no impact on the people we are hoping to help?

STATEMENT ON POTENTIALLY OFFENSIVE AND HARMFUL CONTENT

In the winter of 2022, the Electronic and Technical Services Department did an environmental scan of other libraries' statements addressing the issue of offensive language in their content. Using those other statements as models, especially the one from Brandeis University,[6] the Cataloging Team created multiple drafts of statements supporting the institutional commitment to diversity, equity, and inclusion while acknowledging that by nature, library collections include materials from different cultures and different time periods, some of which may be experienced as offensive. Then we provided a procedure for patrons to report such issues for us to review on a one-by-one basis, "balancing the preservation of original context with an awareness of the effect of language on our users." The full statement, including the procedure for review, reads as follows:

Statement on Potentially Offensive and Harmful Content

In support of Ithaca College's institutional commitment to diversity, equity, and inclusion, the staff of the Ithaca College Library strive to make our collections and services accessible, inclusive, and equitable and to practice the mutual care, respect, and accountability central to the college's vision, mission, and values.

Libraries and archives collect materials from different cultures and different time periods to preserve and make available the historical and scholarly record. As a result, the library's collections may contain materials or descriptions that our community could find offensive, harmful, and counter to the college's vision, mission, and values.

We retain these items in our collections not to endorse the offensive content, but to accurately represent the historic record. We do not censor materials in our care.

Additionally, the language used by libraries to describe materials evolves over time. We are making efforts to create respectful and inclusive descriptions in our catalog and recognize that this is an ongoing process.

We acknowledge that we may not always make the right decisions. If you encounter descriptive language in our catalog that you find offensive or harmful, we welcome you to reach out to us to open dialogue or to share your concerns or questions. Please use the "Report a Problem" button directly from the catalog or send us an email to share your concerns. We will review your request with the goal of balancing the preservation of original context with an awareness of the effect of language on our users.[7]

This statement is posted in the policies section of the Ithaca College Library website and is also linked in every record display in Primo. An assessment of webpage usage shows that this policy gets more views than the new books page, but not as much as the hardware and software page. However, no one has yet submitted a report on offensive or harmful materials. This may be because no one has found any of our materials offensive, or they have but either didn't find the statement or chose not to use the reporting procedure. That website statistic would seem to indicate that people are finding the form but not using it.

Post-Project Assessment

We will wait a year to see if any reports are submitted. If none are submitted, perhaps we can conclude that the policy in and of itself is answering people's concerns. If reports are submitted, we can assess how well we are able to apply the review process on an ad hoc basis.

LESSONS LEARNED

At the time of this writing, I am wrapping up our projects and will give them six months to a year before there is enough data to assess their effectiveness. Assessment is how we measure if our work is creating positive impacts and is not just performative, so post-project assessment will be a critical step. In the meantime, a review of the lessons learned may be useful, especially the value of interim assessments.

At the meta-level, we learned that our work is not always linear. Interim assessments often require re-thinking the original goal and result in a change in a project's direction. This can feel disruptive, but it is actually a good thing. It is better to change gears than to continue investing time and labor going in the wrong direction.

The reclassification project is a good example of how assessment can change a project. Our original impetus was based on how the Cataloger, Dr. Bright, and I thought we might feel about the subject hierarchy, but we knew we would need to check in with members of the LGBTQIA+ community to be sure we were headed in a direction that addressed their needs as they would want them addressed. Those conversations were an interim assessment which

                                                          Karin Wikoff

provided different views we had not considered. I brought his information back to the consultant for a second interim review. She counseled us not to abandon the project because the hierarchy was still philosophically problematic. Instead, the cataloger and I did a fresh (third) review of our original premises and found that the Library of Congress had made changes fairly recently that she and I had missed. Humility proved to be an important factor in the success of this project as well, allowing us to adjust away from our original project goals so that the end result would be more effective at meeting the needs of the community.

Over the course of these projects, we used and will use several different methods of assessment. You will find more formal methods described in other chapters of this book, but most of the methods we used are informal, which works for us with limited staff and resources. Here's our list:

—comparing lists of materials against our holdings
—evaluating lists of materials against specific criteria
—reviewing database, circulation, and website usage statistics
—researching the publishing environment for specific kinds of materials
—investigating the hierarchical structure of a classification system
—having informal conversations with members of impacted communities
—reviewing and weeding outdated materials while looking for any problematic classifications
—reviewing policy using a DEIJA rubric as well as just seeking areas that needed updating
—looking for appropriate places to include a DEIJA perspective in our policies and work
—doing environmental scans of other libraries' policies and what they have done
—sharing drafts with colleagues and others for their input
—reflecting on our work and anything that has changed
—hosting focus groups

CHOOSING PROJECTS

It may seem like our choice of projects was serendipitous, but I would credit the effect of planting seeds. When Renae J. Watson, Khaleedah Thomas, and Kristine Nowak of Colorado State University presented their projects for the Long Island Library Resources Council, they planted seeds. I heard what they were doing and thought we could do something like that too. When I described the projects I was working on at a Librarians' Meeting at Ithaca College, I planted seeds. Other librarians were inspired to suggest additional projects. When I spoke up to ask questions at a Charleston Lively Discussion, I planted seeds.[8] Karen Kohn saw me and asked me to contribute a chapter to this book.

And when this book is published, we will have planted more seeds as readers are inspired to take their own actions.

Many of you reading this book will be looking for ideas of things you can do when DEIJA work is not your sole or primary job responsibility. You need projects you can do with limited resources in terms of time, staffing, and funds. Bringing a DEIJA perspective to all your work is a worthy goal in itself. Beyond that, it will be up to you to find DEIJA-specific projects that fit your needs and resources. There is only one rule I would suggest for whatever projects you choose. In the words of Yulia Navalnaya paraphrasing her late husband, Alexei Navalny, "It's not a shame to do little, it's a shame to do nothing."[9]

NOTES

1. Alyssa Brissett, Diana Moronta, Renae J. Watson, Khaleedah Thomas, and Kristine Nowak, "Practicing Social Justice in Libraries: Building Equitable and Inclusive Collections" (Presented at the LILRC 9th Annual Technical Services Open Forum, Zoom, April 14, 2023), https://web.archive.org/web/20230402114042/https://lilrc.org/event-5158669.
2. Karin Wikoff, "LibGuides: DEIJA Projects: Get Started," accessed June 22, 2024, https://libguides.ithaca.edu/c.php?g=1350943&p=9970367.
3. Library of Congress, "Library of Congress Classification Outline: Class H—Social Sciences," accessed July 25, 2024, https://www.loc.gov/aba/cataloging/classification/lcco/lcco_h.pdf.
4. Kawanna M. Bright, "Policy Review Rubric," accessed April 29, 2024, http://www.kawannabright.info/uploads/1/3/2/6/132654087/policy_review_rubric_shareable.pdf.
5. Ithaca College Library, "Ithaca College Library Collection Development & Management Policy," accessed May 15, 2024, https://library.ithaca.edu/policies/CDP_2024.pdf.
6. Brandeis University, "Statement on Potentially Harmful Language in Collections, Cataloging and Description," last updated August 11, 2021, https://www.brandeis.edu/library/about/services/language.html.
7. Ithaca College Library Cataloging Team, "Statement on Potentially Offensive and Harmful Content," accessed June 22, 2024, https://library.ithaca.edu/policies/offensive.php.
8. Megan Watson, Anne Davis, Je Salvador, Julie Garrison, and Paul Gallagher, "Systemic Change Through Local Action: Advancing DEI and Measuring Impact at the Institutional Level" (Panel Discussion presented at the Charleston Conference 2023, March 1, 2024), https://www.youtube.com/watch?v=QwUpaYvXB7k.
9. Associated Press, "Navalny's Widow Says She Will Continue His Fight against the Kremlin," February 19, 2024, https://www.pbs.org/newshour/world/navalnys-widow-says-she-will-continue-his-fight-against-the-kremlin.

12

Moving Forward

Once you've completed your assessment, there are several things you can do with the results. You'll probably want to share them within your library. You'll almost definitely want to take some steps to improve or keep improving your collection. It would also be a good idea to plan future assessments so you can see how your collection is getting more diverse and can push yourself and your colleagues to do more.

SHARING FINDINGS

There are several reasons it could be useful to share your findings with colleagues within the library. Selectors might use the information to influence their purchases, administrators could use the data to justify budget changes, and faculty or a diversity office on campus might treat your presentation as a prompt to recommend titles or review sources to you. Presenting information about your audit can help build the social justice mindset discussed in chapter 10. Michelle Baildon and Rhonda Kauffman explain how small actions can lead to changes in organizational culture, which lead to larger actions.[1] In the previous chapter, Karin Wikoff called this process planting seeds. In order for the seeds of change to be planted, your colleagues need to know about the work that you are doing.

The arenas or forms of communication that you use to share findings will depend on the structure and norms of your library. You might write an article for a library blog or newsletter or give a presentation at a department meeting. Liaison librarians could forward a brief summary to their academic departments. Administrators may prefer a written report that they can review at their convenience.

Whoever your audience and whatever your communication channel, consider adding some type of visualization of the data, such as a bar graph. Many people get overwhelmed when seeing tables full of numbers and would find a visual representation easier to interpret. In addition, graphs can break up long blocks of text in a blog post or presentation.

When sharing the findings of your audit, remember to describe your data accurately and avoid terminology you know to be offensive. These points have been made in previous chapters but merit a recap here.

An accurate description would use words indicating the methods you used and what you measured rather than the assumptions you are making about what the findings mean. For instance, you can state with certainty that catalog searches for terms related to Native Americans retrieved nine thousand books, whereas "The library has nine thousand books on Native Americans" would be a slight leap to conclusions. Your library may have more books about Native Americans that don't have adequate cataloging for you to discover them. When describing author identities, chapter 8 emphasized stating what you know, for instance, "80 percent of authors are known to be in opposite-sex relationships" rather than "80 percent of authors are heterosexual." Some people in an opposite-sex relationship are bisexual, and some people whose relationship information is not publicly available are heterosexual. If you used a sample and didn't do any statistical tests, be clear that the statements you are making refer to the sample and not to the whole collection, for example "6 percent of the authors in the sample were found to be non-white."

The issue of offensive language is most likely to come up when doing metadata searches, as these rely on a controlled vocabulary that is often outdated and sometimes contains terms not used by the people they describe. For example, a catalog search for books on Native Americans would rely on the official subject term "Indians of North America," which is not a phrase used in ordinary speech. You don't need to use this exact phrase to describe your findings accurately, as you could say that you did a catalog search for subject headings related to Native Americans or North American Indigenous People.

SHAPING FUTURE ACTIONS

When sharing your findings with colleagues, you will often want them to do something specific in response, whether it is changing their selection habits or redistributing the budget. While many librarians make attempts to diversify their collections without doing any assessment and still make positive changes, having data can influence the actions you take.

One way that the data can help shape collection-building is by strengthening requests for more funding or reallocation of funds. Kara Bledsoe and colleagues note that while many different library staff can be involved in the work of collections-building, any initiative that involves a change to the budget or to policies needs support from the top levels of administration and from the person in charge of the collection (a manager or strategist).[2] If the people doing the assessment aren't the ones who allocate the budget, being able to present numbers to those who have this authority can be useful.

Assessment can also help you set goals for future purchasing. In their article on collection-building for justice, equity, diversity, and inclusion (JEDI), Colleen Mullally, Jeremy Whitt, and Kayla Valdivieso write, "libraries should seek to answer the question, 'Which collecting areas will be the focus of our JEDI efforts?' This question provides the opportunity to define, at least initially, which areas or selection criteria the library will focus on with this collection development effort."[3] They suggest looking at student demographics as a guide to what types of representation to seek. If your assessment method allowed you to measure disparities between the student population and different marginalized groups' representation within your collection, this measurement could also help you choose a focus by looking at where the disparities are greatest.

Even if your assessment method did not allow for comparison to your student population, the assessment can help you set goals by serving as a baseline. An example goal could be to have 5 percent more of your purchases be by or about people of color in the next year as were in the past. Even without a target, you can use your findings as a point of comparison against future assessments, watching how the numbers change year to year, as Artemis Vex and Ruth Castillo described in chapter 9.

If your assessment included an evaluation of your actions, in addition to or instead of the collection, the assessment can help you decide which initiatives to continue, make adjustments to projects, or celebrate successes. Whether your assessments have been focused on the existing collection or on your efforts to improve it, they will probably inspire you to find ways to change your selection and purchasing processes.

When aiming to create more diverse, equitable, and inclusive collections, Mullally, Whitt, and Valdivieso advocate for making an action plan. You can use the plan to monitor your progress throughout the year, thus continually assessing yourselves. The plan should clarify whether you want to focus your efforts on specific populations and topics or on many types of diversity. Though the plan should include the time frames in which you intend to accomplish specific things, Mullally and colleagues also note that diversifying collections requires ongoing work. "Inclusive collection building is not an initiative that is achieved in a one-, two-, or three-year period: it is ongoing work requiring steady commitment."[4]

It's important to remember there are usually costs associated with building more diverse collections. Some of the costs are staff time, which might be spent selecting titles that weren't identified by the approval plan or cataloging materials that were purchased from a local bookstore that doesn't provide MARC records. There could also be materials expenditures, such as adding a new subscription package or adding more publishers to an approval plan.

Lori Jahnke, Kyle Tanaka, and Christopher Palozzolo say, "By its very nature, diversity in a system is inefficient and is therefore more costly . . . developing library collections that exemplify the value of diversity requires an additional investment of resources to overcome structural barriers resulting from broader social inequities, market forces, and professional practices that remake or amplify injustices."[5] While assessment data could help you advocate for more funds, limited budgets and staff time will likely still constrain what you're able to do. Still, you should be able to do something, particularly since there are so many strategies libraries have used for making their collections more diverse, equitable, and inclusive.

COLLECTION STRATEGIES

Lists

If you found or created lists of recommended titles so you could check these against your holdings, an obvious place to start adding to your collection is by using these same lists as selection tools. You probably won't be able to buy all the books on the lists, so you might prioritize getting books about populations that have the fewest books according to your assessment. Recommended book lists can work well if you are trying to retroactively build a collection, as most of the other strategies described in this section will mainly discover newly published books. William Walters notes that older books might be out of print, but if you can find them on the online bookstore Alibris they will probably be inexpensive.[6]

Packages

Adding packages to your collection is a common way to quickly expand the number of books that your library holds about marginalized populations. Deborah Lee's toolkit on building an Indigenous Studies library collection lists more than twenty databases, including some that are open access. The content in these databases ranges from primary sources to legal materials to scholarly journals.[7] Alexander Street has many collections focused on particular populations or identities, such as Black Thought and Culture, Border and Migration Studies, LGBTQ Thought and Culture, North American Indian Thought and Culture, and South and Southeast Asian Literature in English. ProQuest, which owns Alexander Street, and EBSCO also have collections centering particular nondominant groups.

If you only have a small amount of money to spend, you may be interested in a package that is more generically focused on diversity, or on ethnic diversity. Walters offers some factors to consider when acquiring general diversity packages. He notes that "some vendors' diversity collections seem to include many titles that are not about particular groups or perspectives, but about diversity itself or the push for diversity."[8] Subscribing to a general diversity package also means you won't be able to customize which groups are represented, and your audit may have shown that you have larger gaps to fill in representation of some groups than others. Other limitations to subscription packages, whether general or population-focused, are that they are limited to books available electronically and may be missing small presses.

Partnerships

If you are able to expand your collections by adding individual books, a useful and important way of getting ideas of what to add is by talking to members of marginalized groups who use your library, or scholars of those groups. MIT's report, Creating a Social Justice Mindset, lists as a strategy, "Partner with members and groups within the MIT community to (1) assess and meet their information needs and (2) welcome their input about our collections and services."[9] Bledsoe and colleagues list as potential partners "researchers in relevant subject areas, instructors who are working to diversify curricula, students, and other relevant community groups such as institutes, clubs, and associations."[10]

There is a wide array of ways librarians have reached out to members of their university communities to solicit feedback. Table 12.1 lists some examples. Outreach to students often involves asking for recommendations from a group that is already a captive audience, such as those working at the library or participating in an instruction session. It is ideal if this captive audience primarily consists of marginalized students, such as the group of first-generation college students that Renae Watson, Khaleedah Thomas, and Kristine Nowak asked for book recommendations.[11] Students might not share a common identity but have a proclaimed interest in diversity, equity, and inclusion, such as those who participated in Bryn Mawr College's "Students Shape the Shelves" internship.[12] Another option for interacting with students is to go to where they are, as Alexis Pavenick and George Martinez did when they approached LGBTQ student groups who were tabling and later set up their own table in LGBTQ student housing.[13]

Many diversification efforts have also involved seeking recommendations from faculty. It is common to do as Brittany Kester did and simply email faculty asking for ideas.[14] More unusual was Dickinson College's summer study group, held in 1991, which paid six faculty members to create annotated bibliographies related to African American Studies.[15]

If your university has a diversity officer, that person could be a resource as well, especially if they have a collection of books in their office. Campus cultural centers are another possible partner.[16]

Table 12.1 Partnerships for Diverse Collections

Partners	Outreach Type	Outreach Activity
Students	Existing Structure	Survey of the student workers who conducted the diversity audit
		Veronica Wells, Michele Gibney, Mickel Paris, and Corey Pfitzer, "Student Participation in a DEI Audit as High-Impact Practice," *The Journal of Academic Librarianship* 49, no. 1 (2023): 102615.
		Class assignment for students in an Education class, "Methods of Teaching Language Arts";
		Mitchell Scott, "Patron Driven DEI Acquisitions: Using Education Students and the Diverse Book Finder to Diversify a Children's Picture Book Collection." Presented at the Acquisitions Institute at Timberline Lodge, 2023, https://acquisitionsinstitute.org/wp-content/uploads /2023/05/Patron-Driven-DEI-Acquisitions_NEW.pptx.
		In-person class activity for student participants in an information literacy program for first-generation students
		Renae J. Watson, Khaleedah Thomas, and Kristine Nowak, "Adhocking It: Overcoming the Overwhelm to Start Creating: Equitable and Inclusive Collections Now," In *Practicing Social Justice in Libraries*, eds. Alyssa Brissett and Diana Moronta (New York: Routledge, 2022), 100–116.
Students	New Structure	Spring break student internship promoting diversity in the collections
		Camilla McKay and Arleen Zimmerle, "Works in Progress Webinar: Diversifying library collections through student-led collection development," presented through OCLC, April 23, 2024, https://www.oclc.org/research/events/2024/diversifying-library-collections-student -led.html.

Students	Solicitation	Whiteboard in the library announcing, "Submit your inclusive STEM recommendations here!" with post-it notes
		Janet Calderon, "Acquisitions for the Sciences—Using a Diversity Assessment to Serve BIPOC Students in STEM," presented at the Acquisitions Institute at Timberline Lodge, 2023, https://acquisitionsinstitute.org/wp-content/uploads/2023/05/Monday_Calderon_s-Presentation_final.pptx
		Visits to tables of student organizations during Club Week
		Librarians tabling in LGBTQ student housing
		Alexis Pavenick and George Martinez, "Hearing and Being Heard: LGBTQIA+ Cross-Disciplinary Collection Development," *Collection and Curation* 41, no. 4 (2022): 109–115.
Faculty	New Structure	Funded summer study group for faculty teaching African American Studies courses
		Steven McKinzie, "A Multicultural Studies Collection Enhancement Group: A Model for Preemptive Collection Development in a Small Academic Library," *The Reference Librarian* 21, no. 45–46 (1994): 187–96.
Faculty	Solicitation	Request sent to faculty
		Brittany Kester, "Diversifying an Academic Library's Children's and Young Adult Collection: A Case Study from the University of Florida's Education Library," *Collection Management* 47, no. 2–3 (2021): 136–56.
		Alexis Pavenick and George Martinez, "Hearing and Being Heard: LGBTQIA+ Cross-Disciplinary Collection Development," *Collection and Curation* 41, no. 4 (2022): 109–115.
Administration	Solicitation	Conversations with Chief Diversity Officer and this person's staff
		Colleen S. Mullally, Jeremy Whitt, and Kayla Valdivieso, "Starting and Sustaining JEDI Acquisitions and Collections in Academic Libraries: Considerations and Strategies for Success," In *Perspectives on Justice, Equity, Diversity, and Inclusion in Libraries* (Hershey, PA: IGI Global, 2023), 104–122.

Dedicated Budget Line

Often projects focused on DEI in collections involve creating a designated fund for DEI purchases. There are downsides to this strategy, as having a separate fund could position DEI as one person's job rather than something selectors across all disciplines should be considering. Those who have created such a fund explain how it can be useful for works that don't fall into a specific person's area of responsibility. A task force at the University of Washington advocated for creating a fund that a variety of selectors could access. They noted,

> our purchasing of diverse materials is hindered by confusion over who is buying material for some ethnic groups in America. For example, the Korean Studies librarian doesn't buy materials on Korean-Americans, even though they have the strongest Libraries connections to that community. The Ethnic Studies selector doesn't buy anything not in English, so who is buying Chinese American materials in Chinese? We suggest a group folder, and a funding source, that Ethnic Studies or another area selector can use to purchase this important category that we routinely overlook.[17]

Jessica Schomberg and Michelle Grace, at Minnesota State University, requested a small fund for purchasing books "by and about Somalia and Somalis."[18] They noted that their traditional curriculum-driven means of collection-building left a gap in serving this growing immigrant group in their state. If you have a specific population in mind that you want to support in ways that fall through the cracks of your collection funds, a designated fund could be a good idea.

New Vendors

MIT's report, Creating a Social Justice Mindset, recommends a strategy of "supporting diversity in the marketplace by identifying alternative vendors (e.g. women- or minority-owned businesses)."[19] This has become a somewhat popular practice. California Lutheran University, as of 2023, was making 80 percent of its purchases through Bookshop.org, an online store that distributes profits to independent bookstores.[20] The University of Nevada Las Vegas has started making a limited number of purchases from five BIPOC-owned independent bookstores, while South Puget Sound Community College makes nearly all its purchases through such stores.[21]

The African American Literature Book Club maintains a list of Black-owned bookstores at https://aalbc.com/bookstores/list.php. Bookshop.org has a directory of affiliated stores, not limited to BIPOC- or woman-owned, at https://bookshop.org/pages/bookstores.

Like with many of these strategies, there are costs associated with working with smaller vendors. The books will not come shelf-ready, adding work for in-house catalogers. The bookstores also probably won't have the systems that larger vendors have for sending invoices that can be loaded into the library's software or offer discounts to library customers. Mullally, Whitt, and Valdivieso note the need to "balance competing values, such as financial stewardship and support for marginalized communities."[22] Some institutions, like UNLV and this author's institution, Temple University, have balanced these priorities by making only a limited number of purchases from independent bookstores. Others have decided instead to focus on ways they can better discover diverse titles through their existing vendors.[23]

Changes to Approval Plans

Approval plans rely on a profile that a library sets up with a vendor to describe which books they want to purchase. Profiles include a variety of criteria such as subject matter, publisher, audience, format, or price. The vendor compares newly published books to the library's profile to determine which books to ship to the customer.

A relatively common and straightforward way to set your library up to regularly acquire more diverse books is to add specific publishers known to focus on marginalized groups to an approval profile. You can discover publishers by looking at whose books win awards or by a directory such as the University of British Columbia's list of indigenous publishers or the African American Literature Book Club's list of Black-owned publishing companies.[24] You'll want to review the publishers to see if they meet other criteria for your library's purchasing.

It is possible that your vendors are not currently including many of the smaller publishers in their profiling processes. In a 2020 article, Sue Phelps describes how she compared a list of African American publishers to a list of the publishers GOBI tracked and found an overlap of only four out of 420 publishers.[25] However, even if your book vendor has not previously been tracking new releases by the publishers you are interested in, they may be able to begin doing so based on your recommendation. Letting vendors know which publishers you want to include can be a form of advocacy.

Approval profiles can also be set up to include winners of awards. Watson, Thomas, and Nowak set up a "Diversity Awards Purchase Plan" for Colorado State University through GOBI, based on thirty-seven awards they selected.[26] Temple University does something similar with ProQuest Clarivate using a list of awards that librarians compiled.[27] A profile can be set up that has a book's award-winning status as one variable, interacting with other criteria, so that you still won't receive books that are above your price threshold or on subjects your library typically doesn't collect. You can also create a separate profile for awards that is looser on the other criteria.

Approval profile criteria can also be applied retroactively to help fill gaps in your collection. Sunshine Carter and colleagues at the University of Minnesota asked GOBI for a list of books published in the last three years that GOBI had tagged with one of several Interdisciplinary Studies tags, such as Asian American Studies, Black Studies, and Chicano or Hispanic Studies. They then compared the list to their existing collection and were able to purchase 1,200 ebooks that they did not previously have access to.[28] Watson, Thomas, and Nowak did something similar at Colorado State University.[29]

Other Selection Strategies

If your purchasing is primarily through title-by-title selection rather than automated programs, there are also a variety of strategies you can use to discover more diverse materials. You can receive alerts for journals that publish book reviews on particular populations or equity issues, such as *Gender & Society* or *Sociology of Race and Ethnicity*. Instead of adding publishers to an approval plan, you could sign up to receive these publishers' catalogs in print or by email. María Emerson and Lauryn Lehman mention using social media to connect with communities of interest and encounter book recommendations.[30] Lee suggests attending events such as pow-wows or finding recommendations of books or media through cultural centers and museums.[31]

At times the intention to build a collection that represents diverse groups could mean purchasing items in formats you might not usually buy. Baildon and colleagues advise, "Because marginalized groups have not had equal access to traditional publishing streams, ensure that the format of materials does not create unnecessary barriers to their acquisition and preservation. Accept unusual formats, including ephemera such as posters, zines, and postcards, as well as student-created objects."[32]

RETURNING TO THE PARKING LOT

Chapter 4 mentioned creating a place to "park" ideas that emerged during an audit, so that you wouldn't get derailed trying to address every thought as it arose. These ideas are ones you do want to address eventually, and once the assessment is complete you might plan some new projects based on ideas you had or additional information you learned while conducting the assessment.

Emerson and Lehman note that their coding project uncovered examples of research fraud and works written by sex offenders, and that these "highlighted the importance of having library-wide discussions about censorship [and] weeding."[33] David Cox's findings were less contentious, as they simply represented gaps in the collection: authors whose classics works were missing despite the library owning other works, incomplete series, or bodies of work with no corresponding literary criticism.[34] Though not necessarily diversity-related, these types of observations can also guide collection decisions.

FUTURE ASSESSMENTS

Acting on the findings from your assessment creates a need for even more assessment. Once you have some strategies in place for trying to collect more diverse materials, you'll want to be able to see how you've improved. Future assessments could be simply descriptive, gathering data to show if you're doing better to some degree, or they could measure whether you've achieved specific goals. You might now be able to set goals where you weren't able to before, as you can aim for the next year's purchases to be somewhat more diverse than what you found in the existing collection.

Libraries that acquire a relatively small number of books each year can commit to coding every book according to the criteria used for the initial audit. Emerson and Lehman note that since completing their coding project, "it is now standard practice at Tredway Library to record this data when cataloging new items, so that reports can be generated annually."[35] The University of West Florida is also now applying codes to new acquisitions.[36]

If your library purchases enough books each year that it is not feasible to code them all, or you want to use a method other than diversity coding, you can still repeat your assessment and will probably find the process easier the second time. If you compiled a list of subject headings for a metadata search, you can re-run the same searches, though it would be good to check whether authorized headings have changed. Be aware that since these searches include the entire collection, adding one more year's acquisitions isn't going to change the results very much, but it could have some effect. If you coded a sample of materials, you can sample from the most recent year's purchases as well. List-checking is the one method that doesn't work well for a repeat assessment, as it will only tell you that you bought some more items from the list. Repeating a list-checking analysis only makes sense if you're using a list that is updated yearly, like the lists from *Resources for College Libraries* that Melissa Gonzalez wrote about in chapter 6.

CONCLUSION

Assessing your collection and the work you've done to diversify it in a regular, ongoing way allows you to acknowledge progress while continuing to keep your commitment to DEI a priority. Bledsoe and colleagues recommend "celebrating wins big and small" as a way to "keep . . . the momentum going" and "demonstrat[e] the library's commitment to operating differently."[37] It is important to acknowledge progress toward diversifying collections because there won't really be an endpoint. As Jahnke, Tanaka, and Palozzolo write, "diversity as it relates to library collections is an ongoing pursuit that requires critical engagement with developing areas of scholarship, emerging social justice issues, and critique and re-evaluation of methods."[38] While working toward a goal that can never truly be completed sounds discouraging, the good news is that the assessment will have given you a lot of ideas of what needs to be done and helped instill habits of focusing on representation of marginalized people, and both of these will better equip you to make changes.

NOTES

1. Michelle Baildon and Rhonda Kauffman, "Diversity, Inclusion, and Social Justice Work in the MIT Libraries' Collections Directorate," OCLC Works in Progress webinar, September 19, 2017, https://www.oclc.org/research/events/2017/09-19.html.
2. Kara Bledsoe, Danielle Miriam Cooper, Roger C. Schonfeld, and Oya Rieger, *Leading by Diversifying Collections* (New York: Ithaka S+R, November 9, 2022), https://sr.ithaka.org/publications/leading-by-diversifying-collections/.
3. Colleen S. Mullally, Jeremy Whitt, and Kayla Valdivieso, "Starting and Sustaining JEDI Acquisitions and Collections in Academic Libraries: Considerations and Strategies for Success," in *Perspectives on Justice, Equity, Diversity, and Inclusion in Libraries*, ed. Nandita S. Mani, Michelle A. Cawley, and Emily P. Jones (Hershey, PA: IGI Global, 2023), 110.
4. Mullally, Whitt, and Valdivieso, "Starting and Sustaining JEDI Acquisitions and Collections in Academic Libraries," 107.
5. Lori M. Jahnke, Kyle Tanaka, and Christopher A. Palazzolo, "Ideology, Policy, and Practice: Structural Barriers to Collections Diversity in Research and College Libraries," *College & Research Libraries* 83, no. 2 (2023): 167.
6. William H. Walters, "Assessing Diversity in Academic Library Book Collections: Diversity Audit Principles and Methods," *Open Information Science* 7, no. 1 (2023).
7. Deborah Lee, *Indigenous Studies Library Collection Development Toolkit* (Saskatoon: University of Saskatchewan, February 21, 2023), https://hdl.handle.net/10388/14484.
8. Walters, "Assessing Diversity in Academic Library Book Collections."
9. Michelle Baildon, Dana Hamlin, Czeslaw Jankowski, Rhonda Kauffman, Julie Lanigan, Michelle Miller, Jessica Venlet, and Ann Marie Willer, *Creating a Social Justice Mindset: Diversity, Inclusion, and Social Justice in the Collections Directorate of the MIT Libraries* (Cambridge, MA: MIT Libraries, 2017), https://dspace.mit.edu/handle/1721.1/108771.
10. Bledsoe et al., *Leading by Diversifying Collections*.
11. Renae J. Watson, Khaleedah Thomas, and Kristine Nowak, "Adhocking It: Overcoming the Overwhelm to Start Creating: Equitable and Inclusive Collections Now," in *Practicing Social Justice in Libraries*, ed. Alyssa Brissett and Diana Moronta (New York: Routledge, 2022), 100–116.
12. Camilla McKay and Arleen Zimmerle, "Diversifying Library Collections through Student-Led Collection Development," OCLC Works in Progress webinar, April 23,

2024, https://www.oclc.org/research/events/2024/diversifying-library-collec-tions-student-led.html.

13. Alexis Pavenick and George Martinez, "Hearing and Being Heard: LGBTQIA+ Cross-Disciplinary Collection Development," *Collection and Curation* 41, no. 4 (2022): 109–115.

14. Brittany Kester, "Diversifying an Academic Library's Children's and Young Adult Collection: A Case Study from the University of Florida's Education Library," *Collection Management* 47, nos. 2–3 (2021): 136–156.

15. Steven McKinzie, "A Multicultural Studies Collection Enhancement Group: A Model for Preemptive Collection Development in a Small Academic Library," *The Reference Librarian* 21, nos. 45–46 (1994): 187–196.

16. Laurel Kristick, "Diversity Literary Awards: A Tool for Assessing an Academic Library's Collection," *Collection Management* 45, no. 2 (2020): 151–161.

17. Moriah Caruso, Faye Christenberry, Anne Davis, Leslie Gascon, Judith Henchy, Claire Kenny, Sarah Schroeder, Zhijia Shen, and Madison Sullivan, "UW Libraries Task Force on Diversity, Equity, Inclusion, and Anti-racism in Collections Final Report," University of Washington Libraries, 2022, 18, https://digital.lib.wash-ington.edu/researchworks/bitstream/handle/1773/49181/DEI%20TF%20Final%20Report.pdf?sequence=1&isAllowed=y.

18. Jessica Schomberg and Michelle Grace, "Expanding a Collection to Reflect Diverse User Populations," *Collection Building* 24, no. 4 (2005): 125.

19. Baildon et al., *Creating a Social Justice Mindset: Diversity, Inclusion, and Social Justice in the Collections Directorate of the MIT Libraries*, 12.

20. Meghan Kwast, "California Lutheran University's Diversity Audit: A Project in Prog-ress," presented at SCELCapalooza, March 2, 2023, https://docs.google.com/pre-sentation/d/1y8ksacioG429UArHHBDK3OQr6715pGSN; Bookshop.org, "About Us," accessed July 9, 2024, https://bookshop.org/info/about-us.

21. Annette Day, Jennifer Culley, and Amy Tureen, "Towards Diversifying Col-lections—Implementing Strategies," OCLC Works in Progress webinar, March 3, 2024, https://www.oclc.org/research/events/2024/diversifying-collections-implementing-strategies.html.

22. Mullally, Whitt, and Valdivieso, "Starting and Sustaining JEDI Acquisitions and Col-lections in Academic Libraries," 114.

23. Caruso et al., "UW Libraries Task Force"; Anne Osterman, Kevin Farley, and Peter Potter, "Building Bibliodiversity in the Collective Collection through Consortial Acquisition of Small Publisher Content," *Against the Grain* 35, no. 5 (2023), https://www.charleston-hub.com/2023/11/building-bibliodiversity-in-the-collective-col-lection-through-consortial-acquisition-of-small-publisher-content/.

24. "Indigenous Publishers, Distributors & News Media," The University of British Columbia, https://guides.library.ubc.ca/indigenouspublishers/publishers, updated June 17, 2024; African American Literature Book Club, "Black Owned Publishing Companies," accessed July 9, 2024, https://aalbc.com/books/black_owned_pub-lishing_companies.php.

25. Sue F. Phelps, "Assessing a Consortium for a Multidisciplinary Subject," *Collection Management* 46, no. 1 (2021): 35–36.

26. Watson et al., "Adhocking it."

27. Karen Kohn, Emily Crawford, Noa Kaumeheiwa, and Jenny Pierce, "Inclusive Collecting, Inclusive Cataloging – Acquiring and Describing Award-Winning Books Honoring Diverse Experiences," *Library Resources and Technical Services* 68, no. 4 (2024).

28. Sunshine J. Carter, Malaika Grant, Wanda Marsolek, and Katherine Nelsen, "Retrospectively Purchasing Ebooks to Amplify Diverse Voices and Perspectives at the University of Minnesota Libraries," University of Minnesota, 2022, http://conservancy.umn.edu/handle/11299/226104.

29. Watson et al., "Adhocking it."

30. María Evelia Emerson and Lauryn Grace Lehman, "Filling in the Gaps: A Diversity Audit Toolkit from Tredway Library," *Library and Information Science: Faculty Scholarship & Creative Works*, 2021, https://digitalcommons.augustana.edu/libscifaculty/14.

31. Lee, *Indigenous Studies Library Collection Development Toolkit.*

32. Baildon et al., *Creating a Social Justice Mindset: Diversity, Inclusion, and Social Justice in the Collections Directorate of the MIT Libraries*, 14.

33. Emerson and Lehman, "Filling in the Gaps," part 3.

34. David B. Cox II, "Introductory Diversity Audits," presented at the Alaska Library Association Conference, March 2021, https://scholarworks.alaska.edu/handle/11122/12642.

35. María Evelia Emerson and Lauryn Grace Lehman, "Who Are We Missing? Conducting a Diversity Audit in a Liberal Arts College Library," *The Journal of Academic Librarianship* 48, no. 3 (2022): 10.

36. Melissa Gonzalez, "Diversity Collection Audit and Assessment," June 25, 2024, https://libguides.uwf.edu/c.php?g=1057279&p=7683515.

37. Bledsoe et al., *Leading by Diversifying Collections.*

38. Jahnke et al., "Ideology, Policy, and Practice," 166.

References

"Aanii / Boozhoo / Osiyo / Halito / Ya'at'eeh / Greetings!" Association for the Study of American Indian Literatures, 2022. https://www.asail.org/.

AAUW (American Association of University Women). "DEI Toolkit: Sexual Orientation." n.d. https://www.aauw.org/resources/member/governance-tools/dei-toolkit/dimensions-of-diversity/sexual-orientation/.

"About WNDB." We Need Diverse Books. Accessed January 30, 2024. https://diversebooks.org/about-wndb/.

Adichie, Chimamanda Ngozi. "The Danger of a Single Story." TED Talks, July 2009. https://www.ted.com/talks/chimamanda_ngozi_adichie_the_danger_of_a_single_story.

African American Literature Book Club. "Black Owned Publishing Companies." Accessed July 9, 2024. https://aalbc.com/books/black_owned_publishing_companies.php.

Ahmed, Sara. *On Being Included: Racism and Diversity in Institutional Life*. Durham, NC: Duke University Press, 2012.

Albertalli, Becky. "I Know I'm Late." *Medium*, August 31, 2020. https://medium.com/@rebecca.albertalli/i-know-im-late-9b31de339c62.

Alexander, David L. "American Indian Studies, Multiculturalism, and the Academic Library." *College & Research Libraries* 74, no. 1 (2013): 60–68.

American Association on Intellectual and Developmental Disabilities. "Defining Criteria for Intellectual Disability." Accessed March 20, 2023. https://www.aaidd.org/intellectual-disability/definition.

American Library Association. "Diverse Collections: An Interpretation of the Library Bill of Rights. Advocacy, Legislation & Issues." July 26, 2006. https://www.ala.org/advocacy/intfreedom/librarybill/interpretations/diversecollections.

American Library Association. "Diversity Counts 2012 Tables." 2012. https://www.ala.org/aboutala/sites/ala.org.aboutala/files/content/diversity/diversitycounts/diversitycountstables 2012.pdf.

American Library Association. "Library Bill of Rights. Advocacy, Legislation & Issues." June 30, 2006. https://www.ala.org/advocacy/intfreedom/librarybill.

Associated Press. "Navalny's Widow Says She Will Continue His Fight against the Kremlin." PBS News Hour, February 19, 2024. https://www.pbs.org/

newshour/world/navalnys-widow-says-she-will-continue-his-fight-against
-the-kremlin.

Backowski, Roxanne Marie and Timothy Ryan Morton. "Something to Talk About: The Intersection of Library Assessment and Collection Diversity." In *Proceedings of the Charleston Library Conference*, edited by Beth R. Bernhardt, Leah Hinds, and Lars Meyer, 170–175. Lafeyette, IN: Purdue University Press, 2019. https://docs.lib.purdue.edu/charleston/2019/collectiondevelopment /2/.

Baildon, Michelle and Rhonda Kauffman. "Diversity, Inclusion, and Social Justice Work in the MIT Libraries' Collections Directorate." OCLC Works in Progress webinar, September 19, 2017. https://www.oclc.org/research/ events/2017/09-19.html.

Baildon, Michelle, Dana Hamlin, Czeslaw Jankowski, Rhonda Kauffman, Julie Lanigan, Michelle Miller, Jessica Venlet, and Ann Marie Willer. *Creating a Social Justice Mindset: Diversity, Inclusion, and Social Justice in the Collections Directorate of the MIT Libraries*. Cambridge, MA: MIT Libraries, 2017. https:// dspace.mit.edu/handle/1721.1/108771.

Baton Rouge Area Foundation. "Criteria & Submission." The Ernest J. Gaines Award for Literary Excellence, 2023. https://ernestjgainesaward.org/ criteria.

Billey, Amber, Emily Drabinski, and K. R. Roberto. "What's Gender Got to Do with It? A Critique of RDA 9.7." *Cataloging & Classification Quarterly* 52, no. 4 (2014): 412–421.

Billey, Amber, Matthew Haugen, John Hostage, Nancy Sack, and Adam Schiff. "Report of the PCC Ad Hoc Task Group on Gender in Name Authority Records." October 4, 2016. https://www.loc.gov/aba/pcc/documents/ Gender_375%20field_RecommendationReport.pdf.

Bledsoe, Kara, Danielle Miriam Cooper, Roger C. Schonfeld, and Oya Rieger. *Leading by Diversifying Collections*. New York: Ithaka S+R, November 9, 2022. https://sr.ithaka.org/publications/leading-by-diversifying-collections/.

Blume, Rachel and Allyson Roylance. "Decolonization in Collection Development: Developing an Authentic Authorship Workflow." *The Journal of Academic Librarianship* 46, no. 5 (2020): 102175.

Bogan, Kelsey. "Diversity Audit: Final Presentation." *Don't You Shush Me* (blog). December 16, 2020. https://dontyoushushme.com/2020/12/16/diversity -audit-final-presentation/.

Bookshop.org. "About Us." Accessed July 9, 2024. https://bookshop.org/info /about-us.

Bosman, Ellen. "The Availability of Gay and Lesbian Materials in Protestant College Libraries." *Collection Management* 41, no. 2 (April 2016): 94–106. https://doi.org/10.1080/01462679.2016.1169963.

Botsford, Frances, Nina Davis-Millis, Robin Deadrick, Mohamed El Ouirdi, Melissa Feiden, Judith Gallagher, Keith Glavash, Rhonda Kauffman, Grace Mlady, Monica Ruiz, Maria Rodrigues, and Greta Suiter. *Diversity, Inclusion, and Social Justice Resource Manual for MIT Libraries Staff.* Cambridge, MA:

MIT Libraries, May 24, 2017. https://libguides.mit.edu/ld.php?content_id =32359042.

Bowers, Jennifer, Katherine Crowe, and Peggy Keeran. "'If You Want the History of a White Man, You Go to the Library': Critiquing Our Legacy, Addressing Our Library Collections Gaps." *Collection Management* 42, nos. 3–4 (October 2, 2017): 159–179. https://doi.org/10.1080/01462679.2017.1329104.

Bradley-Ridout, Glyneva, Kaushar Mahetaji, and Mikaela Mitchell. "Using a Reverse Diversity Audit Approach to Evaluate a Dermatology Collection in an Academic Health Sciences Library: A Case Presentation." *The Journal of Academic Librarianship* 49, no. 6 (2023): 102650.

Brandeis University Library. "Statement on Potentially Harmful Language in Collections, Cataloging and Description." Accessed July 25, 2024. https://www.brandeis.edu/library/about/services/language.html.

Bright, Kawanna. "The Value of a DEI Audit: What an Assessment Can Show You and Why You Should Care." *American Libraries* 53, no. 11/12 (December 11, 2022): 40.

Bright, Kawanna M. "Policy Review Rubric." Accessed April 29, 2024. http://www.kawannabright.info/uploads/1/3/2/6/132654087/policy_review _rubric_shareable.pdf.

Brissett, Alyssa, Diana Moronta, Renae J. Watson, Khaleedah Thomas, and Kristine Nowak. "Practicing Social Justice in Libraries: Building Equitable and Inclusive Collections." Presented at the LILRC 9th Annual Technical Services Open Forum, Zoom, April 14, 2023. https://lilrc.org/event-5158669.

Calderon, Janet. "Acquisitions for the Sciences – Using a Diversity Assessment to Serve BIPOC Students in STEM." Presented at the Acquisitions Institute at Timberline Lodge, 2023. https://acquisitionsinstitute.org/wp-content/ uploads/2023/05/Monday_Calderon_s-Presentation_final.pptx.

Carter, Sunshine J., Malaika Grant, Wanda Marsolek, and Katherine Nelsen. "Retrospectively Purchasing Ebooks to Amplify Diverse Voices and Perspectives at the University of Minnesota Libraries." University of Minnesota, 2022. http://conservancy.umn.edu/handle/11299/226104.

Caruso, Moriah, Faye Christenberry, Anne Davis, Leslie Gascon, Judith Henchy, Claire Kenny, Sarah Schroeder, Zhijia Shen, and Madison Sullivan. "UW Libraries Task Force on Diversity, Equity, Inclusion, and Anti-racism in Collections Final Report." University of Washington Libraries, 2022. https:// digital.lib.washington.edu/researchworks/bitstream/handle/1773/49181/ DEI%20TF%20Final%20Report.pdf?sequence=1&isAllowed=y.

Center for Disability Sports, Health and Wellness. "Sensory Disabilities." Rutgers University: Department of Kinesiology and Health. Accessed July 10, 2024. https://kines.rutgers.edu/dshw/disabilities/sensory/1061-sensory -disabilities.

Chan, Lois Mai and Theodora L. Hodges. "Library of Congress Classification (LCC)." In *Encyclopedia of Library and Information Sciences* (4th ed.), edited by John D. McDonald and Michael Levine-Clark, 2847–2855. Boca Raton, FL: CRC Press, 2018.

Conerly, Tonja R., Kathleen Holmes, and Asha Lal Tamang. *Introduction to Sociology*. Third edition. Houston, TX: OpenStax, 2021. https://openstax.org/details/books/introduction-sociology-3e.

Cox II, David B. "Introductory Diversity Audits." Presented at the Alaska Library Association Conference, March 2021. https://scholarworks.alaska.edu/handle/11122/12642.

Crenshaw, Kimberle. "Demarginalizing the Intersection of Race and Sex: A Black Feminist Critique of Antidiscrimination Doctrine, Feminist Theory and Antiracist Politics." *University of Chicago Legal Forum* 139, no. 1 (1989): 139–167.

Day, Annette, Sarah R. Jones, Amy Tureen, Susan B. Wainscott, Amanda Melilli, Thomas Padilla, and Aidy Weeks. *Inclusive and Anti-Racist Collecting at UNLV: Draft Report and Recommendations*. University of Nevada Las Vegas, September, 2022. https://digitalscholarship.unlv.edu/lib_articles/748.

Day, Annette, Jennifer Culley, and Amy Tureen. "Towards Diversifying Collections—Implementing Strategies." OCLC Works in Progress webinar, March 3, 2024. https://www.oclc.org/research/events/2024/diversifying-collections-implementing-strategies.html.

Delgado, Richard and Jean Stefancic. *Critical Race Theory, Fourth Edition: An Introduction*. New York: NYU Press, 2023.

Duyvis, Corinne. "#OwnVoices" Corinne Duyvis. Accessed January 16, 2024. https://www.corinneduyvis.net/ownvoices/.

EBSCO. "Building a Diverse and Inclusive Collection Using GOBI Spotlight Lists." October 6, 2022. https://www.ebsco.com/blogs/ebscopost/2158243/building-diverse-and-inclusive-collection-using-gobi-spotlight-lists.

EBSCO. "DEI in Campus Libraries: Key Challenges and Opportunities." November 1, 2023. https://www.ebsco.com/resources/dei-campus-libraries-key-challenges-and-opportunities.

Emerson, María Evelia and Lauryn Grace Lehman. "Filling in the Gaps: A Diversity Audit Toolkit from Tredway Library." *Library and Information Science: Faculty Scholarship & Creative Works*, 2021. https://digitalcommons.augustana.edu/libscifaculty/14.

Emerson, María Evelia and Lauryn Grace Lehman. "Who Are We Missing? Conducting a Diversity Audit in a Liberal Arts College Library." *The Journal of Academic Librarianship* 48, no. 3 (2022): 102517.

Ex Libris, Part of Clarivate. "Working with Curated Lists." Knowledge Center, viewed on July 25, 2023. https://knowledge.exlibrisgroup.com/Rialto/Product_Documentation/020Rialto_Selector_Guide/Working_with_Curated_Lists.

Fast, Ashley, Laura Foss, and Steve Hyndman. "Options and Opportunities for Increased Diversity, Equity, and Inclusion in Collection Development." Presented at SUNYLA conference (virtual), June 16, 2021. https://sunyla.org/sunyla_docs/conferences/presentations/sunyla21/D5_SUNYLA2021.pdf.

Fox, Violet B. and Kelly Swickard. ""My Zine Life is My Private Life": Reframing Authority Control from Detective Work to an Ethics of Care." In *Ethical*

Questions in Name Authority Control, edited by Jane Sandberg. Sacramento, CA: Library Juice Press, 2019.

Gibbons, Sarah. "Parking Lots in UX Meetings and Workshops." Nielsen Norman Group, September 8, 2019. https://www.nngroup.com/articles/parking-lots/.

Gibney, Michele, Mickel Paris, and Veronica Wells. "A Diversity, Equity, and Inclusion (DEI) Approach to Collection Development in a University Library." Scholarly Commons. (Pre-print), 2022. http://scholarlycommons.pacific.edu/libraries-articles/121.

Gonzalez, Melissa. "Methods." Diversity Collection Audit & Assessment, 2023. https://libguides.uwf.edu/divassess/methods.

Gonzalez, Melissa. "Results." Diversity Collection Audit & Assessment. 2023. https://libguides.uwf.edu/divassess/results.

Gonzalez, Melissa. "Diversity Collection Audit and Assessment." June 25, 2024. https://libguides.uwf.edu/c.php?g=1057279&p=7683515.

Gonzalez, Melissa. "Diversity Collection Audit & Assessment: Introduction." June 25, 2024. https://libguides.uwf.edu/c.php?g=1057279&p=7682341.

Goodman, Diane. *Promoting Diversity and Social Justice: Educating People from Privileged Groups.* Thousand Oaks, CA: Sage Publications, 2001.

Gross, Hannah. "'Diversity in the Stacks' Initiative Aims to Make All Students Feel at Home in the Library." *The Daily Pennsylvanian: University of Pennsylvania (Philadelphia, PA)*, October 8, 2019.

Hakkola, Leah and Rebecca Ropers-Huilman. "A Critical Exploration of Diversity Discourses in Higher Education: A Focus on Diversity in Student Affairs and Admissions." In *Higher Education: Handbook of Theory and Research*, edited by Michael B. Paulsen, 417–468. Cham, Switzerland: Springer, 2018.

Harrington, Morgan. "Rethinking Diversity beyond Catalogue Representation: Lessons from Efforts to Develop a Methodology to Evaluate Diversity within the National Library of Australia." *Journal of the Australian Library and Information Association* 70, no. 1 (2021): 23–43.

Henry, Carmel. "Social Justice: Racial Diversity." Howard University School of Law – Vernon E. Jordan Law Library. Accessed July 10, 2024. https://library.law.howard.edu/socialjustice/diversity.

Hobart, Elizabeth. "Cataloging Gender Diverse Authors: The MARC Field 386, Gender Identity and Privacy." *Journal of Information Ethics* 31, no. 2 (Fall 2022): 48–46.

Howard, Heather, David Zwicky, and Danielle Walker. "Put Your Money Where Your Mouth Is: A Values-Based Evaluation Tool for Collections Decisions." Collection Management, December 26, 2022, 1–13. https://doi.org/10.1080/01462679.2022.2150733.

Howard, Sara A. and Steven A. Knowlton. "Browsing Through Bias: The Library of Congress Classification and Subject Headings for African American Studies and LGBTQIA Studies." *Library Trends* 67, no. 1 (2018): 74–88.

Immigrants Rising. "Defining Undocumented." August 2023. https://immigrantsrising.org/resource/defining-undocumented/.

International Students and Scholars Office. "What Is a Permanent Resident?" International Students and Scholars Office. Accessed July 10, 2024. https://isso.ucsf.edu/permanent-resident.

Ithaca College Library Cataloging Team. "Statement on Potentially Offensive and Harmful Content." Accessed June 22, 2024. https://library.ithaca.edu/policies/offensive.php.

Ithaca College Library. "Ithaca College Library Collection Development & Management Policy." Accessed May 15, 2024. https://library.ithaca.edu/policies/CDP_2024.pdf.

Iverson, Susan V. "Troubling Diversity: An Intersectional Analysis of Diversity Action Plans at U.S. Flagship Universities." In *Intersectionality and Higher Education: Identity and Inequality on College Campuses*, edited by W. Carson Byrd, Rachelle J. Brunn-Bevel, and Sarah M. Ovink, 242–256. New Brunswick, NJ: Rutgers University Press, 2019.

Jahnke, Lori M., Kyle Tanaka, and Christopher A. Palazzolo. "Ideology, Policy, and Practice: Structural Barriers to Collections Diversity in Research and College Libraries." *College & Research Libraries* 83, no. 2 (2023): 166–183.

Jamison, Andrea. "What Does Diversity Mean?" *American Libraries*, May 3, 2021. https://americanlibrariesmagazine.org/?p=123233.

Jensen, Karen. "Diversity Auditing 101: How to Evaluate Your Collection." School Library Journal. Accessed March 24, 2023. https://www.slj.com/story/diversity-auditing-101-how-to-evaluate-collection.

Johnson, Peggy. *Fundamentals of Collection Development and Management*. Chicago: ALA Editions, 2018.

Kardosh, Rasha, Asael Y. Sklar, Alon Goldstein, Yoni Pertzov, and Ran R. Hassin. "Minority Salience and the Overestimation of Individuals from Minority Groups in Perception and Memory." *Proceedings of the National Academy of Sciences* 119, no. 12 (2022): e2116884119.

Kauffman, Rhonda Y. and Martina S. Anderson. "Diversity, Inclusion, and Social Justice in Library Technical Services." In *Library Technical Services: Adapting to a Changing Environment*, edited by Stacey Marien, 213–236. West Lafayette, IN: Purdue University Press, 2020.

Kester, Brittany. "Diversifying an Academic Library's Children's and Young Adult Collection: A Case Study from the University of Florida's Education Library." *Collection Management* 47, nos. 2-3 (2021): 136–156.

Knowlton, Steven A. "Three Decades Since *Prejudices and Antipathies:* A Study of Changes in the Library of Congress Subject Headings." *Cataloging & Classification Quarterly* 40, no. 2 (2006): 123–145.

Kohn, Karen. *Collection Evaluation in Academic Libraries: A Practical Guide for Librarians*. Lanham, MD: Rowman & Littlefield, 2015.

Kohn, Karen, Emily Crawford, Noa Kaumeheiwa, and Jenny Pierce. "Inclusive Collecting, Inclusive Cataloging - Acquiring and Describing Award-Winning Books Honoring Diverse Experiences." *Library Resources and Technical Services* 68, no. 4 (2024), https://journals.ala.org/index.php/lrts/article/view/8325.

Koob, Amanda Rybin, Arthur Aguilera, Frederick C. Carey, Xiang Li, Natalia Tingle Dolan, and Alexander Watkins. "Beyond the Diversity Audit: Uncovering Whiteness in Our Collections." In *Antiracist Library and Information Science: Racial Justice and Community*, edited by Kimberly Black and Bharat Mehra, 69–86. West Yorkshire: Emerald Publishing, 2023.

Kristick, Laurel. "Diversity Literary Awards: A Tool for Assessing an Academic Library's Collection." *Collection Management* 45, no. 2 (2020): 151–161.

Kwast, Meghan. "California Lutheran University's Diversity Audit: A Project in Progress." Presented at SCELCapalooza, March 2, 2023. https://docs.google.com/presentation/d/1y8ksacioG429UArHHBDK3OQr6715pGSN.

Lawrence, E. E. "The Trouble with Diverse Books, Part I: On the Limits of Conceptual Analysis for Political Negotiation in Library & Information Science." *Journal of Documentation* 76, no. 6 (2020): 1473–1491.

Lawrence, E. E. "The Trouble With Diverse Books, Part II: An Informational Pragmatic Analysis." *Journal of Documentation* 77, no. 1 (2020): 181–197.

Lawrence, E. E. and Diana Floegel. "Creating Award Winners in the Library: An Account of 'Reprizing.'" *The Library Quarterly* 92, no. 1 (January 2022): 39–67. https://doi.org/10.1086/717235.

Lee & Low Books. "Where is the Diversity in Publishing? The 2019 Diversity Baseline Survey Results." 2019. https://blog.leeandlow.com/2020/01/28/2019diversitybaselinesurvey/.

Lee, Deborah. "Indigenous Studies Library Collection Development Toolkit." Saskatoon: University of Saskatchewan, February 21, 2023. https://hdl.handle.net/10388/14484.

Library of Congress. "Frequently Asked Questions About Funnel Projects." Accessed February 16, 2024. https://www.loc.gov/aba/pcc/saco/funnel-faq.html.

Library of Congress. "Library of Congress Classification Outline." Accessed June 14, 2024. https://www.loc.gov/catdir/cpso/lcco/.

Library of Congress. "Library of Congress Classification Outline. Class B – Philosophy. Psychology. Religion." Accessed October 10, 2024. https://www.loc.gov/aba/cataloging/classification/lcco/lcco_b.pdf.

Library of Congress. "Library of Congress Classification Outline. Class H Social Sciences." Accessed July 25, 2024. https://www.loc.gov/aba/cataloging/classification/lcco/lcco_h.pdf.

Library of Congress. "Library of Congress Classification Schedules. Schedule E-F." Last updated June 27, 2004. https://www.loc.gov/aba/publications/FreeLCC/LCC_E-F2024TEXT.pdf.

Library of Congress. *Summary of Decisions, Editorial Meeting Number 12*, December 15, 2014. https://www.loc.gov/aba/pcc/saco/cpsoed/psd-141215.html.

Liebowitz, Cara. "I am Disabled: On Identity-First Versus People-First Language." *The Body is Not an Apology*, March 20, 2015. https://thebodyisnotanapology.com/magazine/i-am-disabled-on-identity-first-versus-people-first-language/.

Maguire, Margaret. From Concept to Practice: Themes of Diversity Within the Strategic Planof Academic Libraries. Master's Paper. University of North Carolina at Chapel Hill, April 2020. https://cdr.lib.unc.edu/concern/masters_papers/s1784r89b.

McCall, Leslie. "The Complexity of Intersectionality." *Signs* 30, no. 3 (Spring 2005): 1771–1800.

McKay, Camilla and Arleen Zimmerle. "Diversifying Library Collections through Student-Led Collection Development." OCLC Works in Progress webinar, April 23, 2024. https://www.oclc.org/research/events/2024/diversifying-library-collections-student-led.html.

McKinzie, Steven. "A Multicultural Studies Collection Enhancement Group: A Model for Preemptive Collection Development in a Small Academic Library." *The Reference Librarian* 21, nos. 45–46 (1994): 187–196.

McNair, Jonda C. and Patricia A. Edwards. "The Lasting Legacy of Rudine Sims Bishop: Mirrors, Windows, Sliding Glass Doors, and More." *Literacy Research: Theory, Method, and Practice* 70, no. 1 (2021): 202–212.

Meehan, William F. III. and Thomas E. Nisonger. "The Rowing Collection in the Free Library of Philadelphia OPAC: A Checklist Evaluation." *Collection Management* 30, no. 4 (2005): 85–104.

Meyers, Jeffrey D. "The Importance of Linguistically Diverse Collections: Decolonizing the Theological Library." *Theological Librarianship* 14, no. 2 (October 1, 2021): 11–28. https://doi.org/10.31046/tl.v14i2.2889.

Middle East Studies Association. "Fatema Mernissi Book Award." Accessed June 17, 2024. https://mesana.org/awards/category/fatema-mernissi-book-award.

Monroe-Gulick, Amalia and Sara E. Morris. "Diversity in Monographs: Selectors, Acquisitions, Publishers, and Vendors." *Collection Management* 48, no. 3 (2023): 210–233.

Mortensen, Annabelle. "Measuring Diversity in the Collection." *Library Journal* 144, no. 4 (2019): 28–30.

Mullally, Colleen S., Jeremy Whitt, and Kayla Valdivieso. "Starting and Sustaining JEDI Acquisitions and Collections in Academic Libraries: Considerations and Strategies for Success." In *Perspectives on Justice, Equity, Diversity, and Inclusion in Libraries*, edited by Nandita S. Mani, Michelle A. Cawley, and Emily P. Jones, 104–122. Hershey, PA: IGI Global, 2023.

Myers, Marianne. "LibGuides: Ethnography Research: Choosing Your Subculture." Accessed July 10, 2024. https://guides.library.tulsacc.edu/c.php?g=1054390&p=7673005.

National Center for Education Statistics. "Table 306.10., Total Fall Enrollment in Degree-granting Postsecondary Institutions, by Level of Enrollment, Sex, Attendance Status, and Race/ethnicity or Nonresident Status of Student: Selected Years, 1976 through 2021." *Digest of Education Statistics*, 2022. https://nces.ed.gov/programs/digest/d22/tables/dt22_306.10.asp.

National Center for Education Statistics. "Table 313.20 Fall Enrollment in Degree-granting Historically Black Colleges and Universities, by Sex of

Student and Level and Control of Institution: Selected Years, 1976 through 2021." *Digest of Education Statistics*, December 2022. https://nces.ed.gov/programs/digest/d22/tables/dt22_313.20.asp.

Nelsen, Kat, K. L. Clarke, Wanda Marsolek, Sunshine J. Carter, Malaika Grant, Nicole Theis-Mahon, and Pearl McClintock. "Finding Our Way Forward: A Roadmap for Anti-racist Collection Development." Charleston Hub., November 22, 2023. https://www.charleston-hub.com/2023/11/finding-our-way-forward-a-roadmap-for-anti-racist-collection-development/.

Office of Engagement and Inclusion. "What Does Being a First-Generation Student Mean? // First-Generation College Students." Marquette University. Accessed July 10, 2024. https://www.marquette.edu/first-generation-students/about.php.

Office of Management and Budget. "Revisions to the Standards for the Classification of Federal Data on Race and Ethnicity." *Federal Register* 62, no. 210 (October 30, 1997): 58782–58790. https://www.govinfo.gov/content/pkg/FR-1997-10-30/pdf/97-28653.pdf.

Oglala Lakota Nation. "Oglala Lakota Nation." Accessed April 22, 2024. https://oglalalakotanation.org/.

Organization of American Historians. "Darlene Clark Hine Award." Accessed June 17, 2024. https://www.oah.org/awards/book-awards-and-prizes/darlene-clark-hine-award.

Osterman, Anne, Kevin Farley, and Peter Potter. "Building Bibliodiversity in the Collective Collection through Consortial Acquisition of Small Publisher Content." *Against the Grain* 35, no. 5 (2023). https://www.charleston-hub.com/2023/11/building-bibliodiversity-in-the-collective-collection-through-consortial-acquisition-of-small-publisher-content/.

"Parking Lot Matrix Template." Miro. Accessed April 12, 2024. https://miro.com/templates/ideas-parking-lot-matrix/.

Pavenick, Alexis and George Martinez. "Hearing and Being Heard: LGBTQIA+ Cross-Disciplinary Collection Development." *Collection and Curation* 41, no. 4 (2022): 109–115.

Penguin Random House. "Diversity, Equity, & Inclusion U.S. Report." 2022–2023. https://randomhouse.app.box.com/s/gu32fxcyozvdmdz0ryohb2fck8gvolkv.

Phelps, Sue F. "Assessing a Consortium for a Multidisciplinary Subject." *Collection Management* 46, no. 1 (2021): 35–36.

Proctor, Julia. "Representation in the Collection: Assessing Coverage of LGBTQ Content in an Academic Library Collection." *Collection Management* 45, no. 3 (2020): 223–234.

ProQuest. "Bowker Book Analysis System." Accessed June 14, 2024. https://about.proquest.com/en/products-services/Bowker-Book-Analysis-System/.

ProQuest. "Resources for College Libraries: Frequently Sked Questions." Accessed June 14, 2024. https://pq-static-content.proquest.com/collateral/media2/documents/rcl-faqs.pdf.

ProQuest, Part of Clarivate. "Curated Topics." Viewed on December 8, 2023. https://about.proquest.com/en/customer-care/curated-topics/.

Ranganathan, S. R. "Library Science and Scientific Method." *Annals of Library and Information Studies* 4, no. 1 (1957): 19–32.

Schomberg, Jessica and Michelle Grace. "Expanding a Collection to Reflect Diverse User Populations." *Collection Building* 24, no. 4 (2005): 124–126.

Scott, Mitchell. "Patron Driven DEI Acquisitions: Using Education Students and the Diverse Book Finder to Diversify a Children's Picture Book Collection." Presented at the Acquisitions Institute at Timberline Lodge, 2023. https://acquisitionsinstitute.org/wp-content/uploads/2023/05/Patron-Driven-DEI-Acquisitions_NEW.pptx.

Shotick, Kimberly. "Uncovering Whiteness in Academic Library Collections: a Study of Author Identities in Journalism Monographs." *Collection Management* 49, no 1-2 (2024): 28–45.

Singh-Mann, Sanjeet. "Lessons Learned from Armacost Library's Collections Audit." Presented at SCELCapalooza, 2023. https://docs.google.com/presentation/d/18sba5D-cwu2fhA1lWnl1dsLuk-FxxO4O.

Singletary, Gilbert, Kenneth Royal, and Kathy Goodridge-Purnell. "Diversity Committees During the Era of Social Justice: Where do we go From Here?" *The International Journal of Information, Diversity, & Inclusion* 5, no. 5 (2021): 48–56.

Speer, Elizabeth. "DEI Collection Evaluation." *Texas Library Journal* 98, no. 4 (Winter 2022): 9–11.

Speer, Elizabeth. Letter to Vendors. January 25, 2021. https://library-apps.hsc.unt.edu/staff/vendor-letter.pdf.

Stone, Scott M. "Whose Play Scripts Are Being Published? A Diversity Audit of One Library's Collection in Conversation with the Broader Play Publishing World." *Collection Management* 45, no. 4 (2020): 304–320.

Taler, Izabella. "The Jewish Studies Book Awards: A Collection Development Strategy for Non-Sectarian Academic Libraries." *Collection Building* 30, no. 1 (January 2011): 11–38. https://doi.org/10.1108/01604951111104998.

Thomas, Peyton. "Did the Mother of Young Adult Literature Identify as a Man?" *New York Times*, December 24, 2022. https://www.nytimes.com/2022/12/24/opinion/did-the-mother-of-young-adult-literature-identify-as-a-man.html.

The Trans Metadata Collective, Jasmine Burns, Michelle Cronquist, Jackson Huang, Devon Murphy, K. J. Rawson, Beck Schaefer, Jamie Simons, Brian M. Watson, and Adrian Williams. "Metadata Best Practices for Trans and Gender Diverse Resources, Version 1.5." June 22, 2022. https://doi.org/10.5281/zenodo.6829167.

U.S. Census Bureau. "Hispanic or Latino Origin." https://www.census.gov/quickfacts/fact/note/US/RHI725222?.

University of British Columbia. "Indigenous Publishers, Distributors & News Media." Updated June 17, 2024. https://guides.library.ubc.ca/indigenouspublishers/publishers.

University of Illinois Counseling Center. "Body Size Diversity and Acceptance." University of Illinois at Urbana-Champaign. Accessed July 10, 2024. https://counselingcenter.illinois.edu/brochures/body-size-diversity-and-acceptance.

University of Sydney Libraries, Nathan Sentance. "Aboriginal and Torres Strait Islander Cultural Protocols." 2021. https://ses.library.usyd.edu.au/handle/2123/24602.

University of West Florida. "Prohibition of Discrimination, Harassment and Retaliation." Last modified March 9, 2020. https://confluence.uwf.edu/display/UP/Prohibition+of+Discrimination%2C+Harassment+and+Retaliation.

Vex, Artemis and Ruth Castillo. "Collection Assessment Codes Toolkit." Google Docs, 2019. http://bit.ly/acq-dei-toolkit.

Voels, Sarah. *Auditing Diversity in Library Collections.* Santa Barbara, CA: Libraries Unlimited, 2022.

Vong, Silvia, Allan Cho, and Elaina Norlin. "The Five Labours of Equity, Diversity, Inclusion, and Anti-racism Work by Racialized Academic Librarians." *The International Journal of Information, Diversity, & Inclusion* 7, no. 3/4 (2023): 1–24. https://jps.library.utoronto.ca/index.php/ijidi/article/view/41002.

Walters, William. "Assessing Diversity in Academic Library Book Collections: Diversity Audit Principles and Methods." *Open Information Science* 7, no. 1 (2023): 20220148. https://www.degruyter.com/document/doi/10.1515/opis-2022-0148/html.

Watson, Megan, Anne Davis, Je Salvador, Julie Garrison, and Paul Gallagher. "Systemic Change Through Local Action: Advancing DEI and Measuring Impact at the Institutional Level." Panel discussion presented at the Charleston Conference 2023, March 1, 2024. https://www.youtube.com/watch?v=QwUpaYvXB7k.

Watson, Renae J., Khaleedah Thomas, and Kristine Nowak. "Adhocking It: Overcoming the Overwhelm to Start Creating: Equitable and Inclusive Collections Now." In *Practicing Social Justice in Libraries*, edited by Alyssa Brissett and Diana Moronta, 100–116. New York: Routledge, 2022.

Wells, Veronica A., Michele Gibney, and Mickel Paris. "Student Learning and Engagement in a DEI Collection Audit: Applying the ACRL Framework for Information Literacy." *College & Research Libraries News*, September 8, 2022. https://doi.org/10.5860/crln.83.8.335.

Wells, Veronica Michele Gibney, Mickel Paris, and Corey Pfitzer. "Student Participation in a DEI Audit as High-Impact Practice." *The Journal of Academic Librarianship* 49, no. 1 (2023): 102615.

Whittaker, Thomas A. "Demographic Characteristics in Personal Name Authority Records and the Ethics of a Person-Centered Approach to Name Authority Control." In *Ethical Questions in Name Authority Control*, edited by Jane Sandberg, 57–69. Sacramento, CA: Library Juice Press, 2019.

"Why We Need Diverse Books Is No Longer Using the Term #OwnVoices." We Need Diverse Books. June 6, 2021. https://diversebooks.org/why-we-need-diverse-books-is-no-longer-using-the-term-ownvoices/.

Wikoff, Karin. "LibGuides: DEIJA Projects: Get Started." Accessed June 22, 2024. https://libguides.ithaca.edu/c.php?g=1350943&p=9970367.

Wilson, William Julius. "The Declining Significance of Race: Revisited & Revised." *Daedalus* 140, no. 2 (2011): 55–69. https://dash.harvard.edu/handle/1/8052151.

Young, Janis L. "Library of Congress Subject Headings (LCSH)." In *Encyclopedia of Library and Information Sciences* (4th ed.), edited by John D. McDonald and Michael Levine-Clark, 2866–2878. Boca Raton, FL: CRC Press, 2018.

Zamudio, Margaret, Christopher Russell, Francisco Rios, and Jacquelyn L. Bridgeman. *Critical Race Theory Matters: Education and Ideology.* New York: Routledge, 2010.

Acknowledgments

In 2022, I reached out to Emily Hopkins at the University of Georgia, with whom I had at the time a slight professional acquaintance, to ask if she wanted to work with me to lead some type of conversation related to collection assessment for diversity, equity, and inclusion. After leading an open discussion on Zoom, we continued to think of ways to keep the conversation going, and one day she had an idea that surprised me. She said, "I think we should write a book." Although Emily eventually had to step away from the book project, it would never have gotten started without her idea or her confidence in me. Emily, I've enjoyed working together and getting to know you.

Many people have helped with specific pieces of the project, either reviewing my work or confirming statements I wanted to make. Stacey Franklin at ProQuest Clarivate verified several sentences about ways her company works with customers. Danielle Cooper and Tracy Bergstrom at Ithaka S+R had ideas that helped me find a guest author. Katy Rawdon, my colleague at Temple University, read and provided feedback on chapter 8. Julie Darken at the University of Georgia read chapter 6 and answered questions about metadata. Larissa Gordon at the University of Pennsylvania provided helpful comments on chapter 10, as she has done for so much of my writing over the years. My sisters, Wendy Kohn and Deborah Ala, reviewed several of my tables and gave advice on layout, and as a bonus told me that the material was even interesting to non-librarians! My editor at Rowman & Littlefield, Erinn Slanina, was always supportive and had the fastest turnaround time I could imagine.

My colleagues at Temple University Libraries and University Press have influenced this book in many ways, such as teaching me about inclusive metadata, the concept of the ideas parking lot, and academic book publishing. I'm afraid if I try to list everyone I'd forget someone, but there are some key people I want to mention by name. I am always appreciative of my supervisor, Brian Schoolar, whose response when I told him I was writing a book was "okay." Andrea Goldstein, Rebecca Lloyd, and Van Tran volunteered to conduct diversity assessments at Temple, not realizing they were providing me with experience that would help me with this book. My heartfelt thanks to Jenny Pierce and Noa Kaumeheiwa, my partners on the DEI in Collections committee, for learning alongside me and collaborating on projects that I'm proud of. It has been great working with you, and I think we work really well together!

I am not the only author of this book. Ruth Castillo, Melissa Gonzalez, Artemis Vex, and Karin Wikoff, the four authors of three guest chapters: I'm so grateful to you for agreeing to be part of this work, for turning in drafts on time (or even early!), responding graciously to my feedback, and for doing assessment projects that I can learn from as well as our readers. Having chapters that showcase your examples of assessment makes the book much stronger—that was Emily's idea.

Index

Page references for figures are italicized.

About the Authors

Karen Kohn is Collections Analysis Librarian at Temple University in Philadelphia, where she serves on the Diversity, Equity, and Inclusion in Collections Committee and the Open Education Group. She also teaches Introduction to Collection Analysis through Library Juice Academy and serves on the editorial board of *portal: Libraries and the Academy*. She has published articles in *College & Research Libraries*, *Journal of Academic Librarianship*, *Journal of Documentation*, *Collection Management*, and *portal*. Her previous book, *Collection Evaluation in Academic Libraries: A Practical Guide for Librarians*, was published in 2015.

GUEST AUTHORS

Ruth Castillo holds a bachelor of science in psychology from Virginia Tech and a master of library and information science from the University of South Carolina. She has served as the director of the Emory & Henry College Library in Virginia and the head of reference and instruction in the library at Charleston Southern University in South Carolina. Ruth has experience in integrated information literacy, providing library services for on-campus and online learning, web services, research support for faculty and students, and government information. Her research focuses on advancing library initiatives to develop inclusive collections and services that support equitable access for diverse academic communities.

Melissa Gonzalez is the collection development librarian and history, philosophy, religion, anthropology, political science, and music subject liaison at the University of West Florida in Pensacola. She holds a master of library and information science and a master of arts in history from the University of Southern Mississippi. She has held leadership positions in the RUSA History section and currently serves on committees for both the Women and Gender Studies and the Anthropology and Sociology sections of ACRL. She also teaches a capstone course for the UWF bachelor of general studies program. Her current professional interests center around collection management and assessment, with a particular focus on building and maintaining diverse collections.

Artemis D. Vex is the public services librarian at Emory & Henry University in Virginia. Her research and work experience includes student outreach and communication, as well as incorporations of diversity, equity, inclusion, and belonging in libraries.

Karin Wikoff grew up just outside Detroit, MI, before moving to rural central New York State. After graduating from Wells College (BA German) and Cornell University (MA German Studies), she continued her education at Syracuse University (MLS). She also has conservation/preservation technician certification from Cornell University Libraries. She started her library career as a cataloger at Wells College, where she worked in every department including the archives. She began her work at Ithaca College Library as the electronic resources librarian and then was promoted to head of Electronic and Technical Services; she also served a year as the interim college librarian. She is the author of the 2011 textbook *Managing Electronic Resources in an Academic Library*. She also believes that she is the only female academic librarian who is also a former professional (WPFL) football player.